XII 10 00

Moving Targets

Moving Targets

NUCLEAR STRATEGY AND NATIONAL SECURITY

Scott D. Sagan

A Council on Foreign Relations Book

PRINCETON UNIVERSITY PRESS

PRINCETON, NEW JERSEY

Copyright © 1989 by Princeton University Press
Published by Princeton University Press, 41 William Street,
Princeton, New Jersey 08540
In the United Kingdom: Princeton University Press, Guildford, Surrey

Library of Congress Cataloging-in-Publication Data

Sagan, Scott Douglas.
Moving targets : nuclear strategy and national security / Scott D. Sagan.
p. cm.
"A Council on Foreign Relations book."
Bibliography: p.
Includes index.
ISBN 0-691-07815-7 (alk. paper)
1. United States—Military policy. 2. Nuclear warfare.
I. Title.
UA23.S215 1989
355'.0217'0973—dc19   88-34038

This book has been composed in Linotron Palatino

Clothbound editions of Princeton University Press books are printed
on acid-free paper, and binding materials are chosen for strength
and durability. Paperbacks, although satisfactory for personal
collections, are not usually suitable for library rebinding

Printed in the United States of America by Princeton University Press,
Princeton, New Jersey

In memory of my grandfather
Bishop J. Waskom Pickett

Contents

Figures and Tables

Acknowledgments

THIS BOOK could not have been written without the support of the Council on Foreign Relations, which provided me with two highly unusual opportunities to study the development of U.S. nuclear strategy. First, in 1984, I was awarded a Council International Affairs Fellowship and—with the generous assistance of Gen. Jack Merritt, then Director of the Organization of the Joint Chiefs of Staff—spent the better part of two years working on the problems of U.S. nuclear strategy as a Joint Staff "action officer" in the Policy and Plans Directorate (J-5). Moving directly from the ivory tower of Harvard to a windowless room in the basement of the Pentagon brought about an abrupt, but intellectually enriching, change in perspective. Although scholars and soldiers approach the complex problems caused by nuclear weapons from very different viewpoints, reflecting their different biases and responsibilities, the experience gave me a greater appreciation of the need for deep and sustained interaction between the academic theorists and the military and civilian practitioners of American strategy. I wish to thank my colleagues in the Nuclear and Chemical Division and the Nuclear Strategy Development Group—especially Col. Robert Irvine, Capt. Donald Knepper, Brig. Gen. Joel McKean, Mr. Franklin Miller, Comdr. Edward Ohlert and Capt. James Shew—for their support and friendship.

Second, the Council sponsored a 1985–1986 Washington Study Group on Nuclear Diplomacy for which I served as a rapporteur and occasional discussion leader. The study group, chaired by Elliot Richardson and R. James Woolsey and including many past, present, and, presumably, future senior American national security officials, met over the academic year to debate and discuss elements of U.S.

nuclear policy and arms control strategy. I profited enormously from these discussions and especially want to thank Alton Frye, director of the Council's Washington program, for encouraging me to write a book developing my own views of U.S. strategy, and not simply a report of the study group's deliberations. In addition, the Council sponsored a meeting to review the manuscript in May 1988. The comments and criticisms of the review group members—Richard Betts, Barry Blechman, Robert Einhorn, Alton Frye, Robert Jervis, Jan Lodal, Michael Mandelbaum, Elliot Richardson, Gregory Treverton, Edward Warner, and R. James Woolsey—were extremely valuable.

The breadth of my understanding of American strategy and military organizations was also enhanced by participation in a series of seminars on U.S. military policy sponsored by the Lehrman Institute in 1985 and 1986. A few of the ideas in chapter 1 appear in germinal form in my chapter "Change and Continuity in U.S. Nuclear Strategy" in the product of that seminar series: Michael Mandelbaum (ed.), *America's Defense* (New York: Holmes and Meier, 1989). I would also like to express my appreciation to the Harvard Center for International Affairs and the Stanford Center for International Security and Arms Control for supporting my research trips to the various archives utilized in this study.

I also want to thank a number of my colleagues from the academic world. The completion of this project was postponed for more than a year by my teaching responsibilities at Harvard University and Stanford University. The delay in publication, however, improved the product immensely as I benefited from the comments and criticisms of the following friends and colleagues from the scholarly community who read all or portions of the draft manuscript: Kurt Campbell, Andrew Carpendale, Ashton Carter, Antonia Chayes, Lynn Eden, Charles Glaser, Joseph Nye, Robert Powell, Edward Rhodes, Condoleezza Rice, Henry Rowen, and Marc Trachtenberg.

In addition, I would like to express my appreciation to

those who assisted in the preparation of the book. Margaret Pinedo provided superb secretarial support. Carolyn Wenger was the copy editor and Eliska Ryznar prepared the index. Ben Hunt and John Shields were excellent student research assistants.

Finally, great credit must be given to my wife, Bao Lamsam, who has had the patience and grace to put up with more discussions about nuclear strategy than anyone who has not chosen to study this subject deserves.

Scott D. Sagan
San Francisco, California

Moving Targets

The Usability Paradox

MANY AMERICANS feared the future at the dawn of the nuclear age. "In that terrible flash 10,000 miles away," James
Reston wrote immediately after the destruction of Hiroshima and Nagasaki, "men here have seen not only the
fate of Japan, but have glimpsed the future of America."[1]
Unless the new weapon was abolished, it was widely believed, nuclear war was inevitable: if not this year, then
the next; if not through deliberate aggression, then by accident. Certainly the prevalence of war in the past offered
little hope that war could be prevented in the future. As a
group of Manhattan Project scientists argued, "The whole
history of mankind teaches . . . that accumulated weapons
of mass destruction 'go off' sooner or later, even if this
means a senseless mutual destruction."[2]

Today, over forty years later, the United States and the
Soviet Union have amassed some fifty thousand nuclear
weapons. Not one of these weapons, however, has been
used—either by accident or in combat—since the summer
of 1945. This is a great achievement: despite the continued
existence of nuclear weapons, the recurrence of crises and
conflicts, and the persistence of deep Soviet-American ri-
valry, nuclear peace has been maintained.

I have never lived in a world without nuclear weapons
and, realistically, I know that I never will. This belief,
however, should engender neither complacency nor despair. For the history of U.S. nuclear policy, reviewed in
this book, suggests that we have maintained a secure nuclear peace precisely because American decision makers
were not complacent about the bomb: secure deterrent
forces were built and maintained at great cost, prudent
changes in nuclear strategy were implemented, and im-

proved weapons' safety programs and arms control agreements were enacted, significantly reducing both the risk
of deliberate Soviet aggression and the danger of accidental war.

Despair about maintaining nuclear deterrence in the future must also be avoided, however, for it can lead to the
false attractions of utopian, unrealizable schemes to eliminate the risk of war. The danger of nuclear utopianism—
whether it takes the form of a belief in the abolition of nuclear weapons, in the total elimination of Soviet and American political rivalries, or in the rapid creation of perfect
strategic defenses—is that it focuses attention away from
the more prudent and practical steps that can be taken in
the near term to reduce the risk of conflict. The policy recommendations offered in this book—proposals for altera-
tions in American nuclear strategy, for superpower arms
control measures and improved U.S. safety systems to reduce the likelihood of accidents, and for the potential development of limited strategic defense capabilities—will
not, therefore, satisfy those who find hope only in radical
solutions to the nuclear dilemma. They do, however, offer
what I believe to be realistic prospects for lessening the
persistent risks we will face in the nuclear future.

THE USABILITY PARADOX

A prudent policy of deterrence has produced a nuclear
world in which a major war between the United States and
the Soviet Union is improbable. Nuclear war is not, however, impossible. Indeed, if the use of nuclear weapons
was impossible, nuclear deterrence could not be effective.

A perpetual dilemma, which has been called the "usability paradox," exists at the heart of U.S. nuclear weapons policy.[3] The two central objectives of U.S. policy—to
deter aggression against the United States and its allies
and to prevent accidental war—require that U.S. nuclear
forces be usable, but not too usable. For the sake of deterrence, nuclear forces must be "usable enough" to convince

the Soviet Union that a potent U.S. nuclear response would actually be forthcoming in the event of a Soviet attack on the United States or its vital interests. To prevent accidental war, however, U.S. weapons must not be "so usable" that they are ever launched through a mechanical error, used by unauthorized or insane military commanders, or operated in such a provocative manner as to cause the Soviet Union to mistakenly "preempt" what it falsely believes is an imminent U.S. attack.

To understand the numerous tensions and trade-offs between these twin goals of secure deterrence and accidental war prevention, it is necessary to delve deeply into the operational details of U.S. *nuclear doctrine*.[4] What do we target with our nuclear weapons and why? When and how does the United States plan to use its nuclear weapons if deterrence fails? What prevents accidental or unauthorized use of nuclear weapons in peacetime, and what military operations would take place in a crisis or conventional war to prepare for authorized use? Until recently, insufficient unclassified information has been available to permit a thorough investigation of these sensitive subjects. This book, however, utilizes numerous recently declassified government documents and builds upon the work of other scholars of the "operational dimension" of U.S. nuclear policy, to present an unusual examination of the inner workings of U.S. nuclear strategy.[5] It documents the severe and persistent difficulty with which senior U.S. political and military officials have grappled with the paradoxes inherent in a policy of nuclear deterrence.

The history is not always reassuring. For while the U.S. government has been successful in achieving its major objectives—nuclear peace has been maintained, no major conventional war with the Soviet Union has occurred, and not a single nuclear weapon has been detonated by accident—senior U.S. officials have not always been in full control of the nuclear machine that they have created. Civilian authorities have often provided new political guidance, changing elements of U.S. nuclear doctrine in an effort to enhance deterrence, but the actual operational results of such changes were often unanticipated and undesired. Senior civilian and military leaders have added many safety features to the U.S. nuclear arsenal to prevent accidental war or inadvertent escalation, but numerous close calls have nonetheless occurred when military operations were inadequately controlled in nuclear crises. If we are to reduce further the risks of nuclear war, we must learn not only from past achievements but also from past mistakes. Nuclear peace has been maintained for over forty years, but it is not assured for the future.

Outline of the Book

This book attempts to bridge the gap between the theory and the practice of nuclear strategy. The first chapter is a study of the evolution of U.S. *nuclear employment policy*: the actual plans the United States has developed to use these weapons if necessary and the nuclear targeting doctrine that has guided the military planners. Many scholarly examinations of deterrence theory exist, and numerous case studies of the U.S. acquisition of individual weapons systems have been written.[6] There are, however, far fewer studies of actual nuclear war planning and targeting doctrine. Yet nuclear war plans and targeting policy can be seen as the critical component of nuclear strategy.

The reason for this is simple. Not only do U.S. targeting doctrine and war plans determine how the United States is likely to respond to an attack, but they can exert a strong influence themselves on the likelihood of war. On this point, American defense analysts agree; they just disagree on which potential U.S. doctrines and plans make nuclear war less likely and which make it more so. American nuclear strategists, for example, vigorously debate whether the United States should develop a capability and plans to destroy Soviet ICBMs in their hardened concrete silos, and the Soviet political leadership itself in its deep underground shelters, because they fundamentally disagree over whether such a capability would be a provocation or a deterrent.

U.S. targeting doctrine also exerts a strong influence on decisions about what weapons we buy. The impact is often indirect, since many political, technical, and bureaucratic factors also affect acquisition policy. But, as chapter 1 demonstrates, some of the most significant historical decisions about the structure of the U.S. nuclear arsenal—decisions to emphasize more survivable submarines and ICBMs rather than bombers in the early 1960s, to reduce dramatically the size of U.S. air defenses in the late 1960s, and to develop increasingly accurate missiles and earth-penetrating warheads in the 1980s—can be seen as having been strongly influenced by developments in nuclear doctrine.

While chapter 1 analyzes the elements of continuity and changes in U.S. nuclear doctrine since 1945, chapter 2 focuses on the rationale and critiques of current U.S. counterforce targeting doctrine. Why does the United States target Soviet nuclear forces and leadership-protection facilities? While the chapter demonstrates that many of the common criticisms of the current "countervailing strategy" are based on a fundamental misunderstanding of the strategy, it nonetheless does recommend that significant changes be made in current doctrine. The strongest criticism of current counterforce targeting concerns its potential negative impact on crisis stability: such U.S. plans and capabilities may be perceived by the Soviet leadership as being designed for a U.S. "damage-limiting" first strike and may therefore increase the probability of Soviet nuclear preemption in a deep crisis or conventional war. The analysis presented in chapter 2, however, suggests that it is possible to maintain a strong *second-strike counterforce* capability, while minimizing crisis stability problems, and outlines how future U.S. nuclear forces could be designed to implement such a strategy.

Chapter 3 reviews the arguments for and against a U.S. decision to deploy highly limited strategic defenses, the only form of an SDI (Strategic Defense Initiative) system that is likely to be feasible over the next five years. What is the potential impact of such limited defenses against ballistic missiles on both the maintenance of mutual deterrence and the prevention of accidental war? Would Limited Strategic Defense make nuclear war more likely or less? The chapter concludes that while the gradual U.S. deployment of highly limited defenses, within the current or slightly renegotiated ABM (Anti-Ballistic Missile) Treaty, may be in American national interests, a rapid movement to larger-scale unrestricted defenses would be highly imprudent in the near future.

Chapter 4 examines the risks of accidental nuclear war. How close have we come to accidental war in past incidents and crises? The chapter presents a brief history of the unilateral U.S. steps and bilateral arms control arrangements that the United States has already implemented that have significantly lessened such dangers, and then critically assesses a number of current proposals for further U.S. actions or arms control agreements intended to reduce accidental war dangers. The operational arms control recommendations in this chapter are designed—when coupled with the revised nuclear doctrine outlined in chapter 2—to reduce the tensions caused by the usability paradox: they attempt to maximize robust nuclear deterrence while at the same time minimizing the problems of crisis instability and the danger of inadvertent escalation or nuclear accidents.

The improvements in U.S. nuclear weapons doctrine that are analyzed in this book are unlikely to come into being unless they both engender public support for U.S. policy and elicit more thorough civilian leadership oversight in the implementation of strategic decisions. The last chapter examines the issues. Can a nuclear deterrent doctrine based on offensive retaliation, not on direct protection by defenses, be sustained in a democracy? How can civilian and military authorities work together more effectively to reduce the risk of war? Such political and organizational dilemmas must be addressed if future U.S. nuclear weapons policy is to be managed better than was often the case in the past.

Moving Targets

Finally, a brief explanation of the title might prove helpful. *Moving Targets* does not refer only to mobile missiles or the analysis of past changes in U.S. nuclear targeting policy and the recommendations I make for further moves in strategic doctrine. It is also an allusion to the central topic. Strategic adversaries constantly monitor each other and react to one another's moves. Neither military technology nor Soviet-American relations are static. The Soviet Union's political and military leadership is currently engaged in a serious debate about the future course of Soviet doctrine. And U.S. political and military leaders, along with their negotiating positions and the strategic concepts they seek to implement, are all constantly in flux. Indeed, as anyone who has written about this exceedingly complex subject understands, U.S. nuclear strategy, in many ways, is itself a moving target.

CHAPTER ONE

The Evolution of U.S. Nuclear Doctrine

THE CLASSICAL Roman adage warns, *Qui desiderat pacem, praeparet bellum*—"If you want peace, prepare for war." For the past forty years of the nuclear age, the government of the United States has followed that advice with a vengeance. This chapter examines the evolution of U.S. nuclear doctrine since 1945. It is the history of senior American political officials, and the complex military organizations beneath them, attempting to maintain a precarious nuclear peace by planning to fight a nuclear war if deterrence fails.

A thorough examination of nuclear war planning and targeting doctrine is central to any discussion of U.S. nuclear strategy. Targeting doctrine is, after all, a reflection of the government's judgments about the requirements of deterrence: What targets inside the Soviet Union must U.S. nuclear forces hold at risk, that is, threaten to destroy in a retaliatory strike, in order to deter Soviet aggression? Should the United States threaten to strike first or only threaten nuclear retaliation? Should the United States maintain nuclear forces capable only of destroying Soviet urban-industrial areas, or should the United States build nuclear forces designed to destroy Soviet military forces, including their offensive nuclear capabilities, and the Soviet leadership itself with its political control apparatus? Finally, if deterrence does fail, how should U.S. nuclear forces be used? Should the United States plan and build the capabilities for limited nuclear wars or only for total conflicts, for prolonged wars or only for a brief spasm of destruction?

This chapter examines how different American administrations have answered these perplexing questions. It traces the evolution of actual U.S. nuclear doctrine and war plans to the extent that the currently unclassified record permits. How and why has American nuclear strategy changed over the past forty years, and what areas of continuity remain? It is important to examine thoroughly this history of U.S. nuclear strategy in order to illuminate our current dilemmas and future choices. It is, in short, necessary to know where we have been in this dangerous arena of nuclear strategy, in order to understand where we should be heading.

Two Myths about MAD

One common perspective on nuclear strategy equates nuclear deterrence with the threat of indiscriminate destruction of cities. This view, that war is best deterred by threats to destroy a significant portion of an adversary's population and industry, is called the doctrine of *Assured Destruction*. The belief that stable deterrence is best maintained when both the United States and the Soviet Union have such a strategy is called the doctrine of *Mutual Assured Destruction*, or MAD. This chapter will dispel two widely held myths about MAD.

The first myth about MAD is the layman's myth—the long-standing and persistent notion that the United States based its security solely on the Assured Destruction threat to attack Soviet cities in the 1960s, but later switched to a "war-fighting" counterforce nuclear doctrine.[1] As this history of U.S. nuclear strategy will demonstrate, this view greatly exaggerates the degree of change in targeting policy over time. For over thirty-five years, the United States has had, to a significant degree, a counterforce nuclear doctrine. Since the Soviet Union first developed nuclear weapons, as Secretary of Defense Harold Brown has acknowledged, "we have always considered it important, in the event of war, to be able to attack the forces that could do damage to the United States and its allies."[2]

The second mistaken view, however, is the expert's

myth about MAD—that Assured Destruction was merely reassuring rhetoric for public consumption and, at most, a force-sizing criterion used by Secretary of Defense Robert McNamara to fend off Air Force and congressional demands for increased counterforce capabilities in the 1960s. In this view, Assured Destruction was merely U.S. *declaratory policy*; it was not a serious element in U.S. nuclear doctrine.[3] This chapter will demonstrate that, in fact, Assured Destruction has influenced U.S. nuclear strategy and targeting doctrine in three important ways.

First, it has shaped war plans indirectly by affecting both the quantity and the quality of U.S. weapons procurement over time. The size of the Minuteman force in the 1960s and the pace of accuracy improvements in the early 1970s, for example, were both influenced by beliefs that meeting Assured Destruction criteria was the primary requirement for strategic deterrence.[4] Second, Assured Destruction had a direct influence on nuclear war planning under Secretary of Defense Robert McNamara. According to a recently declassified top secret 1961 Draft Presidential Memorandum (DPM), the maintenance of "protected reserve forces capable of destroying the Soviet urban society, if necessary, in a controlled and deliberate way" was the "highest priority" in McNamara's nuclear strategy.[5] While the McNamara policy throughout the 1960s did not exclude counterforce targeting, it also clearly included countercity targeting with these withheld nuclear forces. In short, while the McNamara targeting policy was not Assured Destruction *only*, it clearly did have an Assured Destruction component.

Finally, the concept of Assured Destruction also played a critical role in targeting policy in the mid-1970s, when "an important objective of the assured retaliation mission," according to Secretary of Defense Donald Rumsfeld, was "to retard significantly the ability of the U.S.S.R. to recover from a nuclear exchange and regain the status of a 20th century military and industrial power."[6] As will be demonstrated in this chapter, "counter-recovery" targeting was the priority mission of U.S. nuclear forces in the mid-1970s and required very significant numbers of weapons. Although Soviet military forces continued to be targeted during this period, the guidance given to military war planners to "retard" the Soviet Union's recovery from a nuclear exchange moved American nuclear strategy much closer to MAD than is often realized.

The two myths about MAD are mirror images of one another. One overestimates the degree of change in U.S. doctrine; the other exaggerates the degree of continuity. The layman's view, by focusing on McNamara's public statements about Assured Destruction, underestimates the degree to which counterforce remained an important component in U.S. nuclear doctrine in the 1960s. The expert's view, however, by focusing on the discussions of "limited nuclear options" and the maintenance of counterforce capabilities in the 1960s and 1970s, both overlooks the important emphasis placed on counterindustrial targeting in that period and underestimates the significance of the changes in nuclear doctrine implemented in the 1980s. Indeed, as this chapter demonstrates, the United States moved significantly away from such a MAD-oriented doctrine in the 1980s. Under what has been called the "countervailing strategy," U.S. security was no longer based on the ability to retard Soviet economic recovery. Instead, in the words of Secretary of Defense Caspar Weinberger, deterrence was based "on the threat to destroy what the Soviet leadership values most highly: namely, itself, its military power and political control capabilities, and its industrial ability to wage war."[7] The concluding section of this chapter will examine the origins of this doctrine; the next chapter will provide a detailed examination of the current countervailing doctrine and an assessment of its implications for the future of U.S. national security.

1945–1950: THE AMERICAN NUCLEAR MONOPLY

Among some professional military analysts after World War II, there was a tendency to underestimate the destructive potential of atomic weapons. Maj. Alexander P. de

Seversky, for example, told *Reader's Digest* readers in February 1946 that the effect of the bombs that struck Hiroshima and Nagasaki "had been wildly exaggerated." He claimed, "The same bombs dropped on New York or Chicago, Pittsburgh or Detroit, would have exacted no more toll in life than one of our big blockbusters, and the property damage might have been limited to broken window glass over a wide area."[8] As late as 1949 the director of the Navy's Aviation Ordnance Branch similarly reported to the House Armed Services Committee that "you could stand in the open at one end of the north-south runway at the Washington National Airport, with no more protection than the clothes you now have on, and have an atom bomb explode at the other end of the runway without serious injury to you."[9]

At the highest levels of the government, however, U.S. military and political leaders quickly recognized the revolutionary character of atomic power. For example, the Joint Chiefs of Staff (JCS) evaluation board for the Bikini tests reported in July 1947 that "in conjunction with the other mass destruction weapons it is possible to depopulate vast areas of the earth's surface, leaving only vestigial remnants of man's material works."[10] After the Hiroshima and Nagasaki attacks, President Truman also viewed the bomb as a weapon of terror, not a traditional part of the military arsenal. "You have got to understand," he told a group of advisers in July 1948, "that this isn't a military weapon. It is used to wipe out women and children and unarmed people, and not for military uses. So we have got to treat this differently from rifles and cannons and ordinary things like that."[11] Truman's initial impulse, therefore, was to seek an agreement to internationalize the control of atomic weapons through the Baruch Plan in the United Nations, rather than to plan for their potential use against the Soviet Union. Indeed, the early war planning that did take place within the Pentagon was devoid of political guidance. Truman was not even informed of the size of the atomic arsenal from 1945 to the spring of 1947 and, when he was briefed on the JCS nuclear war planning document "Halfmoon" in May 1948, he ordered that an alternative contingency plan be developed that would rely entirely on conventional weapons.[12]

Early War Planning

The Berlin crisis of 1948 forced a change of policy.[13] On June 24, the Soviets shut off all ground access to Berlin, and Truman immediately ordered an airlift of supplies into the beleaguered city. On June 27, the Strategic Air Command (SAC) was placed on initial alert, and in mid-July the Administration resorted to atomic "gunboat diplomacy," sending what government press releases pointedly described as two "atomic capable" B-29 squadrons to Great Britain.[14] Although these specific bombers had not, in fact, been modified to enable them to deliver atomic weapons, few reports of the action noted this fact. At the same time, however, all the SAC B-29s that had been modified to accommodate the arsenal's huge atomic bombs were placed on a twenty-four-hour alert back in the United States.[15]

These readiness measures and atomic "signals" took place in the absence of any agreed-upon plans for potential use of atomic bombs in a war with the Soviet Union. When senior Pentagon and National Security Council (NSC) officials met on June 30 to discuss the U.S. responses to the Soviet placement of barrage balloons in the airlift's flight corridors, the Chief of Staff of the Air Force was not even certain if the Air Staff was studying targeting options. Secretary of Defense Forrestal wondered whether "a reduction of Moscow and Leningrad would be a powerful enough impact to stop a war," and Admiral Souers from the NSC suggested that in the event of war the United States should "just kill ten million people and make them [the Soviets] get a political decision now" to surrender.[16] With the prospect of conflict on the horizon, the critical need for advance planning—and indeed some fundamental strategic thinking—about the potential use of atomic weapons was painfully obvious.

Finally, in September, the National Security Council approved a document (NSC-30, "United States Policy on Atomic Weapons") stating that the "National Military Establishment must be ready to utilize promptly and effectively all appropriate means available, including atomic weapons, in the interest of national security and must therefore plan accordingly."[17] At the same time that it approved the inclusion of the atomic bomb in the military's war plans, NSC-30 explicitly maintained the sole authority of the President to make "the decision as to the employment of atomic weapons in the event of war."[18] Truman wanted to make sure, he told Secretary Forrestal, that the United States did not have "some dashing lieutenant colonel decide when would be the proper time to drop one."[19] If atomic weapons were used against the Soviet Union, it would be Truman's decision alone. On September 13, the President told his advisers "that he prayed that he would never have to make such a decision [to use atomic weapons], but if it became necessary, no one need have a misgiving but [that] he [would] do so," and that night Truman confided to his diary, "I have a terrible feeling . . . that we are very close to war."[20] The Soviet Union did not, however, challenge the U.S. airlift to Berlin and in May 1949 lifted the blockade without further tests of U.S. military capability or political resolve.

The Berlin crisis had forced the U.S. government to recognize that nuclear use would quickly become necessary in the event of a Soviet attack on Western Europe. The major burden in any future war effort, therefore, would have fallen onto the Strategic Air Command and its newly appointed commander, Curtis LeMay. Now that NSC-30 had given the Air Force the green light for nuclear war planning, the critical question for SAC was what to attack in the event of hostilities, and LeMay clearly applied his Pacific War experience with terror bombing against Japan to SAC's new mission against the USSR: "We should concentrate on industry itself *which is located in urban areas,"* LeMay told his war planners in 1951, so that even if the specific target was missed, *"a bonus* will be derived from the use of the bomb."[21]

In December 1948, while the Berlin airlift was still underway, a SAC emergency war plan was formally approved by the JCS calling for "the strategic air offensive" to be implemented "on a first-priority basis" in the event of hostilities. The plan made "the major Soviet urban industrial concentrations" the "highest priority target system": atomic attacks on seventy Soviet cities were planned to take place over an initial thirty-day period producing an estimated 6.7 million casualties. "Destruction of this system," the Joint Chiefs' evaluation of the war plan concluded, "should so cripple the Soviet industrial and control centers as to reduce drastically the offensive and defensive power of their armed forces." Yet, in case this initial air offensive did not end the war, SAC planned a prolonged atomic and conventional bombing campaign against petroleum refining targets in the USSR and Eastern Europe, as well as the Soviet hydroelectric system and inland transportation system.[22]

It is important to note, however, that SAC was not prepared to execute this war plan immediately if the Soviets had invaded Western Europe in the late 1940s, for while Truman had allowed military planning for the use of atomic bombs, he had resisted requests to turn actual possession of the weapons over to the military. Although the U.S. atomic stockpile and delivery capability were growing, U.S. military effectiveness was still extremely limited. Only fifty weapons were in possession of the Atomic Energy Commission (AEC) in July 1948. Each of them took approximately forty men more than two days to assemble once presidential authority was granted, and only around thirty SAC B-29s had been specially modified to carry the weapons.[23] Throughout 1948 and 1949, the Air Force lobbied for increased atomic weapons capabilities and direct military custody of the weapons themselves, but Truman refused to take steps that might compromise civilian control over the awesome new weapon. Under Truman's policy, therefore, SAC anticipated full use of its powerful arsenal in a global conflict, but the planned atomic attack against the USSR would not have been launched until six days after the war had started.[24]

In May 1949, a special high-level military evaluation of U.S. atomic war plans took place. The Harmon Committee report reached highly pessimistic conclusions: not only would the SAC atomic offensive fail to "bring about capitulation, destroy the roots of Communism or critically weaken the power of Soviet leadership to dominate the people," but the capability of Soviet forces to overrun Western Europe and the Middle East "would not be seriously impaired."[25] Civilian authorities did not disagree with this judgment and the National Security Council explicitly expressed concerns that atomic deterrence could fail in the future because of a Soviet "miscalculation of the determination and willingness of the United States to resort to force in order to prevent the development of a threat intolerable to U.S. security."[26] By mid-1949, the U.S. military had developed plans for a large-scale atomic strike against Soviet cities in the event of war, and yet neither civilian nor military leaders were confident that global war could either be prevented or won by the relatively small U.S. atomic arsenal. The U.S. nuclear monopoly had not produced great confidence in American security.

1949–1961: Massive Retaliation

Two events occurred between the summers of 1949 and 1950 that shaped U.S. nuclear strategy throughout the decade: the explosion of the first Soviet atomic bomb and the Truman Administration's decisions to expand the U.S. atomic stockpile and build the hydrogen bomb. The first event forced a major shift in U.S. targeting policy: the requirement for a prompt countermilitary mission against Soviet atomic weapons capability was added to SAC's prolonged city-busting strategy. In addition, as the Soviet nuclear stockpile and delivery capability grew in the late 1950s, the vulnerability of U.S. nuclear forces to a surprise Soviet nuclear attack became an increasingly serious problem. The second event, the decision to increase U.S. nuclear capabilities, was in large part determined by the perceived need for more weapons to cover more targets and to ensure that the Soviet Union did not race ahead in the nuclear competition. The resulting growth of the U.S. nuclear arsenal in the 1950s was massive: only an estimated 250 primitive atomic bombs existed in 1949; by 1960 the U.S. fielded approximately 18,000 atomic and thermonuclear weapons.[27]

The "Blunting" Mission

The Soviet A-bomb test in August 1949 produced two fundamental changes in U.S. nuclear strategy. First, the Soviet Union's atomic weapons, rather than the "war-making" potential of its industries, now posed the greatest threat to the United States. Second, the traditional assumption that the United States could permit an aggressor to decide when and where to start a war, and still have sufficient strength to recover and mobilize for eventual victory, was severely challenged. For example, a February 1950 JCS report, "Implications of Soviet Possession of Atomic Weapons," concluded that "the time is approaching when both the United States and the Soviets will possess capabilities for inflicting devastating atomic attacks on each other. *Were war to break out when this period is reached, a tremendous military advantage would be gained by the power that struck first and succeeded in carrying through an effective first strike.*"[28]

In its major review of U.S. national security policy in April 1950, the National Security Council rejected, on strategic and moral grounds, the idea of *preventive war*, that is, a war deliberately initiated by the United States before the

Soviet Union could become stronger. The critical document, NSC-68, was blunt on this issue:

> It is important that the United States employ military force only if the necessity for its use is clear and compelling and commends itself to the overwhelming majority of our people. The United States cannot therefore engage in war except as a reaction to aggression of so clear and compelling a nature as to bring the overwhelming majority of our people to accept the use of military force.

Furthermore, "It goes without saying that the idea of 'preventive' war—in the sense of a military attack not provoked by a military attack upon us or our allies—is generally unacceptable to Americans."[29] This did *not* mean, however, that the U.S. government had decided that the United States would permit the Soviet Union to strike first in a nuclear conflict. Indeed, NSC-68 explicitly accepted the idea of a U.S. *preemptive* attack, a "counter-attack to a blow which is on its way *or about to be delivered. . . .* The military advantages of landing the first blow become increasingly important with modern weapons, and this is a fact which requires us to be on the alert in order to strike with our full weight as soon as we are attacked, *and if possible before the Soviet blow is actually delivered.*"[30]

At the level of military planning, the JCS responded to the Soviet A-bomb by making Soviet nuclear capability the priority target in U.S. war plans. In August 1950, the JCS approved three objectives for war-planning purposes:

> BRAVO: the *blunting* of Soviet capability to deliver an atomic offensive against the United States and its allies;
> ROMEO: the *retardation* of Soviet advances into Western Eurasia;
> DELTA: the *disruption* of the vital elements of the Soviet war-making capacity.[31]

The critical importance given to the blunting mission against Soviet nuclear forces throughout the 1950s was by no means a secret. For example, in 1953, General LeMay told Congress that while SAC had been willing, before the

Soviet A-bomb test, to "go about leisurely destroying their war potential," now SAC had "to go back to the rulebook and the principles of war and fight the air battle first, which means that we must as quickly as possible destroy their capability of doing damage to us."[32] In 1954, Air Force Chief of Staff Gen. Nathan Twining also publicly stated that the Air Force can "now aim directly to disarm the enemy rather than to destroy him as was so often necessary in wars of the past."[33]

A strategy of "disarming" the enemy would be most effective, however, if the United States was striking first or preempting an imminent attack. Could SAC have executed such a strategy in the mid-1950s? Given the small size of the Soviet strategic arsenal, and its low readiness rate and high vulnerability, there was a strong possibility that a surprise American preventive strike would have been successful in the early-to-mid 1950s. Indeed, LeMay now maintains that "there was a time in the 1950s when we could have won a war against Russia . . . [that] would have cost us essentially the accident rate of the flying time."[34] Such an attack would have been most effective, of course, if the United States struck first against an unalerted Soviet adversary. Did American political and military leaders seriously contemplate such a bolt-out-of-the-blue attack?

In the first year of the Eisenhower Administration, there were, in fact, numerous examinations of the preventive war option, and in May 1954 the President was briefed on a Joint Chiefs of Staff Advance Study Group report that specifically recommended that the United States consider "deliberately precipitating a war with the U.S.S.R. in the near future," before the Soviet nuclear forces became "a real menace" to U.S. security.[35] Senior military advisers were not, however, uniformly supportive of such considerations. Army Chief of Staff Matthew Ridgway argued to Eisenhower, for example, that deliberately precipitating a war with the Soviet Union would be "contrary to every principle upon which our Nation had been founded" and "abhorrent to the great mass of American people."[36] In

December 1954, the National Security Council finally rejected, as a policy option, "the concept of preventive war or acts intended to provoke war."[37]

Preemption, however, was clearly not ruled out. If warning that a war was imminent existed in a crisis or if actual combat broke out, Eisenhower was apparently quite certain about the appropriate response. At a December 1954 meeting, the President "expressed his firm intention to launch a strategic attack *in case of alert of actual attack*," adding that a "major war will be an atom war."[38] A March 1955 National Security Council report listed a number of specific tactical warning indicators that would, it was maintained, provide "clear evidence that Soviet attack upon the continental U.S. is certain or imminent": the penetration of the U.S. air warning system by Soviet aircraft in hostile flight patterns; a Soviet attack against U.S. overseas territories, military bases, or NATO allies; the concentration of Soviet submarines "in a position and in sufficient numbers to permit effective attacks on major U.S. ports"; or the laying of Soviet minefields near U.S. ports or continental shipping routes.[39] Throughout the 1950s, Eisenhower repeatedly emphasized the need for immediate U.S. action under extreme emergency conditions. Strategic Air Command bombers would be launched, he told the JCS in March 1956, "as soon as he found out that Russian troops were on the move."[40] SAC must understand, the President repeated in November 1957, that "we must not allow the enemy to strike the first blow."[41] Eisenhower apparently maintained this position until he left office, telling a State Department official in late 1960 that he could not "see any chance of keeping any war in Europe from not becoming a general war," and that "for this reason he thought we must be ready to throw the book at the Russians should they jump us."[42]

"To Retaliate Instantly"

Publicly, the Eisenhower Administration's strategy became known as the "massive retaliation" doctrine. President Eisenhower and Secretary of State John Foster Dulles, convinced that their threat to use atomic weapons in Korea had ended the stalemate there, believed future conventional wars could also be deterred by the threat of rapid escalation. As Dulles argued in a speech at the Council on Foreign Relations in January 1954, nuclear weapons offered "more security at less cost," and the best way to deter aggression, was "to depend primarily upon a great capacity to retaliate instantly by means and at places of our own choosing."[43] Eisenhower privately was more blunt in his description of massive retaliation, telling a congressional delegation in late 1954 that the basic idea of the strategy was "to blow the hell out of them in a hurry if they start anything."[44]

By the mid-1950s, the rapid growth in the U.S. nuclear arsenal and delivery capabilities permitted SAC to build a war plan that targeted both Soviet nuclear forces and industry in a massive fashion. In 1955, SAC's BRAVO mission included attacks on 645 Soviet bloc airfields, with twenty-five weapons aimed to destroy Soviet atomic energy installations. Under the DELTA mission against urban-industrial targets, SAC planned attacks on 118 of the 134 major cities in the Soviet Union. Overall "Sino-Soviet bloc" casualties were expected to be seventy-seven million, of which approximately sixty million would be fatalities. "Such casualties, coupled with the other effects of the atomic offensives, may have an important bearing on the will of the Soviets to continue to wage war," the JCS were coolly informed in April 1955. In the 118 major Soviet cities, fatalities were estimated to range from 75 to 84 percent. Given such high levels of fatalities in urban areas, it was reported that "industries located in such heavily damaged cities are assumed to have no production or recuperative capability during the period D to D + 6 months [D-Day plus six months] regardless of what plant capacity survives." The ROMEO mission against the Red Army in Europe received the lowest priority in terms of weapons allocated, and it was estimated that such attacks could not prevent the Soviet Union from overrunning Western defenses.[45]

SAC's capability to strike rapidly—preempting Soviet nuclear attacks against the United States and Western Europe—was absolutely critical to the success of the plan. Air Force Intelligence maintained that the Soviet Union could launch sufficient one-way long-range aircraft on missions to deliver its entire estimated arsenal of 284 atomic weapons against the United States. Therefore, as SAC war planners noted, "The factor of timing is of vital importance in the blunting mission. . . . [I]f the Soviets launch such a strike before our offensive is begun, or before our bombs fall on targets, the U.S. offensive may not materially reduce the Soviet atomic capabilities."[46] Privately, General LeMay was adamant on the need for preemption: "I want to make it clear that I am not advocating a preventive war," he told a top secret military planning group in March 1954; "however, I believe that if the United States is pushed in the corner far enough we would not hesitate to strike first."[47] Gen. Thomas White was only slightly less direct in his public testimony to Congress in February 1959: "the first priority" if the United States took the initiative after receiving "tactical or strategic warning" would be to "destroy the enemy's capability to destroy us."[48]

SIOP-62

The Eisenhower Administration, in its final years, presided over a major effort to restructure the massive retaliation war plan. Prior to 1960, each U.S. Commander in Chief (CINC) of a unified or specified command had in essence prepared his own nuclear war plan, and the Administration sought to rationalize the highly redundant targeting under the newly created Joint Strategic Target Planning Staff (JSTPS).[49] The first *national* nuclear war plan, SIOP-62 (Single Integrated Operational Plan), was produced by the JSTPS in 1960 and 1961, under civilian guidance, to cover the "optimum mix" of military and urban-industrial targets in the Sino-Soviet bloc. When the war plan was finally completed, however, its rigid over-kill proportions, Eisenhower admitted to an aide, "frighten[ed] the devil out of me."[50]

A recently declassified military briefing for President Kennedy fully reveals the stunning inflexibility of SIOP-62.[51] The plan permitted retaliation if necessary and preemption if possible, but both on an utterly massive scale. If the United States was attacked or war appeared imminent, the President would have, ostensibly, fourteen "options." Each so-called option, however, simply pro-vided for alerting more U.S. nuclear missiles and bombers and then launching *all* available forces against *every nation* in the Sino-Soviet bloc. If sufficient strategic warning ex-isted to alert all U.S. forces, and a decision was reached to preempt or retaliate before Soviet forces reached the United States, the entire force of 3,267 nuclear weapons would be launched against the Soviet Union and the Peo-ple's Republic of China, plus the satellite nations of East-ern Europe, North Korea, and North Vietnam. The first SIOP maintained no readily available reserve forces, and had no provision for completely avoiding attacks on any individual enemy nation. Although only approximately 15 to 20 percent of the DGZs (Designated Ground Zeros) in SIOP-62 were urban-industrial targets, such nuclear at-tacks, coupled with the significant collocation of military targets and population centers, ensured that Communist bloc casualties would have been horrendous beyond his-torical precedent.

It is critical to note, however, that despite the lopsided nuclear balance at the time (see fig. 1-1), the Joint Chiefs of Staff could not be confident that SIOP-62 forces would completely protect the United States from a Soviet attack if deterrence failed. Not only might the Soviets launch their nuclear bombers and missiles against the United States first, but even if the United States preempted a So-viet attack, the size and unknown location of some Soviet nuclear forces prevented the American military from being certain that the entire Soviet nuclear arsenal would be destroyed. "Under any circumstances—even a preemptive attack by the U.S.—it would be expected that some portion of the Soviet long-range nuclear force would strike the United States," the Chairman of the Joint Chiefs of Staff appropriately warned the President in September 1961. He did not, however, provide the President with estimates of U.S. casualties under the different scenarios for a nuclear exchange, but only noted that "clearly the most important factor affecting damage to the U.S. is that of whether the U.S. acts in retaliation or preemption."[52]

Nevertheless, President Kennedy was also informed that execution of SIOP-62 "should permit the United States to prevail in [the] event of general nuclear war."[53] What did the Joint Chiefs mean by this? The available evidence suggests that this judgment was based upon a very narrow military perspective: to prevail meant to be able to carry out U.S. war plans successfully. The military planners had been ordered to construct plans that would give the United States a 75-percent probability of delivering a weapon on each Soviet target in order to "destroy or neutralize" Soviet nuclear delivery capability as well as urban-industrial centers. These war objectives could be met regardless of who struck first. Therefore, in this narrow military sense, the JCS believed that the United States would prevail in any nuclear war against the Soviet Union.[54]

1961–1974: Assured Destruction and Damage Limitation

Fundamental problems with the Eisenhower Administration's nuclear strategy were made apparent to President John F. Kennedy within his first year in office. In July 1961, when the Berlin crisis forced a high-level review of U.S. nuclear options in the event of war, McGeorge Bundy, the Special Assistant for National Security Affairs, reported to Kennedy that "in essence, the current plan [SIOP-62] calls for shooting off everything we have in one

FIGURE 1-1
The U.S. and USSR Nuclear Balance, 1961

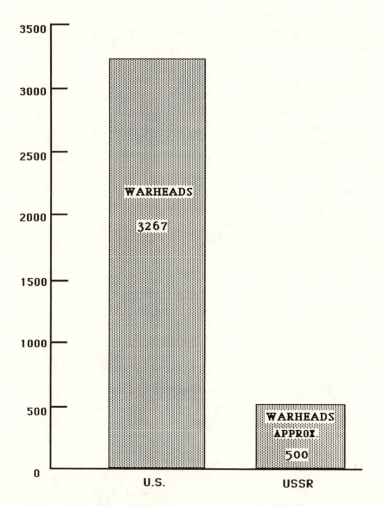

Source: Derived from "SIOP-62: The Nuclear War Plan Briefing to President Kennedy," Scott D. Sagan, *International Security*, vol. 12, no. 1, Summer 1987, pp. 23–29.

shot, and is so constructed as to make any more flexible course very difficult."[55] At the height of the crisis, when Kennedy was briefed on SIOP-62 by the Chairman of the Joint Chiefs, according to a witness he "emerged thoroughly persuaded that there was insufficient capability for the President to exercise discrimination and control should nuclear conflict come."[56]

In early 1961, Secretary of Defense Robert McNamara requested that the JCS assess the feasibility of building controlled responses and negotiating pauses into the war plan. McNamara's objectives were made clear in a memorandum drafted for the President that September. In this document, McNamara explicitly rejected "minimum deterrence," a posture in which, "after a Soviet attack, we would have a capability to retaliate, and with a high degree of assurance be able to destroy most of Soviet urban society, but in which we would not have a capability to counter-attack against Soviet military forces." Minimum deterrence should be rejected, McNamara recommended, for two basic reasons:

> Deterrence may fail, or war may break out for accidental or unintended reasons, and if it does, a capability to counter-attack against high-priority Soviet military targets can make a major contribution to the objectives of limiting damage and terminating the war on acceptable terms;
> By reducing to a minimum the possibility of a U.S. nuclear attack in response to Soviet aggression against our Allies, a "minimum deterrence" posture would weaken our ability to deter such Soviet attacks.[57]

At the same time, however, McNamara also rejected the opposite extreme, the Air Force's preferred posture of a "full first-strike capability" that would enable the United States "to attack and reduce Soviet retaliatory power to the point at which it could not cause severe damage to U.S. population and industry." There were three arguments against U.S. acquisition of such a "full first-strike capability," McNamara wrote: it was extremely costly; U.S. efforts to achieve it would risk "the provocation of an arms race"; and it was "almost certainly infeasible" since the Soviets could counter it by deploying invulnerable submarines and hardened ICBMs. McNamara's alternative was to plan to attack only Soviet military targets in any initial strike, but to maintain a capability to destroy Soviet cities if necessary. Thus, the memorandum reported:

> The forces I am recommending have been chosen to provide the United States with the capability, in the event of a Soviet nuclear attack, first to strike back against Soviet bomber bases, missile sites, and other installations associated with long-range nuclear forces, in order to reduce Soviet power and limit the damage that can be done to us by vulnerable Soviet follow-on forces, while, second, holding protected reserve forces capable of destroying the Soviet urban society, if necessary, in a controlled and deliberate way.[58]

McNamara, therefore, rejected Air Force requests for more bombers, but recommended the initial acquisition of more ICBMs and SLBMs (submarine-launched ballistic missiles). Although vulnerable bombers could *not* be "held in reserve to be used in a controlled and deliberate way," McNamara noted that "Polaris is ideal for counter-city retaliation." Moreover, the speed of the missile force was very advantageous for the counterforce mission: "In the case of the military targets, the missiles reach their targets much faster than do bombers, and therefore would be more effective in catching enemy bombers and missiles on the ground."[59]

Guidance drafted by McNamara's assistants in 1961 was used by the JSTPS to build a new nuclear war plan, SIOP-63, which separated the "optimum mix" into three target sets—(1) nuclear-threat targets, (2) other military targets, and (3) urban-industrial targets—and provided new options, including the capability to withhold direct attack against urban industrial targets and withhold nuclear attacks against any individual country.[60] The counterforce and countermilitary options in SIOP-63, however, required the use of massive numbers of nuclear weapons, and civilian damage would have been enormous, even without direct attacks on urban-industrial targets.[61] Finally, McNamara explicitly maintained the option of launching the whole SIOP "to strike back decisively at the entire Soviet target system simultaneously."[62]

Counterforce and Countercity Targeting

The outlines of this new strategy were made public by McNamara in his address at the University of Michigan commencement in June 1962 in Ann Arbor:

> The U.S. has come to the conclusion that to the extent feasible, basic military strategy in a possible general nuclear war should be approached in much the same way that more conventional military operations have been regarded in the past. That is to say, principal military objectives, in the event of nuclear war stemming from a major attack on the Alliance, should be the destruction of the enemy's military forces, not his civilian population.[63]

The new McNamara nuclear doctrine became known as the "no-cities" strategy, a misleading term since the strategy explicitly included the option of attacking the urban-industrial centers of the Soviet Union if U.S. cities were attacked. In addition, despite the Administration's public emphasis on its "second-strike" policy, the new SIOP did not eliminate the option to strike first or preempt. The U.S. counterforce capability "would be used," the JCS reported to McNamara in late 1963, "in case of pre-emption, to provide a first strike option of reasonable size against the Soviet military targets," and SIOP-63 included counter-military options specifically designed for a preemptive response.[64] Although McNamara reported to President Kennedy in 1962 that he believed the U.S. "would not be able to achieve tactical surprise, especially in the kinds of crisis circumstances in which a first strike capability might be relevant,"[65] the senior members of the

Administration were undoubtedly aware that the Soviet Union remained very vulnerable to a U.S. first strike. Indeed, despite the changes in the nuclear war plan, the Kennedy Administration was not unwilling to emphasize American nuclear superiority and the fear of a massive U.S. first strike for coercive political purposes. During the Cuban Missile Crisis in October 1962, for example, Kennedy publicly threatened a "full retaliatory response" against the USSR if a single missile was launched from Cuba against any country in the Western Hemisphere.[66]

Given both the great numerical inferiority of Soviet nuclear forces, and their extraordinary low state of day-to-day readiness (neither Soviet bombers nor ICBMs were kept on day-to-day alert in the early 1960s),[67] under many scenarios an American counterforce strike would have significantly limited damage to the United States in the early 1960s. Even if the United States refrained from preempting a Soviet attack, counterforce retaliation might still destroy many Soviet nonalert, follow-on, or reserve nuclear forces. This was especially the case with respect to the Soviet long-range bomber force, which, in the early 1960s, held the largest number of Soviet nuclear weapons then believed capable of reaching the United States. U.S. prompt counterforce threats against Soviet bomber bases would be highly effective, since to mount a bomber attack against the United States, as McNamara explained to Congress in early 1963, the Soviets would first be required either to deploy their bomber force to their Arctic air bases or stage them through those bases in successive waves. "Such action," the Secretary of Defense reported, "would greatly jeopardize their chance of surprising us and, equally important, their bombers would become vulnerable to our missile attack during the staging operation."[68]

The available evidence is clear, however, that McNamara remained opposed to the development of a "full first-strike capability" and did not believe the United States had such a capability in the early 1960s. As early as December 1963, McNamara argued that a disarming first-strike capability was not only extremely expensive and probably infeasible, but that excessive U.S. counterforce might actually be detrimental to U.S. security. If the United States had such a "full first-strike capability," *crisis stability* might be undermined, it was argued, since the Soviets might then be more likely to launch first in a tense crisis out of fear that a disarming American attack was imminent. As McNamara wrote in his December 1963 top secret Draft Presidential Memorandum to President Johnson, decreased Soviet vulnerability to an American counterforce attack "may be desirable from the point of view of creating a more stable posture, reducing their incentive . . . to make a preemptive strike against us."[69] With respect to the U.S. inability to disarm the USSR in a first strike, McNamara's position was clear in his classified testimony to Congress in February 1962: "Even if we attempted to destroy the enemy nuclear strike capability at its source, using all available resources, some portion of the Soviet force would strike back."[70]

Nevertheless, McNamara maintained in his 1963 memorandum for the President, counterforce strikes, under any condition of war initiation, "might help to limit the damage to the United States by destroying some of the Soviet nuclear delivery systems, and by disrupting the coordination of the rest, thereby easing the task for our defensive forces."[71] Even without a disarming first-strike capability, initial counterforce strikes were useful, as McNamara put it, "to make the best of a bad situation": the goal of such an attack would be "to knock out most of the Soviet strategic nuclear forces, while keeping Russian cities intact, and then coercing the Soviets into avoiding attacks on our cities (by the threat of controlled reprisal) and accepting peace terms."[72]

At the same time that McNamara insisted on the utility of counterforce, he also developed specific Assured Destruction criteria to help measure the adequacy of planned strategic forces: the official *minimum* requirements during the 1960s ranged from the capability to destroy 20 to 30 percent of the USSR's population and also 50 to 66 percent of its industrial capability.[73] These specific criteria were not based on thorough studies of the Soviet leadership's values or the Soviet military's war plans. Instead, the Assured Destruction criteria represented the "flat of the curve" on the nuclear damage charts at the Pentagon: for every marginal increase in destructive capability after that point, increasingly larger and more expensive U.S. nuclear forces would be required. If all U.S. nuclear forces remaining after a Soviet first strike were targeted against Soviet urban-industrial areas, which McNamara argued the Soviets would have to postulate under conservative worst-case planning assumptions, the Assured Destruction criteria could easily be met by projected U.S. nuclear forces. Throughout the mid-1960s, McNamara utilized such arguments in his efforts to fend off congressional and Air Force requests for further offensive forces: after a certain point, extra missiles would add so marginally to U.S. Assured Destruction capabilities, he argued, that their cost could not be justified.

What was the "operational" significance of the Assured Destruction criteria? Certainly, as has been demonstrated, under the Damage Limitation strategy not *all* U.S. nuclear forces would be used against Soviet cities. Unless responding in kind to a Soviet attack on U.S. cities, *initial* attacks would be designed to destroy counterforce targets, with *withheld* forces used to threaten Soviet urban-industrial society. Although the specific guidance given to the war planners is not available, it is important to note that the numbers of nuclear weapons expected to be assigned to this withheld countercity reserve force (what could be called the Assured Destruction force) were planned to be sufficient to achieve the overall Assured Destruction criteria. McNamara's December 1963 Draft Presidential Memorandum provides the best evidence. The specific Assured Destruction criterion given in DPM-63 was "30% of their population, 50% of their industrial capacity, and 150 of their cities."[74] Each year, McNamara provided a "projected

Soviet-Bloc target list," which he described as "an approximate expression" of how projected U.S. forces "might be allocated to targets."[75] The 1963 DPM projected target list (see table 1-1) for fiscal year 1969 had 533 U.S. missiles (332 Polaris, 75 Minuteman, 54 Titan, and 72 Atlas missiles) capable of being withheld in initial attacks and specifically targeted against 150 Soviet "Urban Industry and Government Control" targets. Use of these forces in a retaliatory strike was expected to result in destruction of 60 percent of Soviet industrial capability and fifty million prompt urban fatalities.[76]

The full projected assignment of U.S. nuclear forces against Soviet targets under the McNamara strategy can be seen in this Soviet bloc target list. In this war plan projection, approximately 16 percent of the U.S. nuclear weapons available would have been targeted directly at Soviet urban-industrial areas. In contrast almost 50 percent of the weapons were assigned to Soviet strategic nuclear targets.

Disillusion with Damage Limitation

Even in the late 1960s, by which time Assured Destruction criteria were widely used in declaratory policy and in bureaucratic battles over the nuclear forces budget, U.S. nuclear *employment* policy maintained a heavy emphasis on counterforce for initial attacks on the Soviet Union, with capabilities for urban-industrial destruction to be held in reserve. "Our Assured Destruction capability does not indicate how we would use our forces in a nuclear war," the January 1968 Draft Presidential Memorandum stated. "If we failed to deter nuclear war, we would want to be able to follow a policy of limiting our retaliatory strikes to the enemy's military targets and not attacking his cities if he refrained from attacking ours."[77] Yet, although such counterforce nuclear options were maintained throughout the 1960s, the ability to limit damage through offensive strikes declined significantly as the rapid growth in the numbers and survivability of the Soviet ICBM and SLBM force made

TABLE 1-1
Soviet Bloc Target List
(Projected for FY 1969)

Targets	No. of Targets	ICBMs & SLBMs	Air-to-Surface Missiles[a]	Gravity Bombs[a]
		Weapons Assigned		
Urban Industry & govt. controls	150	533		
Satellites	65	27[b]		
Strategic Nuclear				
Bomber bases	210	309		
ICBM soft	122	179		
ICBM hard	100	147		200
IR/MRBM	125	184		
IR/MRBM-hard	113	166		226
Sub bases	35	51		35
Offensive control	45	66		
Defensive and Other Military				
Air defense fields	115	96	65	
Unco-located SAMs	140		280	
Aircraft disp. bases	110			220
Strat./tac. wpns. storage	240			249
Other mil./ interdiction	220			220
Total	1,790	1,758	345	1,150

Source: Draft Memorandum for the President, Recommended FY 1965–1969 Strategic Retaliatory Forces, December 6, 1963, p. I–37 (McNamara Recommended Forces), OSD-FOI.

[a] The air-to-surface missiles and gravity bombs are associated with the alert bomber force only.

[b] These forces could possibly be augmented by missiles in an emergency combat condition, part of the alert bomber force, and the bomber positive control backup force.

the Soviets far less vulnerable to U.S. attack. Moreover, U.S. counterforce options remained extremely large. After the initial efforts to add more flexibility to the war plan, McNamara did not instruct the war planners to build more limited options into the SIOP. Saving his political capital for other fights with the JCS, he gave up on preplanned small options, hoping that such nuclear plans could be prepared, if necessary, in the course of a crisis or war.[78]

McNamara went through a similar disenchantment in the 1960s with the prospect of strategic defense against nuclear attack. In his first years in office, he was a strong advocate of improved American defenses: civil defense fallout shelters, continental air defense against Soviet bombers, and ballistic missile defense. Although there was no expectation that such programs would provide an impenetrable "shield," defenses were a critical component of the original Damage Limitation strategy. "Under any circumstances, even if we had the military advantage of striking first, the price of any nuclear war would be terribly high," McNamara acknowledged in an interview with Stewart Alsop in late 1962. Yet he also argued in the same interview that "you have to recognize that there is a tremendous difference, a vital difference, between say, thirty percent fatalities and sixty percent," adding that "a serious national fallout shelter program could make that sort of difference."[79] Spending on civil defense, however, became increasingly politically unattractive in the 1960s as Congress deeply cut Administration requests. The strategic significance of continental air defense also decreased rapidly as the Soviet Union placed its major emphasis on land-based ICBMs. As McNamara noted in 1968, "Even a very strong air defense could not save many lives. . . . [because] the Soviets could simply target cities with their missiles."[80] Finally, despite keen initial interest in the Army's Nike-Zeus anti-ballistic missile system, McNamara soon determined that cost-effective Soviet countermeasures could be easily developed to overcome U.S. defenses. By 1967, the American ABM effort was being justified solely as a potential defense against a future Chinese nuclear threat, not against an overwhelming Soviet attack.

By the end of the decade, official views on the prospects for limiting damage in a nuclear exchange were bluntly pessimistic: "Achieving a significant Damage Limiting capability against the Soviet Union," the Secretary of Defense's January 1969 DPM stated, "does not appear to be feasible with current technology."[81] The Soviet nuclear arsenal was still considerably smaller than the U.S. arsenal (see fig. 1-2). But, for the foreseeable future, it was expected that each side could retain the capability for massive destruction against the other even in a retaliatory second strike.

Flexible Response in NATO

The other major area of change in nuclear strategy under McNamara was in NATO. Under the Eisenhower Administration's Massive Retaliation doctrine, the United States threatened an immediate and massive nuclear response to a Warsaw Pact conventional attack on Western Europe. This strategy, however, came under increasing criticism during the late 1950s and early 1960s as many European and American analysts expressed deep skepticism over the credibility of the U.S. commitment to Europe. McNamara's proposal for a Flexible Response doctrine in NATO explicitly maintained the U.S. commitment to use nuclear weapons first if NATO's conventional defense faltered. "The United States is prepared to respond immediately with nuclear weapons to the use of nuclear weapons against one or more members of the Alliance," McNamara told the NATO defense ministers in a restricted session in May 1962. Furthermore, he added, "the United States is also prepared to counter with nuclear weapons any Soviet conventional attack so strong that it cannot be dealt with by conventional means."[82]

Flexible Response did, however, call for two important changes in NATO nuclear doctrine. First, nuclear escala-

FIGURE 1-2
The U.S. and USSR Nuclear Balance, 1968

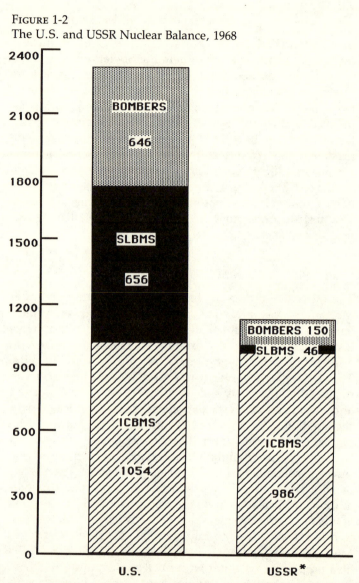

Source: Melvin Laird's statement before the House Armed Services Committee, *Department of Defense Authorization for FY 1971*, March 2, 1970, OSD-FOI, National Security Archives, Washington, D.C.

* Soviet SLBMs include nuclear-powered submarines only.

tion was to come as late as possible, only after considerable efforts at conventional defense had failed. Second, the planned nuclear response at the tactical level would be far more limited in nature than had been planned under Massive Retaliation. Throughout the 1960s, McNamara called for improved NATO conventional capabilities and conventional war plans to enable the alliance to forgo nuclear escalation against all but the most massive Soviet attack. Pentagon studies of the period convinced the Secretary of Defense that NATO conventional forces would be adequate to defend Western Europe against most plausible Warsaw Pact attacks. McNamara acknowledged in a January 1964 memorandum that "despite my confidence in the feasibility and desirability of a major nonnuclear option, we cannot exclude the possibility that, under heavy pressure, NATO's nonnuclear defenses might begin to crumble."[83] The American first-use commitment could not, therefore, be abandoned. Although the United States was able to get formal NATO endorsement of Flexible Response in 1967, after the French had pulled out of the alliance's military organization, NATO's conventional strength in the 1960s was not sufficient to quell allied concerns about the need for a nuclear first-use threat. In short, Flexible Response was officially adopted, but doubt about the U.S. commitment to initiate the use of nuclear weapons remained a serious problem.

1974–1980: LIMITED NUCLEAR OPTIONS AND COUNTER-RECOVERY TARGETING

Just as the Kennedy Administration had rapidly revised its predecessors' nuclear policy in 1961, the Nixon Administration came into office determined to resolve what it saw as three related, fundamental problems in the existing U.S. nuclear strategy. The first was the continuing problem of the credibility of extended deterrence in Europe. Although Secretary McNamara had consistently maintained in public that the United States remained committed to use nuclear forces first to defend NATO, if necessary, under the Flexible Response doctrine, lingering doubts had been raised by his repeated emphasis on Mutual Assured Destruction as the likely outcome of any nuclear war. (Indeed, these doubts may not have been unfounded. McNamara now states that "at that time, in long private conversations with successive Presidents—Kennedy and Johnson—I recommended, without qualification, that they never initiate, under any circumstances, the use of nuclear weapons. I believe they accepted my recommendation.")[84] There was, in essence, a deep underlying tension between McNamara's statements on mutual nuclear deterrence and NATO military doctrine. As Henry Kissinger, Nixon's national security adviser, queried: "How could the United States hold its allies together as the credibility of its strategy eroded? How would we deal with Soviet conventional forces once the Soviets believed that we meant what we said about basing strategy on the extermination of civilians?"[85]

A second, and related, problem remained. How should the United States respond if directly attacked by the Soviet Union? President Nixon emphasized the dilemma in his 1970 Report to Congress: "Should a President in the event of a nuclear attack be left with the single option of ordering the mass destruction of enemy civilians, in the face of the certainty that it would be followed by the mass slaughter of Americans?"[86]

This question was partly caricature, for virtually no one supported restricting the President to the "single option" of massive destruction, and—as has been shown—McNamara had already added the SIOP option, under the "no-cities" doctrine, of attacking Soviet nuclear forces promptly while withholding attacks on urban-industrial targets. Yet Nixon's statement was not entirely spurious, for, given the size of both the Soviet and American arsenals by the 1970s, the U.S. counterforce option was massive. Indeed, because there were no options in the McNamara SIOPs that were designed as responses below the level of a major counterforce attack, a number of questions about what to do if deterrence failed remained unanswered.[87] If the Soviets attacked in a limited nuclear strike, how should the United States respond? In the event that conventional defense failed in a war in Europe, and escalation moved beyond the use of tactical nuclear weapons, how should U.S. strategic forces be used?

The third major problem in nuclear strategy confronting the Nixon Administration was the danger that the Soviet Union might eventually build such a potent combination of offensive forces and strategic defenses that U.S. Assured Destruction capabilities would be threatened. McNamara had not originally foreseen such a possibility. Indeed, he publicly announced in 1965: "The Soviets have decided that they have lost the quantitative [arms] race and they are not seeking to engage us in that contest. . . . There is no indication that the Soviets are seeking to develop a strategic nuclear force as large as ours."[88]

It was apparent to most observers by 1969 that McNamara had been wrong. The Soviet ICBM arsenal had rapidly expanded in the late 1960s, surpassing that of the United States in numbers of launchers (though not in total warheads) by the time Nixon came into office. In addition, an anti-ballistic missile complex was being constructed around Moscow. The Soviets had clearly not settled for inferiority and the new administration was concerned that they would not settle for strategic parity either. Improvements in the U.S. offensive and defensive forces were now considered critical; as Henry Kissinger put it, "The USSR would accept a stabilization of the arms race only if convinced it would not be allowed to achieve superiority."[89]

To counter these Soviet programs, the Nixon Administration pursued a dual track of force modernization and arms control. Most significant, it continued the major program, begun in the Johnson Administration, to add MIRVs (Multiple Independently targetable Reentry Vehicles) to a large portion of the ICBM and SLBM force and pushed the Safeguard ABM Program, a defense of ICBM sites, through Congress. Finally, in May 1972, Nixon reached a major arms control agreement with the Soviets: under the ABM and SALT (Strategic Arms Limitation Talks) I Interim Agreement on offensive arms, both sides agreed to limit their ABM systems to two sites of one hundred launchers each and froze the number of ICBM and SLBM launchers in both arsenals. The Nixon Administration believed that such an agreement was very much in the United States' interest, since there was little domestic support for an ABM buildup, and therefore was willing to limit U.S. defenses in exchange for restrictions on Soviet offenses and defenses. Thus, by 1972, the emerging threat to the overall American deterrent capability was considered to be relatively contained.

The Schlesinger Doctrine

Early in his tenure in office, President Nixon requested that the Defense Department examine alternative targeting policies and, four years later, after a prolonged Defense Department and interagency study process, National Security Decision Memorandum (NSDM) -242 was signed. The new nuclear doctrine—publicly presented by Secretary of Defense James Schlesinger and soon known as the Schlesinger Doctrine—had two major components. The first was the effort to provide more credible deterrence and escalation control through the development of a wider array of planned limited nuclear options. Schlesinger acknowledged in his public presentations that several response options had existed since the early 1960s, but emphasized that the "limited" nature of such options was more apparent than real:

> In the past, we have had massive preplanned nuclear strikes in which one would be dumping *literally thousands of weapons on the Soviet Union*. Some of these strikes could, to some extent, be withheld from going directly against cities, but that was limited even then.

With massive strikes of that sort, it would be impossible to ascertain whether the purpose of a strategic strike was limited or not. *It was virtually indistinguishable from an attack on cities.* One would not have had blast damage in the cities, but one would have considerable fallout and the rest of it.

So what the change in targeting does is give the President of the United States, whoever he may be, the option of limiting strikes down *to a few weapons.*[90]

Schlesinger's public defense of limited nuclear options emphasized the twin purposes of the new strategy: to enhance the credibility of the NATO threat to use nuclear weapons first, if conventional defense failed, and to provide appropriate responses to limited Soviet nuclear attacks against the United States or NATO allies. Although European governments remained concerned about the reliability of the American nuclear guarantee to NATO, they were generally receptive to the Schlesinger Doctrine. In the United States, however, there were numerous strategic analysts and members of Congress who argued that the development of limited nuclear options was destabilizing, increasing the likelihood of nuclear war.[91] To the degree that such critics were narrowly focused on an American strategic nuclear *response* to a Soviet conventional invasion of Western Europe, they were right: it was precisely because limited options were more likely to be used that the credibility of the American extended deterrent threat was considered to be improved. Schlesinger emphasized precisely this point in an interview on BBC radio in October 1974: "The recognition that a high level of conventional conflict may elicit a nuclear response, be it tactical, or be it strategic, is, I think, a major contributor to the deterrent." Therefore, he insisted, U.S. strategic nuclear forces are "certainly still coupled to the security of Western Europe; that is a major reason behind the change in our targeting doctrine during this last year."[92]

Schlesinger strongly disagreed, however, with the criticism that limited counterforce options were destabilizing because they might increase American or Soviet incentives to launch a *full-scale* nuclear attack. Limited counterforce or countermilitary options could not, Schlesinger maintained, significantly limit damage to the United States. "There is simply no possibility of reducing civilian damage from a large-scale nuclear exchange sufficiently to make it a tempting prospect for any sane leader," he insisted to Congress in 1974. Limited options might, however, make Soviet conventional aggression less likely and prevent an adversary from "exercising any form of nuclear pressure."[93]

The second major component of the Schlesinger doctrine—the new guidance for the Assured Destruction mission emphasizing the destruction of Soviet *economic recovery capabilities*—received far less public attention than did the limited nuclear options policy. Schlesinger consistently maintained that the ability to destroy urban-industrial targets was indispensable. In the 1975 Defense Department annual report, for example, he noted that "even after a more brilliantly executed and devastating attack than we believe our potential adversaries could deliver, the United States could retain the capacity to kill more than 30 percent of the Soviet population and destroy more than 75 percent of Soviet industry."[94] Evidence that there was new guidance for this Assured Destruction mission, however, was not publicly presented until Schlesinger's successor, Donald Rumsfeld, entered office. Under the new rubric of "assured retaliation," Rumsfeld rejected the approach that would "simply target major cities" in favor of one that emphasized the ability to destroy the Soviet Union's capacity "to recover politically and economically" from a nuclear exchange:

> If the Soviet Union could emerge from such an exchange with superior military power, and could recuperate from the effects more rapidly than the United States, the U.S. capacity for assured retaliation would be considered inadequate. . . . [A]n important objective of the assured retaliation mission should

be to retard significantly the ability of the USSR to recover from a nuclear exchange and regain the status of a 20th-century military and industrial power more rapidly than the United States.[95]

Under this "counter-recovery" strategy, NSDM-242 provided guidance to military planners mandating the capability to destroy 70 percent of the Soviet industry that would be needed to achieve economic recovery after a nuclear exchange.[96] For the next six years the counter-recovery mission was the highest priority for the war planners: according to Air Force testimony to Congress, the counter-recovery mission was "the most specific task outlined in the national guidance," which had to be met "under all conditions." In contrast, with respect to the counterforce mission, the Air Force testified that "to the extent we can, we are supposed . . . to attack his forces which threaten us."[97]

Why was this guidance developed and what were the results of this "counter-recovery" emphasis? The authors of NSDM-242 did not anticipate that the new definition of the Assured Destruction mission would significantly alter the SIOP. McNamara's guidance throughout the 1960s, after all, had similarly placed highest priority on the destruction of urban-industrial targets in the Soviet Union.[98] But destroying 66 percent of the Soviet industrial capability, which was McNamara's definition of Assured Destruction, required relatively few weapons. (Original Pentagon estimates of expected destruction of Soviet industry were calculated using a combined index of war support industries and gross industrial product. Because war support industries were very concentrated geographically, a relatively small number of weapons produced a very high damage estimate.)[99] The NSDM-242 guidance was meant simply to rationalize—that is, to add some political purpose—to the Assured Destruction component of the force. The results, however, were not as expected.

This priority counterindustrial recovery strategy produced a huge analytic effort to understand Soviet economic recovery capabilities after a nuclear war.[100] The resulting studies showed that significantly larger numbers of weapons were required to achieve the counter-recovery objective. Moreover, although the United States had officially abstained from targeting "population per se" since 1973, the pristine econometric models of the Soviet economy that were developed for targeting purposes belied the gruesome nature of the counter-recovery strategy. To give the most dramatic example, fertilizer factories were widely reported to be one of the industrial targets to be destroyed to impede economic recovery. Plans to attack such factories may not have been targeting the Soviet population per se, but since the purpose was to destroy the Soviet postwar food supply, in reality the population was being targeted indirectly.

An abbreviated list of the kinds of economic targets, as well as military targets, that were included in the SIOP under NSDM-242 guidance was released by the Defense Department in March 1980, and is presented in table 1-2. Because the actual plans remain classified, an estimate of the precise emphasis placed on the economic recovery mission is not available. Yet, in open congressional testimony, Under Secretary of Defense William Perry testified that "a significant portion of the forces . . . are dedicated to being able to accomplish that mission."[101]

The general scope, though not the precise degree, of the counter-recovery emphasis can be seen in the targeting assumptions used in official government studies of the period. For example, table 1-3 presents the targeting assumptions used in an Arms Control and Disarmament Agency (ACDA) study on Soviet civil defense. Just as estimates given in McNamara's 1963 Draft Presidential Memorandum (table 1-1) outline the heavy 1960s counterforce emphasis (16 percent of the weapons were aimed at urban targets), this ACDA study suggests the degree to which there was a very significant shift toward urban-industrial

Table 1-2
Unclassified U.S. Nuclear Targeting List, March 1980

War Supporting Industry
  Ammunition factories
  Tank and armored personnel carrier factories
  Petroleum refineries
  Railway yards and repair facilities

Industry That Contributes to Economic Recovery
  Coal
  Basic steel
  Basic aluminium
  Cement
  Electric power

Conventional Military Forces
  Caserns
  Supply depots
  Marshaling points
  Conventional airfields
  Ammunition storage facilities
  Tank and vehicle storage yards

Nuclear Forces
  ICBMs/IRBMs and launch facilities and launch command
    centers
  Nuclear weapon storage sites
  Long-range aviation bases (nuclear-capable aircraft)
  SSBN bases

Command and Control
  Command posts
  Key communications facilities

Source: *Department of Defense Authorization for Appropriations for Fiscal Year 1981*, Hearings before the Committee on Armed Services, U.S. Senate, 96th Congress, 2d session, part 5, p. 2721.

targeting (over 50 percent industrial targets in the fully generated case, *in this ACDA study*) by the late 1970s.

Thus, ironically, although the Nixon Administration de-emphasized the rhetoric of MAD and Assured Destruction, it produced guidance that apparently resulted in a

TABLE 1-3
Counter-Recovery Targeting

	Generated Case	Day-to-Day Alert Case
Nuclear	2,018	1,761
OMT (other military targets)	1,603	935
Leadership	736	423
E/I (economic-industrial)	4,400	2,300
	8,757	5,419

Source: U.S. Arms Control and Disarmament Agency (ACDA), *Effectiveness of Soviet Civil Defense in Limiting Damage to Population* (Washington, Nov 16, 1977), pp. 18–20, cited in Desmond Ball, "Development of the SIOP, 1960–1983," in Desmond Ball and Jeffrey Richelson (eds.), *Strategic Nuclear Targeting* (Ithaca: Cornell University Press, 1986), p. 81.

war plan that put greater emphasis on urban-industrial targets than had been the case under McNamara.

1980–1987: CARTER'S COUNTERVAILING STRATEGY AND THE REAGAN REFINEMENTS

When the Carter Administration entered office in January 1977, disturbing trends in the military balance had emerged. Despite its adherence to the 1972 ABM Treaty restrictions on active ballistic missile defense, the Soviet Union was continuing vigorous strategic defensive programs in air defense against U.S. bombers and in civil defense leadership-sheltering capabilities. Soviet offensive improvements had also continued despite the SALT process. Most important, the huge Soviet MIRVed-ICBM force was rapidly achieving sufficient accuracy to threaten a large portion of the American Minuteman ICBMs. Because the United States had, of course, also MIRVed its ICBM and SLBM force, adding thousands of warheads to its arsenal in the 1970s, there was little doubt that the United States retained the capability, even after receiving a massive Soviet first strike, to retaliate against large numbers of

Soviet urban-industrial targets. But further doubts were emerging among senior officials about whether this capability was a sufficient deterrent upon which to base American security.

In August 1977, the Carter Administration gave temporary endorsement to the war-planning guidance in NSDM-242, but simultaneously called for a major review of U.S. nuclear targeting policy. Over the next eighteen months, a comprehensive reexamination of targeting policy took place under the Nuclear Targeting Policy Review (NTPR). In June 1980, the study effort resulted in a new guidance for nuclear targeting—Presidential Directive (PD) 59—and in August Secretary of Defense Harold Brown publicly presented the outlines of what he called "the countervailing strategy." This concept remains at the center of U.S. nuclear strategy today, for while the Reagan Administration did not use the "countervailing" title and altered some of the details of nuclear planning guidance in its nuclear force employment policy (as distinct from its arms control and strategic defense policy), the Administration followed its predecessor relatively closely.

What is the countervailing strategy and why was it adopted? According to Leon Sloss, the director of the NTPR, perhaps the most important contribution of the review effort was "an extensive survey of Soviet nuclear doctrine and plans, including recent developments in their defensive program."[102] These studies convinced American political leaders that a new strategic doctrine was necessary, one more directly designed to take into account the specific values of the Soviet leadership, and specific operations for which the Soviet military prepares, in an effort to deny the perceived war aims of the Soviet government. "The biggest difference . . . that PD59 introduces," Secretary of Defense Harold Brown explained to Congress in September 1980, "is a specific recognition that our strategy has to be aimed at what the *Soviets* think is important to them, not just what *we* might think would be important to *us* in their view."[103] As Brown explained the policy:

What we have done in the past three and a half years is to look more closely at our capabilities, our doctrine and our plans in the light of what we know about Soviet forces, doctrine and plans. The Soviet leadership appears to contemplate at least the possibility of a relatively prolonged exchange if war comes, and in some circles at least, they seem to take seriously the theoretical possibility of victory in such a war. We cannot afford to ignore these views—even if we think differently, as I do.[104]

The NTPR and subsequent examinations of Soviet military writings, exercises, and force deployments thus focused on Soviet plans for nuclear war and Soviet political-military objectives in such a conflict. In his first public presentation of the countervailing strategy, Harold Brown emphasized that the U.S. capability to deny the Soviets confidence in achieving these specific war aims was now considered an essential component of nuclear deterrence:

We must have forces, contingency plans, and command and control capabilities that will convince the Soviet leadership that no war and no course of aggression by them that led to use of nuclear weapons—on any scale of attack and at any stage of conflict—could lead to victory, however they may define victory. Firmly convincing them of that fundamental truth is the surest restraint against their being tempted to aggression.[105]

Leadership, Military, and Industrial Targets

Three specific changes were implemented after PD-59 to ensure that no Soviet government could believe that "victory" was possible in a nuclear war. The first change was to increase the emphasis given to *counterleadership targeting*. This was by no means an entirely new concept. Indeed, as early as 1955 the United States targeted the Soviet political and military leadership under the BRAVO mission, which included "military headquarters and government control centers," and McNamara's definition of the Assured Destruction targets in his 1963 Draft Presidential

Memorandum included "the Soviet government and military controls."[106] What was new was both a recognition that this objective was becoming increasingly difficult, because of extensive Soviet efforts to protect the country's leadership cadre from the effects of nuclear attacks, and a belief that the existence of this leadership-cadre sheltering program provided an important insight into Soviet values and war objectives. Brown's testimony to Congress best presented the new view of what the Soviet leadership valued most highly:

> I believe that they are motivated by all the same human emotions as the rest of us. They love their kids and so forth, and they don't want to see their country destroyed. What motivates them most, however, is their personal power in a way that is not easily understood by someone who has come up through the American system. . . . In a time of great crisis what they must need to be deterred by is the thought that their power structure will not survive. That is even more important to them than their personal survival or survival of 10, 20, or 30 million, or even 50 million of their fellow countrymen.[107]

Brown also went public with the first estimate of the scope of the leadership-targeting problem—and an admission of the intelligence problem that existed at the time—in his fiscal year 1981 annual report:

> Hardened command posts have been constructed near Moscow and other cities. For the some 100,000 people we define as the Soviet leadership, there are hardened underground shelters near places of work, and at relocation sites outside the cities. The relatively few leadership shelters we have identified would be vulnerable to direct attack.[108]

The Reagan Administration shared this belief in the necessity of holding the Soviet leadership directly at risk, and released updated estimates of the Soviet program in 1985. According to official CIA testimony to Congress, "There are at least 800, perhaps as many as 1,500 relocation facilities for leaders at the national and regional levels.

Deep underground facilities for top national leadership might enable the top leadership to survive—a key objective of their wartime management plans."[109] By 1987, according to the Defense Department publication *Soviet Military Power*, there were estimated to be approximately fifteen hundred hardened alternative facilities for over 175,000 key party and government personnel throughout the USSR.[110]

The second major change resulting from PD-59 was in *countermilitary targeting*. As has been shown, U.S. nuclear strategy under both McNamara and Schlesinger continued to target Soviet military forces, including nuclear forces. Given the growth of the Soviet nuclear arsenal and the increased hardness of its ICBM force, however, U.S. counterforce capabilities decreased significantly in the 1970s.[111] The total nuclear warhead count still favored the United States by the end of the decade, but the number of Soviet launchers, especially ICBMs, had long surpassed that of the U.S. arsenal. The countervailing strategy called for improvements in the American counterforce capability to attack both Soviet nuclear and conventional military targets and improvements in capabilities (including especially the command and control capabilities) to be able to fight if necessary (and therefore, it was hoped, deter) a prolonged nuclear war. Such counterforce programs as the MX and Trident D5 were accelerated as both the Carter and Reagan administrations sought to make force-acquisition policy better serve the purposes of U.S. targeting doctrine.[112]

The primary objective behind this reemphasis on countermilitary, nuclear and conventional, targeting was not, however, to limit damage to the United States.[113] It was to enhance deterrence by denying Soviet war aims. There was an increased concern, resulting from the NTPR and related studies, that the Soviet military was developing plans and capabilities to fight a prolonged war in the event that deterrence failed. Many Soviet ICBM launchers could be reloaded and fired again, and sufficient numbers of weapons had come into the arsenal to provide large reserve forces and capabilities for sequential attacks. Moreover, according to the Defense Department, Soviet military doctrine called for forces able to occupy the NATO countries as well as deter, if possible, and defeat, if necessary, Chinese military forces in a global war.[114] Improved U.S. counterforce capabilities against nuclear and conventional targets would, it was hoped, deny the Soviet Union the ability to achieve such goals.

The third and final change in U.S. nuclear doctrine was the reduced emphasis and new objectives with respect to *industrial targeting*. The Carter Administration, as part of its review of targeting policy, had examined and rejected an alternative strategy that would "rely more heavily on assured destruction."[115] Instead, the annual reports of both Harold Brown (after PD-59) and Caspar Weinberger suggest that a smaller subject of economic targets—"the economic base needed to sustain a war" (Brown) or "the industrial ability to wage war" (Weinberger)—eventually came to be considered critical, rather than the larger set of "economic recovery" assets stressed under NSDM-242.[116] The studies of the NTPR had revealed that not only were the analytic tools for understanding how to impede Soviet recovery very weak, but also that very large numbers of U.S. nuclear weapons would be required. Therefore, under the countervailing strategy, as Leon Sloss noted, "instead of targeting to impede recovery, economic targeting focused on the better understood problems of destroying logistics and industries providing immediate support to the enemy war effort."[117]

The precise changes in targeting emphasis caused by this change in guidance are not available in unclassified sources, but the number of industrial targets is considerably smaller and the planned attacks correspondingly more discriminate. Indeed, Gen. Larry Welch, Air Force Chief of Staff, told a Harvard University seminar in March 1987 that "literally thousands of industrial targets have been dropped from the SIOP."[118] Thus, it appears that urban-industrial targeting receives considerably less emphasis in U.S. war plans than was the case in the late 1970s. In addition, Secretary of Defense Caspar Weinberger also stressed that the Reagan Administration "accelerated the development of more selective, discriminate, and controlled responses" and specifically rejected the belief that "deterrence must rest on the threat to destroy a certain high percentage of the Soviet population."[119]

American nuclear strategy changed considerably during the 1980s. If NSDM-242 produced war plans that were closer to Mutual Assured Destruction than is usually recognized, PD-59 and the subsequent Reagan Administration refinements of the countervailing strategy moved further away from MAD than is often realized. Although urban destruction and civilian casualties would undoubtedly be massive in a full nuclear exchange, U.S. nuclear doctrine is no longer deliberately designed to threaten the Soviet population directly, as under extreme Assured Destruction calculations, or indirectly, by retarding Soviet recovery from a nuclear attack.

Continuity, Change, and Control

This examination of the evolution of U.S. nuclear doctrine has revealed strong currents of both continuity and change. The two central objectives of U.S. nuclear strategy have remained quite constant over the past forty years. First, every administration has sought to utilize the threat of nuclear retaliation to deter Soviet aggression against both the United States and its allies. Second, each administration has developed plans to protect U.S. interests and limit the damage, to the degree possible, if war occurs despite all efforts to prevent it.

The means by which the U.S. government has sought to achieve these twin objectives have, however, changed considerably over the past forty years. Although there has been considerable continuity in the general categories of targets that the United States has threatened to attack—from the BRAVO, DELTA, and ROMEO missions in the

1950s to the set of Soviet nuclear forces, industrial, and other military targets today—the relative emphasis given to those different kinds of targets has changed. Urban-industrial targets received moderate emphasis in the optimum-mix strategy of early SIOP planning, heavier emphasis in the 1970s, and, again, reduced emphasis in the 1980s. Although the Soviet leadership was targeted as early as 1955, much greater weight has been placed on this objective in the 1980s. Soviet conventional force capabilities have also been a U.S. strategic nuclear target for many years, but increased emphasis has again recently been placed on this targeting objective. Finally, the targeting of Soviet nuclear forces has always taken place since 1949, but higher prominence was given to this mission in the early 1960s and 1980s than in the decade in between.

Why has the United States maintained significant counterforce capabilities and plans over the past decades? The evidence presented in this chapter suggests that, contrary to widespread academic opinion, the continuation of U.S. counterforce doctrine was not driven primarily by the parochial interests of the U.S. military services.[120] Indeed, American civilian authorities—including every Secretary of Defense—have consistently believed that it was in the U.S. national interest to maintain a significant counterforce capability and have provided, accordingly, such guidance to military officers. Although U.S. military services have undoubtedly sought to maximize their budget under different variations of counterforce, civilian authorities have approved of the basic targeting doctrine for a mixture of three reasons: to limit damage in the event of war, to maximize the credibility of the extended deterrent commitment to NATO allies, and to enhance central deterrence by denying Soviet war aims. Significant shifts have occurred, however, with respect to the relative importance of these motives, as well as in the flexibility and discrimination available in counterforce options. U.S. war plans in the 1950s and early 1960s sought to limit damage to the United States and its allies through massive prompt counterforce strikes, upon receipt of unambiguous warning of imminent attack, if possible. Starting in a very limited fashion under McNamara's "no-cities doctrine," and increasing under the guidance of the Schlesinger Doctrine, the U.S. shifted to a strategy of protecting its interests and limiting damage through escalation control and early war termination. Many limited options were made available to the President in the event of an initial nuclear strike against the United States or, in the more likely scenario, in response to nuclear or conventional attacks against NATO Europe.

In the 1970s, counterforce strikes were still an important part of war plans, but the ability of the United States to limit damage to itself through counterforce attacks had become diminishingly small as the Soviet nuclear arsenal became larger and less vulnerable. Although there was a consensus within the U.S. government during the past decade that the Soviet government seeks to avoid nuclear war, if possible, a widespread conviction also grew that, in the event that war occurs, the Soviet leadership would attempt to survive and prevail, leaving itself and its political control apparatus intact, Soviet residual conventional and nuclear military power still in existence, and Soviet forces prevailing in Eurasia. The increased emphasis placed on counterforce and counterleadership targeting in the 1980s was, therefore, designed less to limit damage to the United States than to enhance deterrence by convincing the Soviet leadership that the belief in a possible Soviet "victory" in a nuclear war —however theoretical the belief and however strained the definition of "victory"—remains a dangerous illusion.

Finally, while civilian authorities have consistently approved of a U.S. counterforce doctrine, strong elements of both continuity and change can be seen in the degree to which civilian officials have controlled the details of U.S. nuclear doctrine and operational plans. A central and disturbing continuity is obvious: each major shift in U.S. doctrine since 1960 has produced operational plans that did not fully meet the desires and expectations of civilian leaders. Eisenhower certainly provided guidance calling for a large, simultaneous nuclear offensive under the Massive Retaliation strategy, but was nonetheless shocked by the enormous overkill in SIOP-62. In the 1960s, McNamara was able to get a modicum of flexibility built into the plan, but the counterforce strikes were so large that they were "virtually indistinguishable" from countercity attacks. The Schlesinger Doctrine, in the 1970s, did produce many more limited options, but it also resulted in an unanticipated excessive emphasis on urban-industrial targeting because of the counter-recovery guidance. In short, American political authorities made their own nuclear doctrine, but they did not make it just as they desired.

A positive element of change, however, exists in the depth of civilian involvement and oversight in the development of U.S. nuclear operational plans. There was minimal civilian guidance given to military planners in the late 1940s and 1950s, and less than adequate oversight of the implementation of employment policy guidance existed in the 1960s and 1970s. In the 1980s, civilian Pentagon officials gradually became much more deeply involved in the details of nuclear doctrine and war planning. This increase in civilian involvement and oversight certainly increases the likelihood that further doctrinal improvements will be properly designed and implemented to meet the security interests of the United States. It does not, however, guarantee that we will make the right decisions in developing U.S. nuclear strategy for the 1990s.

Second-Strike Counterforce

DETERRENCE is in the eye of the beholder. If U.S. nuclear doctrine is to influence the decisions of the Soviet political and military leadership, it must be designed to affect their perceptions of how a nuclear war would be fought and their vision of the conflict's gruesome outcome. Current U.S. nuclear doctrine does not base deterrent strength on the Assured Destruction threat to annihilate an arbitrarily chosen percentage of the Soviet population and urban industry. Instead it seeks to deny the specific war aims of the Soviet military and to hold at risk what the U.S. government believes the Soviet political leadership values most highly: itself, its political control apparatus, and its military and industrial capability to wage war.

The current U.S. nuclear strategy, the countervailing doctrine, has been extremely controversial. The first purpose of this chapter is to examine contemporary U.S. nuclear doctrine and assess the arguments of its major critics. What does it mean to "deny Soviet war aims" and why might that be important? Does the renewed emphasis on counterforce—especially counter-ICBM capabilities—enhance deterrence or increase the likelihood of war? Is targeting the Soviet leadership a critical requirement for deterrence; or is it, at best, unnecessary and possibly extremely dangerous?

I will argue that the central elements of contemporary U.S. nuclear doctrine are fundamentally sound. Yet, just as the McNamara innovations in the 1960s and the 1974 Schlesinger Doctrine did not produce the precise changes in operational policy originally envisioned by civilian authorities, current operational policy must be further refined to make it more consistently serve the key objectives of the countervailing doctrine. The second purpose of this chapter, therefore, is to examine a number of potential further changes in targeting policy, designed to increase the ability to differentiate a U.S. second-strike counterforce posture from a preemptive first-strike capability, in an effort to enhance crisis stability while maintaining a strong nuclear deterrent.

The conclusions of this chapter, therefore, attempt to move beyond what, in my opinion, has become a rather sterile debate between the advocates of Mutually Assured Destruction and the proponents of improved nuclear counterforce capabilities. The MADvocates often project their beliefs about the requirements of deterrence onto the Soviet leadership, and have ignored the evidence that officials in Moscow do not share their assumptions about nuclear strategy. The extreme counterforce proponents, however, pay inadequate attention to the possibility that excessive prompt U.S. counterforce capabilities could increase the danger that the Soviets might mistakenly preempt what they believed to be a likely U.S. first strike in a crisis or conventional war. The second-strike counterforce posture outlined in this chapter is therefore designed—when coupled with the operational arms control measures discussed in chapter 4—to maximize the ability of the United States to maintain both robust deterrence and crisis stability into the 1990s and beyond.

Denying Soviet War Aims

By the late 1970s, it became clear that the Soviet Union was building an enormously powerful ICBM force, capable of destroying the majority of American land-based ICBMs in a first strike. Increased evidence emerged that the Soviet government had invested heavily in a major elite-shelter-protection program, in the apparent hope that the top leadership and Communist party cadre could survive a nuclear war. Alarming Soviet military writings—suggesting that a Soviet victory was at least theoretically possible in a nuclear war—were widely circulated in the West. The resulting debate among American strategists concerning the significance of these developments, however, was quite misleading. Among more hawkish analysts, there was a tendency to dismiss the continued and obvious destructive power of the U.S. nuclear arsenal: perhaps the most widely read critique of the Assured Destruction strategy was Richard Pipes's provocatively titled essay, "Why the Soviet Union Thinks It Could Fight and Win a Nuclear War,"[1] and one of the most exuberant counterforce proponents, Colin Gray, went so far as to assert that a U.S. retaliatory strike against the USSR might not prove "even seriously embarrassing, to a Soviet recovery effort."[2] Among more dovish analysts, however, there was a tendency to dismiss too easily the emerging evidence of the concerted Soviet effort to acquire counterforce and damage limitation capabilities. Soviet military programs were explained away as the mere outputs of military bureaucracies uncontrolled by central authorities, and every quotation from a Soviet military journal—suggesting that victory was possible in nuclear war—could be countered with a statement by a Soviet political figure stressing the horrors of a nuclear exchange.[3]

It would be misleading, however, either to dismiss the long-standing Soviet political statements on the horrendous costs of nuclear war as mere propaganda or to treat the Soviet military literature's traditional emphasis on nuclear victory as simple military morale-building. Instead, both positions logically can be held—and often have been held—simultaneously by senior military and political authorities. Thus, most Soviet military writers, even while stressing the *objective* of achieving victory in a nuclear war, do not ignore its likely catastrophic consequences. Writing in the 1979 *Soviet Military Encyclopedia*, for example, Chief of the General Staff Marshall Nikolay Ogarkov presented the following assessment:

> Soviet military strategy is based on the fact that should the Soviet Union be thrust into a nuclear war, the Soviet people and

their armed forces need to be prepared for the *most severe and protracted trials*. In this case the Soviet Union and fraternal socialist states, in comparison to the imperialist states, will have definite advantages stemming from the just goals of the war and the advanced nature of their social and state system. *This creates objective possibilities for them to achieve victory.*[4]

Soviet political authorities have also held the twin beliefs that it is imperative to avoid nuclear war if possible and win it if necessary. Thus Nikita Khrushchev, who would publicly proclaim that "nuclear war is stupid, stupid, stupid," could also argue that "if the enemy starts a war against you, then it is your duty to do everything possible to survive the war and to achieve victory in the end."[5]

New Thinking and Old Doctrine?

During the 1950s and 1960s, Soviet military writings were quite explicit on the need for nuclear preemption, to limit damage to the Soviet Union in the event that a nuclear exchange was unavoidable.[6] Obviously military technology and the nuclear balance have changed considerably since that time, and every Soviet leader since Brezhnev has publicly emphasized the importance of avoiding nuclear war. Despite such pronouncements however, there are several reasons to suspect that the long-standing Soviet interest in maintaining a preemptive offensive option under a damage-limiting strategy has not—and will likely not be—completely overturned. As Stephen Meyer noted in 1985:

> Soviet history and domestic politics prevents any Soviet leader from advocating a military doctrine whose guiding principle is accepting the enemy's first blow—a repeat of the disaster of 22 June 1941. . . . Indeed, there is ample evidence that the Soviet political leadership has authorized the military to pursue a damage limitation strategy, combining strategic offensive and both passive and active strategic defense, within set economic constraints. This includes a preemptive component.[7]

In fact, a careful review of Soviet military exercises, leadership-protection programs, arms control strategy, and military writings suggests that preemptive options and damage limitation have remained an important component of Soviet strategy in the 1980s. In June 1982, for example, the Soviet Union conducted an integrated nuclear war-fighting exercise in which an antisatellite test was performed, and two ICBMs, an SLBM, an IRBM, and two ABM interceptor missiles were launched within seven hours. Some U.S. intelligence analysts believed that because the ABM interceptors were launched well *after* the Soviet ICBMs, a preemptive option was being exercised.[8] In the early 1980s, a major construction program was also started on the Soviet deep-underground leadership-protection bunkers, a critical element in a damage limitation strategy.[9] Moreover, although the Soviets have been more willing in the late 1980s to accept reductions in their most threatening ICBM forces, their arms control proposals have consistently permitted maintenance of sufficient modern and accurate ICBM warheads to hold at risk, in a preemptive strike, U.S. land-based forces.

Finally, Soviet military writings in the 1980s, while much less bellicose than during earlier periods, have still displayed apparent interest in preemptive options. For example, a 1985 Soviet Ground Forces field handbook provided insights into possible warning indicators that might also be used at the strategic level by Soviet General Staff officers:

> Warning of troops of the immediate threat of the enemy's employment of weapons of mass destruction is carried out by the staffs based on intelligence data on the enemy's moving up missile troops and artillery, on its laying out firing positions, suspending tactical aviation, on the concentration of artillery, missile launchers, and aviation in certain areas, on the enemy's implementing measures to protect its own troops, on the activities of the enemy's staffs to organize the employment of weapons of mass destruction, on detecting the mass scram-

bling of enemy aviation and on the launching of missiles and other data.[10]

More recently, General Secretary Mikhail Gorbachev, as part of the "new political thinking" promoted under *perestroika* and *glasnost*, has called for a fundamental reexamination of Soviet security policy and military doctrine. Given the increasingly open and vigorous doctrinal debate developing in the Soviet military and political journals, there is little doubt that "new thinking" is present in some quarters. There remains considerable uncertainty, however, about whether such new thinking will remain only at the level of debate about strategic thought, or whether it will have a deep and sustained impact on actual Soviet military operational plans and targeting policy.[11]

Indeed, while the new developments may eventually produce a less-offensive-oriented Soviet strategy and should therefore be encouraged, the history of the evolution of *U.S.* nuclear doctrine presented in chapter 1 suggests a number of strong reasons to expect that fundamental changes in Soviet nuclear doctrine, at the operational level, are not likely to take place. There have been many periods in the evolution of American nuclear strategy in which the gap between declaratory policy and actual operational plans was severe. This gap was less often the result, at least in the U.S. experience, of the use of deliberately misleading declaratory policy for propaganda purposes than of the use of declaratory policy by political leaders to influence weapons-spending programs and the serious difficulty that political authorities had in translating their general political desires into actual plans and procedures. In this sense, the Soviet General Secretary's preferred goal of "reasonable sufficiency" in Soviet strategic forces in the late 1980s may be very much like Robert McNamara's promotion of the Assured Destruction criteria in the late 1960s: both can be seen primarily as efforts to limit the resources spent on offensive strategic forces while exerting only a modicum of influence on the actual operational plans. Indeed, Gorbachev's promotion of "new thinking" in Soviet nuclear policy faces similar, and probably even more intractable, problems in forwarding and implementing serious doctrinal change: the Soviet General Secretary cannot push military reform too far beyond the professional military's tolerance without arousing potentially potent forces of political opposition, and, even if some doctrinal changes are agreed upon, the Soviet institutional mechanisms for civilian involvement in the details of implementing military strategy remain relatively weak.

Second, there is a structural reason to expect that a preemptive element in Soviet nuclear strategy will continue to exist in the future. Because of the commitment to NATO, the United States maintains the threat of nuclear first-use in case conventional defense fails in a war in Europe, as well as the threat of nuclear escalation in response to attacks on NATO allies. As was discussed in chapter 1, this alliance commitment has been a fundamental cause of U.S. development of limited nuclear options. The Soviet government has consistently maintained, however, that any attack on the Soviet homeland will result in full retaliation against the United States. The continued U.S. maintenance of limited strategic options thus provides a strong incentive for Soviet military planners to retain preemptive options for what they call the "first decisive use" of nuclear weapons.

Finally, it is worth noting that Soviet military authorities apparently continue to hold quite conflicting views on the wisdom of significant shifts toward more defensive strategies. On the one hand, some senior officers do emphasize the need for major reform. For example, Col. Gen. Makhmut Gareyev, the Deputy Chief of the Soviet General Staff, while incidentally acknowledging that many of the Western concerns about Soviet nuclear strategy have been justified, recently called for changes in Soviet military doctrine:

Previously, military doctrine was defined as a system of views on the preparation for and conduct of war. Now military doctrine concentrates on the prevention of war. . . . [A] change in the very character of war and a deeper analysis of its course and consequences have shown that the task of preventing armed conflicts which may lead to global holocaust should be given priority without any reservation. Not only a profound political comprehension of both the international and domestic situations, but also a military-strategic analysis of today's realities have convinced us in the need to correct some provisions of our military doctrine.[12]

On the other hand, despite the calls for development of a more "defensive" Soviet military doctrine, some military authorities appear to be reluctant to move completely away from their traditional emphasis on the offense. Indeed, some Soviet military writers have explicitly maintained the continued need for offensive operations even within the Gorbachev guidance for a more defensive doctrine. For example, Gen. A. Gribkov, Chief of Staff of the Warsaw Pact forces, argued in 1987:

Should an attack take place, the armed forces of the Warsaw Treaty countries will act with exceptional resoluteness. In the course of repulsing the aggression they will also conduct counter-offensive operations. This will not contradict their military doctrine because, as the experience of the Great Patriotic War and of local wars shows, within the framework of defensive operations and battles in certain sectors such operations are not only feasible but necessary.[13]

Moreover, at the tactical level, the official basic Soviet military text includes the following description of doctrinal preference in its 1987 edition: "The offensive is the main form of battle. It has decisive significance for victory over the enemy. Only a decisive offensive, conducted at high tempo and in great depth, achieves a complete defeat of the enemy."[14]

In short, there are strong reasons to expect that change

in Soviet military strategy, at the operational level, will be incremental at best. In the past decades, Soviet history and ideology have apparently led the Moscow leadership to take a rather traditional perspective on the revolutionary weapon: nuclear war against the imperialist West is possible, however undesirable given the likely consequences, and it is the responsibility of Soviet officials to ensure that the Soviet state survives and prevails in such a war. The tensions implied in that formulation are likely to continue in the future. It is clear that, despite potential civil-military conflicts, an emphasis in some of the Soviet "military-technical" literature on the requirement to win a nuclear war and the focus of "sociopolitical" writings on the need to avoid a nuclear war can exist simultaneously under normal peacetime circumstances.[15] The critical question is how such tensions might be played out at the brink, influencing Soviet behavior in a severe crisis or during a conventional conflict, or if nuclear weapons are used in a highly limited strike.

ORGANIZATIONS AND DETERRENCE

What are Soviet war aims? How does the Soviet military define "victory" in a nuclear war? And why should the United States be concerned with denying the Soviets the ability to achieve such wartime objectives?

It should be acknowledged from the start that analysis of Soviet nuclear strategy is a very uncertain enterprise. Western observers know a great deal about Soviet military doctrine, but they are by no means omniscient. Many professional Soviet military writings, including Soviet classified journals obtained and released by the U.S. government, are available, but it is always difficult to predict the precise impact of military doctrine on specific strategic decisions. U.S. intelligence services pay constant attention to Soviet force deployments and military exercises, but even when good information exists, it is often difficult to assess and usually subject to conflicting interpretations. In short, the U.S. government knows a great deal about Soviet nuclear capabilities and military doctrine, but Soviet "intentions" are inherently less observable and less "knowable."

Indeed, because different Soviet decision makers maintain individual perspectives on nuclear issues, and would probably defer final judgments and difficult decisions until the moment of absolute necessity, *they* cannot know their intentions in all circumstances. For this reason, thinking about Soviet "proclivities" rather than "intentions" may better capture the inherent uncertainty involved in estimating future Soviet crisis behavior.[16] An understanding of Soviet military leaders' plans and war aims may not illuminate their precise "intentions," but it can suggest the proclivities and pressures that would exist in Moscow at the brink of a major nuclear conflict.

War Aims and Proclivities

If one takes a more complex approach to nuclear deterrence—replacing the common assumption that Soviet leaders are pristine rational actors, in possession of full and unbiased information about nuclear issues, with a greater sense of the degree to which Soviet military organizations can structure and influence decisions about war-initiation—it is not difficult to understand the importance of being able to deny Soviet war aims.[17] Military capabilities and war plans, guided by specific military objectives, provide available options. Military options that have been thoroughly thought through and exercised in peacetime are much more easily implemented in crisis or war. If the specific objectives, which guided the plans, are judged to be achievable, the likelihood of such options being chosen or otherwise implemented is increased.

Four specific characteristics of modern military organizations produce this result. First, nuclear war plans are exceedingly complex and, as a practical matter, only options that have been rehearsed can be expected to be executed with success. The plans that exist, therefore, often will determine the bounds of the possible in a crisis. Second, the war plans that exist and the exercises based on those plans can create or strengthen leaders' beliefs that this reflects what *ought* to be done in all future contingencies. Third, military organizations must develop numerous standard operating procedures, based on the war plans, which are to be implemented during crises or war. The complexity and decentralized character of these organizations make it extremely difficult for central decision makers to understand or control the details of such activities. Fourth, the production of the complex nuclear war plans is guided by specific targeting objectives and is based on a series of analytic assumptions concerning enemy capabilities and reactions. It is often difficult for civilian authorities to understand the complex methodologies and assumptions embedded in the planning process. It is not unusual, therefore, for narrow military criteria of success or failure to become more important—that is, have a greater affect on political decisions—than would otherwise be the case.[18]

Such insights, stemming from the organization theory literature, may be particularly relevant to the Soviet Union. Soviet operational plans are designed by the Soviet military under the *general* guidance of political authorities. There are, however, far fewer domestic political impediments to coherent Soviet military planning than is the case in the United States. Although civilian involvement in Soviet strategy is slowly growing, there are still no equivalents to the large civilian staff of the Office of the Secretary of Defense or the well-established civilian think tanks and academic strategists to provide alternative sources of information and advice on military issues to Soviet political leaders. Because of the relative autonomy of the Soviet General Staff, its influence on strategy is much less diluted than is the case with the professional military in the United States.

The importance of such organization theory ideas on the U.S. countervailing nuclear doctrine is clear. Lt. Gen. William Odom, one of the primary architects of PD-59 under the Carter Administration, has been especially direct on this point:

> [The] organizational model rested on the assumption that you can do what you are *organized* to do. If you are *not* organized to do a particular thing, then it is very unlikely that a government can exercise that choice. I think that is a terribly relevant insight for military affairs. . . . [The Soviets] are going to do what they've designed and trained to do. . . . After a war starts, to try to change everybody's doctrinal view about such employment—that's virtually incomprehensible.[19]

Does It Matter?

Given the size and diversity of the U.S. strategic nuclear arsenal, even a massive Soviet first strike would not, in all likelihood, entirely eliminate the United States' capability to retaliate. Even if the U.S. National Command Authority (NCA) chose not to launch the vulnerable land-based ICBMs on warning (or failed to make such a decision in time), alert U.S. bombers would escape destruction and U.S. submarines would remain largely invulnerable at sea. Even if initial missile attacks were designed to cripple American command and control capabilities (along the lines, for example, of the scenario posited in the next section of this chapter), the redundancy of the U.S. command system, and inherent uncertainty about potential covert capabilities, prevent the Soviet military from having high confidence that execution orders to retaliate would not *eventually* reach invulnerable forces.[20] The Soviets' advantage from striking first, in a situation in which they believe nuclear war is inevitable, would therefore be restricted to two possibilities: first, if the Soviet preemptive attack was purely against counterforce targets, there is at least some chance that the U.S. NCA would decide not to order a major retaliatory strike for fear of receiving an even more devastating Soviet nuclear response against U.S. urban areas; second, the coordination and timing of any large-scale planned U.S. nuclear strike might be disrupted, thereby limiting damage to the Soviet Union.

Before discussing these specific possibilities, it is worth raising a more fundamental question. In such a situation, what difference would it make if Soviet military planners believed they could execute preemptive war plans effectively? Would it influence Soviet behavior in a crisis or conventional war, or increase the likelihood of a Soviet decision to strike first in the event of ambiguous warning of an imminent U.S. attack? These questions cannot be answered with confidence, of course, for we lack sufficient information on Soviet civil-military decision making in crisis or war to anticipate precisely how war planning would influence the central leadership in Moscow. There is, however, an analogy—admittedly a highly imperfect one—that can at least suggest why it is worth being concerned about the Soviets' perceptions of their ability to achieve their specific military aims.

In the early 1960s, the nuclear balance was such that American military leaders believed that the United States could achieve victory in a nuclear war. In September 1961, the Chairman of the Joint Chiefs of Staff reported to President Kennedy that execution of the SIOP-62 war plan "should permit the United States to prevail in [the] event of general nuclear war," even though "under any circumstances—even a preemptive attack by the U.S.—it would be expected that some portion of the Soviet long-range nuclear force would strike the United States."[21] Therefore, as noted in chapter 1, this JCS position—that the United States would "prevail" in a nuclear war—was *not* limited to the case in which the United States preempted a Soviet attack, severely limiting damage to the United States. Instead, it appears to have been based on the most narrow of military criteria: under any condition of war-initiation, even if the Soviets struck first, execution of SIOP-62 would achieve the specific damage expectancy (DE) against Soviet targets that national guidance had ordered. The ability to achieve these war aims, very narrowly defined, meant to the U.S. war planners that the United States would "prevail."[22]

Although such beliefs obviously did not lead the United States to launch a nuclear attack during the Berlin Crisis of 1961 or the 1962 Cuban Missile Crisis, there are three reasons to believe that the perception of the U.S. ability to "prevail" was not entirely inconsequential. First, as was discussed in chapter 1, U.S. war plans in the 1950s and early 1960s included specific counterforce preemptive options. Although war was avoided during the severe Cold War crises of the Kennedy Administration, it is known that high-level political and military officials did secretly discuss a special counterforce first-strike plan during the 1961 Berlin Crisis,[23] and both privately discussed and then publicly threatened a preemptive nuclear attack against the Soviet Union during the Cuban Missile Crisis one year later.[24] Second, the nuclear balance apparently influenced the military advice given to civilian leaders during the Cuban Missile Crisis: on October 26, 1962, the JCS reported to the Secretary of Defense that "we have the strategic advantage in our general war capabilities" and advised him that "this is no time to run scared,"[25] and on October 27, the JCS officially recommended that the United States launch an air strike and invasion of Cuba.[26]

Third, although the currently declassified military exercise reports of the early 1960s provide no evidence that the U.S. military expected to be authorized to launch a first strike, they do demonstrate a strong *proclivity* to launch the SIOP promptly on the basis of quite ambiguous warning that a Soviet attack was underway. For example, in an April 1961 exercise, the Secretary of Defense ordered (with simulated presidential authority) the execution of the SIOP based upon a single warning from NORAD (North American Air Defense Command) that Soviet bombers had penetrated to the DEWline (Distant Early Warning line) radars.[27] In light of current evidence, therefore, it appears that a U.S. preemptive strike, or prompt "response" under ambiguous warning, was made more likely by U.S.

leaders' perceptions in the 1960s that the United States might "prevail" or at least severely "limit damage" under such conditions.

This is an imperfect analogy, of course, since the nuclear balance is nowhere near as lopsided against the United States today as it was against the Soviet Union in the early 1960s. My point, however, is *not* to suggest that the Soviet Union has that degree of nuclear superiority. The issue is more subtle: even if the Soviet leadership fully expects the consequences of nuclear war to be horrendous, the belief that the Soviet Union could "prevail," even according to narrow military logic, could increase the likelihood of a preemptive strike in a crisis or conventional war. We know relatively little about how decisions would be made in the Soviet Union at the brink of war or about what options would appear to be the least unattractive among the horrible alternatives. Although Soviet war planners prepare for a variety of possible contingencies, an alarming doctrinal "proclivity" toward massive preemption as a preferred strategy *if* a major nuclear war appears virtually unavoidable is likely to persist. Understanding Soviet nuclear strategy, war aims, and judgments about damage limitation, therefore, appears to be as critical as it is difficult.[28] The effort to design a U.S. strategy that can convince Soviet military and political leaders that they cannot achieve their war aims—cannot achieve even "victory" as they define it—is a sound and prudent policy.

TARGETING SOVIET NUCLEAR FORCES

Perhaps the most worrisome aspect of the strategic balance during the late 1970s and 1980s has been the emergence of very significant Soviet ICBM counterforce capabilities. Given the size and accuracy of the Soviet ICBM force in the late 1970s, it became at least theoretically possible for a Soviet counterforce attack—using only a portion of the most effective Soviet ICBMs—to destroy the majority of American land-based nuclear forces.[29] The asymmetry in *prompt* counterforce capability between the two superpowers is being significantly decreased by the U.S. strategic modernization program. (The balance of prompt counterforce capability will depend on the number of MX and Trident D5 missiles that are eventually deployed by the United States, and the number of mobile missiles eventually deployed by the USSR.) What is the purpose of having U.S. forces that are capable of attacking Soviet ICBMs? What are the advantages and disadvantages of such a strategy?

Why Counterforce?

Many defense analysts have, erroneously in my view, equated the counterforce emphasis in current American doctrine with a damage-limiting first-strike strategy.[30] This misperception is in part understandable. After all, U.S. counterforce doctrine in the 1960s, as has been demonstrated, was designed to limit damage to the United States in the event of nuclear war, and U.S. war plans included specific preemptive options. Moreover, the blustery rhetoric of some Reagan Administration officials during the first term—especially public pronouncements about the need to "prevail" in a nuclear war—reinforced the view that the administration sought a return to the U.S. nuclear superiority of the 1960s.[31] Finally, the emergence of the SDI program furthered this perception, since a counterforce offensive, if coupled with defensive systems, might produce a significant damage limitation capability.

The second historical rationale for the maintenance of U.S. counterforce capabilities—discussed by every recent Secretary of Defense, as shown in chapter 1—was to enhance the credibility of the U.S. extended deterrent commitment to NATO. This objective remains an important one. Although some scholarly critics of the current U.S. doctrine have argued that anything less than a completely disarming U.S. first-strike capability cannot make NATO's nuclear escalation threat more credible (since U.S. cities would still be vulnerable to Soviet retaliation), senior Pentagon officials have not shared this view.[32] The likelihood of a major U.S. strategic counterforce response to any Soviet nuclear or conventional attack is clearly less today, given the significant changes in the military balance, than it was in the early 1960s when the prospects for direct damage limitation were greater. Yet the absence of U.S. counterforce capabilities or limited options would only serve to further decrease the credibility of the U.S. nuclear commitment to NATO. Each recent Secretary of Defense has sought to maximize the options available, given the grave uncertainties involved in war scenarios in Europe: NATO tactical weapons may be preempted or otherwise unavailable when needed; increasing the number of European-based aircraft on nuclear alert also decreases NATO's conventional defense capability; and a secure capability to attack the Soviet homeland has been considered essential under many escalation scenarios. Thus, the extended deterrence commitment remains an important driving force behind U.S. counterforce capabilities.

The strongest, and most widely discussed, rationale for current U.S. nuclear counterforce capabilities, however, is their role in *denying Soviet war aims*. Although this theme began under Harold Brown in the late 1970s, it was most often expressed by Caspar Weinberger under the Reagan Administration:

> It has been our belief that deterrence is best served by the possession of forces and plans for their use, which make Soviet assessments of possible war outcomes, under any contingency, so uncertain and dangerous as to create strong disincentives for initiating attack or aggression against us or our allies. This requires that we be convincingly capable of responding in such a way that they would be denied their political and military objectives and, hence, could not achieve their war aims.[33]

There is evidence, however, that this interest in denying Soviet war aims is *not* a reflection of U.S. adoption of a major first-strike option. Weinberger, for example, explicitly ruled out strategic preemption as part of U.S. strategy in his 1984 report to Congress: "Our strategy is defensive. . . . [U.S. policy] excludes the possibility that the United States would initiate a war or launch a preemptive strike against the forces or territories of other nations."[34] The Commander of the Strategic Air Command also testified to Congress in 1985 that "there are no preemption options" in the SIOP.[35] (This statement does not mean that SAC could not launch ICBMs on warning or under any other condition if so ordered by the National Command Authority. It does suggest that SIOP options are no longer, as they were in the 1960s, specifically designed to maximize preemptive effectiveness.)

How might U.S. counterforce capabilities contribute to deterrence by denying Soviet war aims? To answer this question, it is necessary to examine the role of the Soviet ICBM force in Soviet military doctrine.

War Aims and Strategy

Soviet Military Power 1987 presents the Pentagon's assessment of specific Soviet war aims in a global conflict as follows:

> defeat European NATO forces at any level of conflict, occupy NATO countries, and use Europe's surviving economic assets to assist Soviet recovery;
>
> neutralize the U.S. and its allies by disrupting and destroying their military forces;
>
> deter China's entry against the USSR, and if deterrence fails, neutralize Chinese capability to interfere with the USSR, while avoiding land war in Asia;
>
> limit damage to vital Soviet political, military, and economic structures; and
>
> dominate the postwar world in which socialism would become the basic politico-economic system in all nations.[36]

The Soviet ICBM force is configured in a manner consistent with the objective of achieving such goals in the event of global war. It is often noted that the Soviets have larger nuclear forces than would be necessary to attack American urban-industrial areas in a second strike. This is neither surprising nor alarming. Both superpowers recognize the need for redundancy in strategic forces, and the United States, even in the McNamara years, sought to have some redundant forces held in each leg of the strategic triad of bombers, submarines, and ICBMs. What is disturbing, however, is the size of the Soviet ICBM force, as well as particular characteristics of Soviet force posture and apparent operational war plans. Sufficient ICBM warheads now exist, as discussed earlier, to attack American land-based forces effectively, with significant Soviet forces still held in reserve. Estimates of Soviet ICBM effectiveness vary, of course, and there are considerable uncertainties concerning how the Soviets might utilize their missiles in a counterforce attack. (For example, would they target each U.S. ICBM with two or three warheads?) But given the size of the Soviet ICBM arsenal—the estimated 3,080 SS-18 warheads, capable of attacking the 1,000 U.S. ICBM silos, are less than half of the total Soviet ICBM warheads—experts agree that after a counterforce first strike against the United States, many Soviet ICBM warheads would remain. "The Soviets have a significant capability with their numbers of land-based ICBMs," Gen. Bennie Davis testified to Congress in 1983:

> With the number of re-entry vehicles, they do not need to execute even half that force to accomplish good results against the United States. So, the idea—and, of course, we know about the Soviets from reading their literature and observing their exercises—and the thought that everything would be launched in one attack, I do not believe is an accurate assumption. So, there certainly will be missiles remaining in silos in the Soviet Union.[37]

Moreover, according to *Soviet Military Power 1987*, the Soviet military has stored extra missiles, missile fuel propellent, and nuclear warheads for ICBM silos and its submarines throughout the USSR: "Some ICBM launchers could be reloaded, and provisions have been made for the de-contamination of those launchers. Plans for the survival of necessary equipment and personnel have been developed and practiced. Resupply systems are available to reload SSBNs in protected waters."[38]

For what purpose does the Soviet military maintain such large missile forces, reserve forces, and reload capability? The answer is by no means clear. Three related possible objectives, however, can be identified.

1. *"Deterring Our Deterrent."* First, the Soviet Union may have acquired large numbers of ICBMs in part as an attempt to deter, if possible, any NATO threat of nuclear escalation. For example, since the 1970s, the United States has threatened to initiate limited nuclear attacks against the Soviet homeland, in the event that NATO conventional forces are defeated. The maintenence of large Soviet counterforce capabilities could be designed, in part, to enhance the credibility of the Soviet counterthreat to retaliate massively against the United States in response to any NATO limited nuclear attack. A recent declaration on Soviet nuclear strategy, by the commander of the Soviet Strategic Rocket Forces, appears to have precisely such a scenario in mind: "A potential opponent must know that the launch of *even a group* of his missiles from any basing area *toward our territory* will be *immediately* followed by inevitable retaliation."[39]

A related objective could be to deter the United States from responding with further escalation in the event of a Soviet "counterforce-only" preemptive strike. This scenario—one version of which was popularized by Paul Nitze in the mid-1970s[40]—posits a decision by the Soviets to attack American nuclear forces during a crisis or war when they believe an American major first strike is likely, with the hope that American political leaders will not retaliate against Soviet urban-industrial or leadership targets for fear that the Soviets will then respond in kind. The large arsenal of Soviet ICBMs is necessary in this scenario to ensure that the damage expectancy against American ICBM silos is very high (by placing two or three warheads against each U.S. ICBM silo) and to keep an adequate, secure ICBM reserve force to help deter American retaliatory attacks.[41] Faced with the choice of responding with an ineffective countermilitary retaliation, or escalating to what was likely to become a mutually devastating nuclear exchange, the American President might, it is assumed, decide to capitulate.

Critics of this scenario have emphasized that the Soviet leaders could not be certain that the U.S. would not respond with a major retaliatory attack against the Soviet Union.[42] This is true: the Soviet leadership could not be *certain* that the United States would not retaliate against Soviet cities, and such a coercive counterforce strike would therefore be an extremely risky venture. But that does not mean that such a desperate decision would not be made *if* Soviet leaders believed nuclear war was likely; nor does it necessarily suggest that the Soviets have not prepared for such a possibility.

Indeed, statements that such a Soviet attack plan is implausible should be strongly tempered by the knowledge that precisely such a "counterforce-only" strike was included in U.S. war plans in the early 1960s, as was shown in chapter 1. Again, an American counterforce-only attack in the 1960s, even if used preemptively, was not expected to disarm the Soviet Union completely. Instead, the objective was, as Robert McNamara put it in a top secret memorandum to President Kennedy in 1962, to "coerce the Soviets into avoiding our cities (by the threat of controlled reprisal) and accepting our own peace terms."[43] The fact that the United States maintained such a coercive counterforce plan in the 1960s does not, of course, prove that the Soviets have a similar strategy in the 1980s. It should, however, at least force strategists to consider seriously the possibility of Soviet interest in such restricted counterforce options.[44]

2. *Damage Limitation and Sequential Strikes.* An alternative strategy in the event that a nuclear war appears unavoidable, one that more closely conforms to the Soviet military writings on the importance of the first *decisive* use of nuclear weapons in war, is to launch a massive attack against all U.S. nuclear forces and command, control, and communications (C^3) targets. Western analysts have long been particularly concerned about the possibility of what has become known as a "decapitation attack." For example, Soviet ballistic missile–launching submarines, from launch positions off both U.S. coasts, could destroy Washington, other critical command targets, and strategic bomber bases in an initial attack before the massive Soviet ICBM force could destroy U.S. ICBMs. In addition, initial Soviet ICBM weapons could be targeted against U.S. command and control. Any such precursor C^3 attack would not, in all likelihood, completely eliminate the U.S. capability to retaliate: the Soviets could not be confident that airborne and ground mobile command posts and reconstitutable or covert communications assets would fail to get execution orders off to surviving U.S. forces. But any initial command and control strike might severely disrupt the complex coordination of an American retaliatory strike, enhancing a Soviet damage limitation strategy. Thus not only is there at least some possibility that U.S. command confusion and disruption of communications after a Soviet SLBM attack would foil a U.S. attempt to launch the ICBMs before they were destroyed, but U.S. bomber and SLBM attacks might be rendered less effective. If large portions of the U.S. arsenal were destroyed preemptively, and the timing and scale of the retaliation by remaining forces were disrupted, for example, U.S. bombers might not be able to rely on precursor missile attacks on Soviet air defenses to enhance bomber penetration. Furthermore, unanticipated "fratricide" (one U.S. warhead destroying another) could ensue in a ragged retaliatory missile strike.

Although damage to the USSR would still be severe under any form of the "decapitation" scenario, destruction might be significantly less than that of a coordinated U.S. retaliation or full first strike.[45] Soviet military writings clearly display strong interest in priority targeting of U.S. political and military command and control. Evidence also exists that the specific SLBM precursor attack scenario, described here, has not gone unnoticed in the Soviet Union.[46]

Moreover, Soviet military planners do not believe that the ICBM force's mission would be completed after the initial launch of nuclear weapons. Soviet military writings and nuclear force deployments suggest that the Soviet General Staff considers it possible that a nuclear war could continue over a relatively prolonged period of time and that the Soviet Union must be prepared for such a contingency.[47] This consideration would add several counterforce requirements for Soviet war planners. First, the Soviet military would require the capability to launch follow-on ICBM attacks against specific targets to compensate for missiles that failed to launch for technical reasons in an initial strike. (U.S. officials estimate Soviet ICBM reliability rates to be in the .80–.85 range,[48] which is one reason to use more than one warhead against each target. Any target left uncovered by such failures would become a priority target for follow-on attacks.) Second, the Soviet military would want to strike U.S. forces and command and control repeatedly to disrupt any delayed retaliation attempt. According to CIA testimony:

> We believe the Soviets would launch continuing attacks on the United States and allied strategic command, control and communications to prevent or impair the coordination of retaliatory strikes, thereby easing the burden on Soviet strategic defenses and impairing United States and allied abilities to marshal military and civilian resources to reconstitute forces.[49]

Finally, the Soviet military would want to be able to ensure that sufficient reserve forces existed to cover any unanticipated targets that emerged during the course of a prolonged war.

3. *Deter and Defeat Other Adversaries.* The United States is not, of course, the only nuclear adversary of the Soviet Union; not only do the Soviets have to take into account the growing French and British nuclear arsenals in Europe, but also the now considerable Chinese nuclear arsenal. Great Britain maintains four strategic submarines, each with sixteen Polaris missiles, and 148 Tornado aircraft. France has six submarines, each with sixteen missiles, as well as eighteen IRBMs, four test silos, and 133 nuclear-capable combat aircraft. China has an estimated six ICBMs, sixty IRBMs, and fifty MRBMs, as well as two strategic submarines, each with twelve SLBMs, and up to 120 medium-range bombers.[50] These arsenals, moreover, are being modernized and greatly expanded: a 1987 Soviet academic publication, utilizing a variety of Western sources, estimated that the combined British and French nuclear arsenals could contain as many as 1,428 strategic warheads in the 1990s.[51]

A strategy to deter such adversaries if possible, but to destroy their land-based forces and command and control if necessary, would require significant Soviet nuclear long-range missile reserves and possibly reload missile capabilities. (One estimate states that there are nine hundred to eleven hundred strategic targets for Soviet planners in Europe and Asia, about 15 percent of which are hardened.[52]) Without the ability to attack such targets, *after* a war with the United States, the Soviet Union could not deter other powers, and might not emerge from a nuclear war as the preeminent military power in the world, apparently a wartime objective. Denying such a capability to the USSR played an important role in the development of the countervailing strategy. For example, Harold Brown argued in 1980 that "if the Soviets think they can destroy the United States, but then can't hold off the Chinese and can't conquer Europe, that will help deter them." "If they don't think that," Brown maintained, "if they think that the United States will be destroyed, much of the productive capability of the Soviet Union will be destroyed, but the

Soviet Union would still be the world's predominant military power, then they might not be so deterred."[53]

Prohibiting "Victory"

In Soviet military thought, these purposes would not be in conflict with one another: large counterforce capabilities can best deter adversaries if they can defeat them when deterrence fails. From the American perspective, the purpose of targeting Soviet ICBM silos, *even in a retaliatory second-strike strategy*, becomes more clear when these possible Soviet military objectives are considered. A Soviet ability to hold large reserves, retarget and launch follow-on missile attacks, and reload and reconstitute ICBM forces, would increase the likelihood that the Soviet military could achieve the specific objectives that apparently guide its war-planning process. A U.S. ability to deny such war aims is necessary to ensure that no Soviet military authority can credibly argue that a Soviet preemptive strike, even if it could not destroy all U.S. retaliatory forces, might nonetheless permit the Soviet Union to "prevail," as Soviets define it, in the event of global war.

TARGETING THE SOVIET LEADERSHIP

The recognition that the Soviet leadership actively sought to protect itself, and preserve its capability to control Soviet society and manage its painful reconstruction after a nuclear war, was one of the most important factors leading to the PD-59 revision of U.S. nuclear strategy in 1980. Numerous intelligence sources have pointed to the development of an extensive leadership-protection program: estimates range from at least eight hundred to as many as two thousand shelters existing at the national and regional level in the Soviet Union.[54] In 1982 the Defense Department reported to Congress that approximately 110,000 Soviet government officials and management personnel could be placed in hardened shelters during a conflict: an estimated 5,000 key party and high-ranking government officials, 63,000 lower-level leaders, 2,000 managers of key defense installations, and 40,000 members of civil defense staffs.[55] In 1987 the Pentagon updated the estimate, stating that more than 175,000 party and government personnel could be protected.[56]

These are not, in the most important cases, austere bomb shelters like those still found in the basements of some American apartment buildings. (Nor are they as obviously inadequate as the civil defense infrastructure the Soviets have developed for the general civilian population.) Instead, according to Defense Department congressional testimony, some of these shelters "appear to be able to hold hundreds of people," and "some appear to be surrounded by very, very nice homes for the big wigs to live in, in case they want to move into that area, and be able to get into those facilities quickly"; moreover, some of the most deeply buried government shelters are estimated to be up to a thousand feet below ground and are hardened to withstand the effects of a U.S. nuclear attack up to the level of several thousand pounds per square inch.[57] Other sources attest to the seriousness of the program. Soviet military technical literature has revealed the development of special communications systems—including satellite links, underground cable networks and extensive radio relays—for the shelter facilities.[58] Finally, published Soviet defector reports of secret leadership evacuation subway lines in Moscow and extensive hardened relocation sites in rural areas have been confirmed by the Defense Department.[59]

This program has presented a severe challenge to U.S. efforts to hold the Soviet leadership at risk. Obviously, any shelters that remained undiscovered could not be targeted. Moreover, the hardness of the deepest leadership shelters presents a very serious problem for current U.S. strategy: according to official CIA testimony to Congress, "Deep underground facilities for the top leadership might enable the top leadership to survive—a key objective of their wartime management plans."[60]

Criticism and Confusion

U.S. programs to hold Soviet leadership targets at risk—such as the improved hard-target-kill capability of the MX and the development of an earth-penetrating warhead[61]—have been among the most controversial aspects of the Reagan strategic modernization program. Three specific criticisms of leadership targeting have emerged. Each of them, however, either misinterprets the U.S. targeting strategy or misunderstands the Soviet Union's purpose in developing such a leadership-protection program.

The first, and most severe, criticism has been that the new emphasis on leadership targeting really reveals that the United States has secretly adopted a first-strike nuclear war plan. This argument suggests that the United States now has a "decapitation" strategy, with preemptive attacks against leadership and command and control targets designed to prevent retaliation against the United States by eliminating the ability of the Soviet central authorities to communicate orders to their strategic forces. For example, Daniel Ford, former Executive Director of the Union of Concerned Scientists, has asserted that "the primary emergency plan" in the SIOP now involves a "massive first-strike" designed to "kill Soviet leaders and thereby paralyze the highly centralized Soviet war machine."[62] Ford's evidence for this provocative statement is the open admission of the U.S. government that it seeks the capability to destroy Soviet leadership and political and military control targets in the event of nuclear war. This must reflect a first-strike decapitation plan, according to Ford, since "there wouldn't be much point in planning to disable their command system only after it had fulfilled its mission."[63]

This critique both confuses a decapitation strike against Soviet command and control and broader counterleadership targeting, and ignores the deterrent function of having the clear capability to ensure that the Soviet leadership would not survive a full nuclear exchange. If the United States sought a decapitating strike force, it would not require the ability to destroy the large set of Soviet *regional* and national lower-level-leadership relocation sites; a smaller set of National Command Authority targets would suffice. Nevertheless, according to government sources, it is beyond the current capability of the United States, even if it did strike first, to prevent the Soviet Union from launching a devastating retaliation. The Soviet Union has constructed not only the extensive underground shelter system and an extensive network of buried land-line communications but also a currently untargetable *mobile* command system: airborne command posts, ground mobile units, and train cars especially designed as command posts.[64] Thus, according to the CIA, even a dedicated attack against the Soviet command and control system could not prevent significant retaliation:

> Although United States attacks could destroy many known fixed command control and communication facilities, the Soviets' emphasis in this area has resulted in their having many key hardened facilities and redundant means of communication; thus it seems highly likely that the Soviets could maintain overall continuity of command and control.[65]

Ford's critique also ignores the central deterrent purpose of holding the Soviet leadership at risk. Contrary to his assertion that a retaliatory strike against such targets would clearly make no sense, American authorities have consistently argued that destruction of the Soviet leadership and political control system would negate a vital Soviet war objective. To the degree that the Soviet leader believed that full-scale nuclear retaliation would destroy their own lives and their ability to control Soviet society during its prolonged and painful recovery effort, Soviet initiation of major nuclear attacks would appear even more useless and dangerous.

The second criticism of counterleadership targeting is that it is unnecessary. The MAD threat to attack a large portion of the Soviet population (so-called countervalue targeting) should, according to this logic, be sufficient to deter Soviet leaders under all conditions. "Surely mechanisms for control, apart from the objects of control, have little political meaning to those who possess them," argues Robert Art. "And since the leaders need the civilians to control, why go after them the hard way (counterforce) rather than the easy way (countervalue)?"[66]

This argument is based on the assumption that destruction of Soviet cities would render the Soviet political control apparatus meaningless. As Art argued, "Extensive countervalue attacks . . . would kill so many Russian citizens that there would be little left to control."[67] There is, however, no evidence that the Soviet leadership shares this assessment and at least some evidence, although unavoidably inconclusive, that they do not.

The Soviet leadership certainly appears to believe that protecting itself and its political control apparatus is extremely important under any circumstances. Official Soviet military writings, for example, have long suggested that protection of "major administrative and political centers" is critical in a nuclear war.[68] It is also worth noting that a massive leadership rural evacuation program existed during World War II.[69] Perhaps most important, the current underground leadership-protection program has been one of the most expensive elements of the Soviet Union's military budget, according to the Defense Department, rivaling "Soviet offensive strategic weapons programs both in scale and level of commitment."[70] No better evidence of the value structure of the Soviet leadership is likely to exist. And if robust deterrence is to be based on holding at risk the things that it values most, it would be imprudent to ignore such evidence of what the Soviet leadership values and seeks to protect.

Assured Destruction of What?

The third criticism of leadership targeting is that implementing the threat would eliminate the hopes of war termination short of a major exchange. Again, Robert Art has been the most vehement critic: "The deliberate extensive targeting of Russian command, communications, control and intelligence facilities is absurd," he argues, since "we (and they) need someone who is in control and with whom we can negotiate."[71] This point is essentially correct. Attacking the Soviet leadership and its political and military control system would almost certainly end the prospects of a negotiated settlement before the United States had suffered the consequences of a major nuclear attack. To the degree that some American nuclear strategists forget that, the reminder is necessary. Yet this "criticism" is also fully consistent with the reading of the "countervailing" strategy as explained by one of its chief proponents, Harold Brown: "PD-59 is very clear on this. It says that you need the option [to destroy the Soviet leadership] but you certainly wouldn't want to use it, except if you had gone to an all-out strategic nuclear war on both sides."[72]

In short, the deliberate targeting of the Soviet leadership is best seen as the Assured Destruction component of current U.S. nuclear doctrine. Just as attacks against Soviet urban areas would not make strategic sense under the 1960s McNamara doctrine, *except in retaliation* after an attack on American cities, destruction of the Soviet leadership and control structure would not make sense under the current doctrine, *except in retaliation after a massive attack against American urban-industrial areas, including the capital.* In response to any other form of aggression or attack, American decision makers would have a great interest in sparing the Soviet central decision makers. Defense Department testimony that the President has a capability in U.S. war plans to withhold an attack against the Soviet "National Command and Control" during a U.S. retaliatory strike[73] supports this interpretation. Under current U.S. nuclear doctrine, the threat to the Soviet leadership should be seen as the paramount deterrent in peacetime and only the final option in the event of war.

CRISIS STABILITY AND SECOND-STRIKE COUNTERFORCE

Under the countervailing doctrine, the United States requires a retaliatory capability to deny Soviet war aims by threatening Soviet nuclear forces and holding at risk the Soviet leadership and political control apparatus. One important final criticism of contemporary U.S. nuclear doctrine, however, remains valid: current counterforce doctrine reduces crisis stabilty. A U.S. ability to threaten attacks on Soviet military and leadership targets in a *second strike* might appear to the Soviet Union as preparation for a U.S. *first strike*. If the American force posture, and military actions taken to ensure that effective counterforce retaliation was possible in a crisis, were misperceived by the Soviet leadership as U.S. preparations for initiating nuclear war, they would inadvertently increase the likelihood of Soviet preemption.

Although American civilian authorities have explicitly ruled out a preemptive nuclear strike, the difficult problem of assessing potential trade-offs between crisis stability and robust deterrence has received inadequate attention in both government circles and among academic strategists. A variety of factors has contributed to this lack of focus on crisis stability under current U.S. doctrine. First, the professional military—by the nature of its responsibility—pays much more attention to the requirements of war fighting than those of crisis stability. "Thinking the unthinkable" is their job, and it is not surprising that they view crisis stability as primarily a concern for diplomats and civilian authorities. An alarming, and unintended, consequence of the changes in U.S. doctrine in the 1980s, however, has been to push this tendency to great extremes. Indeed, by the end of the decade, statements by senior U.S. military officers have occasionally become disturbingly similar to some of the worst elements of Soviet military writings in the 1970s. In 1987, for example, Air Force Chief of Staff Gen. Larry Welch argued that the whole concept that prompt hard-target capabilities might be destabilizing was "nonsense." "He maintained that those weapons hold at risk those assets most essential to Soviet war aims and are therefore a more powerful deterrent and [hence] stabilizing."[74] In congressional testimony in early 1987, the Commander of the Strategic Air Command also bluntly stated his belief in the need for nuclear U.S. war-winning capabilities: "If deterrence should fail, obviously we have to be in a position where we win."[75] Among civilian strategists, and especially among some of the most prominent proponents of improved U.S. counterforce capabilities, there is, moreover, a belief that the Soviet Union simply would not fear a U.S. first strike in a severe crisis or conventional war. The United States did not launch a first strike under conditions of vast nuclear superiority in the past, it is argued, and Soviet concerns about U.S. preemption caused by such details in the U.S. military doctrine would therefore be minimal.[76] Other civilian strategists prefer to maximize doubts in Soviet calculations about a U.S. large counterforce first-strike option, believing that it, rather than more limited nuclear options, is needed to enhance the credibility of extended deterrence in NATO. Yet other strategists do not believe the effort to differentiate between a first- and second-strike counterforce posture is worth making, preferring to depend on MAD threats to the Soviet population or lesser threats to Soviet conventional military power rather than accept the inherent ambiguities involved in the current targeting doctrine.[77]

Reasonable people can disagree, given the great uncertainties involved, on the proper balance between robust deterrence and crisis stability. It would be possible, however, if greater attention is given to this matter, to create a second-strike counterforce posture that would maintain the robust deterrent of the countervailing strategy and yet minimize the crisis stability problem. The key force planning objectives would be to design a force posture that would enable the Soviet Union to differentiate between a U.S. second-strike and first-strike counterforce capability and to differentiate between a counterleadership retaliatory posture and a U.S. "decapitation" threat. Coupled with the proposals to reduce the risk that U.S. nuclear operations in a crisis might lead to inadvertent escalation or mistaken preemption that are discussed in chapter 4, these targeting policy refinements could significantly lessen the risk of a Soviet preemptive attack.

Slow versus Prompt Retaliation

If the U.S. nuclear planning efforts focused more vigorously on the critical difference between prompt and slow counterforce requirements, the crisis instability problem inherent in counterforce targeting could be significantly reduced. U.S. strategic bombers, and the ALCMs (airlaunched cruise missiles) many of them carry, are highly effective as counterforce weapons against hardened Soviet targets. Yet, because bomber delivered weapons require many hours to arrive on target, providing adequate warning of an attack, they are not very useful as a disarming first-strike force. (This is likely to be the case, with respect to a *full-scale* counterforce attack, even with future stealth bomber aircraft and cruise missiles.[78]) To the degree that Soviet targets need not be attacked promptly—even under current doctrine—a less destabilizing counterforce posture, emphasizing strategic bombers and ALCMs, could be adopted.

What are the prompt and slow counterforce requirements under a second-strike counterforce doctrine? With respect to Soviet ICBMs, one can differentiate between four distinct categories: reloads, launch failures, refires (or "second-wave" forces), and reserves. Reload capabilities—the empty ICBM silos that the Soviet military would seek to reload for the purposes described earlier—need not be struck with prompt U.S. counterforce weapons, since U.S. bombers and cruise missiles could destroy the targets in sufficient time to prevent reloading.[79] Soviet launch failures—ICBMs that were part of a Soviet first strike but failed to launch because of mechanical failure—would not, in theory, need to be struck promptly. In practice, however, it would be impossible to discern which remaining missiles were launch failures and which were deliberately withheld for other missions.

The other two Soviet ICBM categories—refires and reserves—do require prompt destruction under a second-strike counterforce doctrine. Refires are the ICBMs that the Soviet military would use for "second-wave" follow-on attacks, to compensate for launch failures, to attack enemy forces discovered not to have been destroyed in the initial strike, and to continue strikes against U.S. command and control in an effort to disrupt nuclear retaliation. U.S. ability to deny the Soviets the ability to execute such a refire mission would require prompt retaliation. Similarly, the United States would require prompt retaliation against Soviet reserve forces—ICBMs intended to be held in reserve for postwar purposes or to deter other Soviet adversaries. Not only would it be impossible for the United States to differentiate between reserve and other remaining ICBMs (both would appear as fully loaded silos), but the prompt destruction of such forces would also deny the Soviets the ability to respond quickly to actions taken by other nuclear powers. In short, second-strike counterforce could be more easily identified as such—and less readily viewed as part of a first-strike plan—if a simple principle was followed: there is no need for the United States to be able to destroy empty silos promptly.

It is not possible to spell out in detail the precise numbers and kinds of U.S. forces needed for this second-strike countermilitary mission. (A thorough analysis requires more information on Soviet nuclear forces and operations, and estimates of U.S. capabilities against hardened targets, than is available in open sources.) But four general characteristics of such a force posture are clear. First, the number of *prompt* counterforce weapons required for this strategy would be significantly less than those needed for a damage-limiting first-strike capability. Although the precise mixture of U.S. systems—the D5 SLBM, Minuteman III, MX, or a smaller ICBM—could be determined by future considerations of survivability, reliability of communications, and relative costs under this doctrine, there would be significant scope to reduce the numbers of vulnerable U.S. fixed-based ICBMs, since the total number of prompt counterforce warheads required *for this mission* could be kept near one thousand. Such a limited counterforce posture need neither produce great crisis instability nor prove prohibitively expensive.

Second, although this second-strike counterforce doctrine would be compatible with targeting Soviet *conventional* forces, it would require fewer prompt strategic forces than would a nuclear doctrine designed primarily to attack all of the so-called other military targets (OMT).[80] Given the immense size and dispersed character of Soviet conventional forces, a nuclear doctrine that focused primarily on OMT would likely lead to large increases in the number of warheads required. To the degree that prompt, accurate strategic forces were deployed, such large numbers might also inadvertently heighten Soviet fears of a major counterforce first strike. Bomber weapons, less accurate systems, and shorter-range systems could, nonetheless, be usefully targeted at Soviet conventional forces under this doctrine.

Third, movement toward a second-strike counterforce posture would require major improvements in U.S. intelligence, communications, and retargeting capability. The current ability to limit prompt counterforce requirements is restricted, in part, by an inadequate U.S. capability to determine precisely which Soviet ICBMs have been launched and which have been withheld.[81] U.S. acquisition of a near-real-time intelligence and retargeting capability could greatly enhance movement toward a more unambiguous second-strike counterforce posture.

Fourth, it should be noted that one common argument against U.S. second-strike counterforce—that it might not destroy the remaining Soviet silo-based missiles because the Soviets could, in reaction, launch their reserve forces on warning of a U.S. retaliation[82]—is not a compelling critique of this strategy. The purpose of the limited, prompt second-strike counterforce capability is *not* to destroy Soviet missiles. It is to enhance deterrence by denying the Soviet military the option of launching prolonged or sequential follow-on strikes and holding large ICBM forces in reserve. The proposed emphasis on less destabilizing bombers and cruise missiles, with restrictions on prompt counterforce capabilities, would serve that more limited objective.

Restrictions on Leadership Targeting Capabilities

The precise character of a U.S. nuclear arsenal designed to hold the Soviet leadership at risk cannot be determined without further information on the exact numbers and hardness of the bunker facilities. Nevertheless, a similar approach could enhance the ability of Soviet observers to distinguish between a second-strike counterleadership capability and a "decapitation" plan. Most important, deterrence under the proposed second-strike doctrine requires only that such leadership targets be threatened with *eventual*, not prompt, destruction in retaliation after a Soviet attack against American cities.

Three potential restrictions on U.S. nuclear capabilities would further clarify the second-strike intention of the counterleadership strategy. First, the assignment of ICBMs to the counterleadership mission can be severely restricted. Because the requirements for *prompt* attacks on Soviet command bunkers are minimal under this doctrine, bombers and cruise missiles could be used for the major proportion of this targeting mission instead of ballistic missiles. Moreover, although the development of very accurate, earth-penetrating warheads may be necessary, the eventual number of such weapons can be kept relatively low since, according to Defense Department estimates, Soviet wartime command posts are "mostly near surface bunkers."[83] Second, if the development of earth-penetrating weapons is required to threaten the deepest shelters, careful consideration of their deployment mode could reduce misperceptions. If earth-penetrating gravity bombs are to be developed for the future U.S. strategic bomber force, as has been reported, the potential destabilizing effect of having a prompt counterleadership capability could be significantly reduced.[84] At a minimum, designing and testing such warheads *only* for deployment on less vulnerable U.S. systems such as the small mobile ICBM or the D5 SLBM—and not on fixed-based ICBMs—would be prudent. Third, there is no requirement under this doctrine to attack airborne or ground mobile command posts promptly. Mutual restrictions on the development of such capabilities—through testing and acquisition of advanced maneuverable warheads—would appear to further U.S. interests by reducing *mutual* fears of a decapitation strike in a crisis or conventional war.

DEEP CUTS AND MOVING TARGETS

A final advantage of moving toward a more distinguishable second-strike counterforce doctrine is that such a strategy is quite compatible with an arms control agenda emphasizing *reductions* in strategic forces and, indeed, might be enhanced by a properly designed deep cuts regime. The strategic force reductions that are achievable in the near future—the outlines of an agreement to limit each arsenal to sixteen hundred missiles and bombers, with a total of between six thousand and nine thousand total warheads, was reached at the 1986 Reykjavik Summit—will not eliminate the danger of nuclear war or even, by themselves, significantly lessen the current vulnerability of U.S. ICBMs.[85] A deep cuts regime could, however, improve the ability of the United States to make mobile missiles invulnerable to a Soviet first strike. Moreover, if final START (Strategic Arms Reduction Talks) agreement counting rules favor renewed emphasis on less destabilizing bomber forces over ballistic missile warheads, they would be compatible with the restrictions proposed on prompt counterforce weapons.

Enhanced Survivability and Stability

For over a decade, the United States has been unable to muster the political resolve to solve the problem of ICBM vulnerability. While the Soviet Union reacted quickly to its emerging vulnerability problem by deploying rail and road mobile systems—absent arms control restrictions on mobility, estimates are that over one-third of its ICBMs will be mobile SS-24s and SS-25s by the mid-1990s[86]—the United States has debated numerous basing schemes for mobile systems, but has actually built none of them. The Reagan Administration rejected the Carter Administration's MX multiple protective shelter "shell game" system, but was unable to get congressional support for its preferred MX alternatives, either "dense-pack" basing or the deployment of one hundred MX missiles in Minuteman silos. By the end of the Reagan second term, both recommended mobile systems—the "rail-garrison" mobile MX and the SICBM (single-warhead ground-mobile small ICBM), or "Midgetman"—were under severe political fire. The rail-garrison MX plan would put fifty MX missiles on railroad cars stationed at Air Force bases and move them onto the nation's commercial rail tracks only in a crisis. Such missiles, however, would be vulnerable to any surprise Soviet first strike against their bases and would be very vulnerable to sabotage of rail lines during a crisis. The dispersed SICBM force would be less vulnerable in peacetime, but would be extremely expensive at approximately $40 billion, and would face the potential danger of vulnerability to a barrage missile attack if the number of Soviet warheads was increased.

START reductions and adoption of the second-strike counterforce doctrine could, potentially, help resolve the U.S. mobile missile vulnerability problem in two ways.

First, by restricting the number of missile warheads the Soviets are permitted, a START regime can significantly reduce the danger of successful barrage attack against the deployment areas of U.S. mobile missiles. This would not reduce the surprise attack or sabotage problem of the MX rail-garrison plan. But it would make ground-mobile small ICBMs, either roaming over U.S. military reservations or deployed to "dash" away from current ICBM silo locations on warning of attack, a more attractive alternative. Second, a second-strike counterforce doctrine, by reducing the required number of prompt hard-target warheads, would encourage deployment of a moderate-sized invulnerable missile force. A small SICBM force might prove more politically acceptable if it was clearly part of a less destabilizing force posture.

START cuts are also compatible with the emphasis given, under this doctrine, to strategic bombers. Bomber gravity bombs and SRAMs (short-range attack missiles) are heavily discounted under the agreed-upon START rules, both because of verification difficulties and because such slowly arriving weapons are considered less useful for a first strike. Bombers exclusively carrying such weapons will, therefore, be counted for START purposes as if they had only a single weapon on them, when, in fact, such bombers are usually estimated to carry approximately twelve nuclear weapons. This feature of the START regime gives both the United States and the Soviet Union a great incentive to place greater emphasis on such less destabilizing forces. If our nuclear doctrine emphasizes the need for a large prompt hard-target capability, strategic bombers and cruise missiles will be of diminished utility. Under a second-strike counterforce doctrine, however, such forces would be encouraged. Indeed, both because they pose less of a threat of a disarming first strike and because they appear to offer the most effective prospect for attacking Soviet mobile ICBMs, a modernized U.S. bomber force would be a critical component of a second-strike counterforce posture.

Preemptive Attack Dangers

Given the awesome destructive power of the U.S. nuclear arsenal, no sane Soviet leader *wants* to start a nuclear war. That danger—that the Soviet Union's leadership would deliberately launch a bolt out of the blue surprise attack—is not the problem we face. The danger is the possibility that in a severe crisis or conventional war, the twin beliefs that the Soviet military could achieve its wartime operational objectives and that the Soviet political leadership could survive to manage the painful reconstruction of Soviet society, could encourage a desperate decision to launch a preemptive strike against the United States. The countervailing doctrine is an attempt to reduce the chance that the Soviet leadership would believe that a preemptive option would be "successful," even in such a desperate situation. These further refinements to that strategy, and the potential restrictions in forces outlined under the second-strike counterforce doctrine, are designed to lower the likelihood that Soviet leaders would believe the U.S. possesses a disarming first-strike threat. The unilateral changes in U.S. military operations and the bilateral arms control measures analyzed in chapter 4 are designed to reduce the risk of a Soviet misperception that an American first strike was imminent and unavoidable in a crisis. Such a delicate balance of strategies is required if the United States is to enhance deterrence as well as maximize crisis stability.

CHAPTER THREE

Limited Strategic Defense

ON MARCH 23, 1983, at the conclusion of a television address devoted primarily to defense budget proposals, President Ronald Reagan shared with the American people what he called a "vision of the future which offers hope." Instead of simply continuing the long-standing American policy of deterrence through the threat of offensive nuclear retaliation, Reagan proposed that "we embark on a program to counter the awesome Soviet missile threat with measures that are defensive." Although it was acknowledged that such a formidable technical task "may not be accomplished before the end of the century," his speech was pervaded by optimism and faith. It concluded with an enthusiastic announcement: "Tonight we're launching an effort which holds the promise of changing the course of human history . . . I believe we can do it."[1]

The March 1983 speech revolutionized the strategic debate in the United States, without changing the world's nuclear arsenals in the slightest. Since that time, dozens of books and countless articles have been devoted to the debate over President Reagan's vision of the Strategic Defense Initiative ending the nuclear threat. Critics have relentlessly attacked this defensive ideal, seeking to demonstrate that the hope of "rendering these nuclear weapons impotent and obsolete," however desirable, is illusory. Administration spokesmen and SDI supporters have vigorously defended the long-range vision of building a perfect defense, arguing that the task is formidable but not impossible. As a result, the public has been confused, alarmed, and comforted at the same time.

THE FALSE DEBATE

It is both understandable and unfortunate that the strategic debate focused on President Reagan's hope of an "Astrodome" defense to protect the American people. It is understandable because it is the distant vision of perfect defense, not the more realistic possibility of highly limited strategic defenses deployed during this century, that has captured the public imagination. Although the SDI speech did not change the nuclear arsenals, it did alter the political landscape. By presenting a "vision of the future which offers hope," the Administration stole the moral high ground from the anti–nuclear freeze movement and, moreover, did so in a manner that appealed to the perennial American isolationist impulse and the technological optimism of our "can do" society. A public emphasis on perfect defenses also united the feuding factions of moderates and hard-liners within the Administration. Moderate arms control advocates supported the President's soaring rhetoric on SDI because it promised a potential bargaining chip, an incentive for the Soviets to agree to deep cuts in their offensive nuclear arsenal. Hard-liners publicly supported building perfect defenses because privately they believed it would be the best way to get actual progress toward defenses of a more limited nature, which they believed were both technologically feasible and militarily necessary to counter growing Soviet offensive and defensive strengths.[2] Finally, it is also understandable that the critics of SDI initially focused on debunking the perfect defense ideal. Because the initial domestic political appeal of SDI was in its idealistic vision, critics naturally sought to temper the public's optimism.

The idealistic nature of the SDI debate has also been unfortunate, however, because it has obscured the central issues the United States will face in the coming years concerning strategic defense and arms control. The most relevant question for future U.S. security is not whether we should build the perfect defenses that are desirable in an ideal world; it is whether it is in our interest to pursue the defenses of limited effectiveness that are possible in the real world. The future debate will be about Limited Strategic Defense, not Star Wars.

The excessive attention placed on Star Wars has meant that many issues concerning strategic defense have been underanalyzed and are consequently poorly understood. For example, the Reagan Administration has developed criteria by which to judge the appropriateness of movement toward highly effective defenses: Ambassador Paul Nitze's three criteria of (1) *technological effectiveness*; (2) *survivability*, to ensure that the defenses themselves cannot be destroyed in the initial attack; and (3) *cost effectiveness at the margin*, to ensure that offensive countermeasures are not cheaper and therefore more likely to be built than the defensive components.[3] Yet it is by no means clear that such criteria are appropriate for decisions to deploy highly limited defenses, since their purpose may be, for example, to protect U.S. command and control (C^2) sites or protect against accidental missile launches, and *not* to counter the large-scale offensive options of a determined Soviet opponent. Similarly, there is no consensus about the methodology to use in assessing the effects of limited defenses and remaining offensive forces on strategic stability or in judging the advisability of various arms control proposals that would permit limited defenses.[4] For over fifteen years after the 1972 ABM Treaty, strategic analysts debated the merits of offensive modernization activities and arms control constraints within what grew to be a familiar framework. Limited Strategic Defense, however, raises new questions in new strategic frameworks.

Although a number of major strategists in both the government and scholarly communities have started to address the complex issues involved in Limited Strategic Defense,[5] the excessive rhetoric of the public debate on perfect defense could soon have an unfortunate political effect. The realistic choices the United States will have to make in the coming years and, indeed, coming decades concerning decisions about both offenses and defenses will entail trade-offs in different approaches to enhancing deterrence. Yet the rhetoric of the SDI debate has all too often included assertions about the basic immorality of nuclear deterrence. To the degree that careless language and logic among both fervent SDI supporters and critics has an impact on popular opinion, it will make prudent security improvements, whatever the mixture of offense and defense decided upon in the near future, far more difficult to achieve.

This chapter will assess the strategic implications of the development of Limited Strategic Defense. Are U.S. deployments of such strategic defenses feasible and desirable? The answer clearly depends on the strategic goals defenses are meant to serve and the kinds and levels of defenses one is discussing. This chapter will, therefore, examine three different perspectives on the strategic defense initiative. It will first present a brief discussion of SDI 1—the President's dream of the perfect defense of population centers—and explain why there is near consensus among serious analysts that such defenses are not possible for the foreseeable future. The main part of the chapter examines SDI 2, which embodies the hope of some Pentagon analysts that a U.S. decision to deploy even limited defenses will enhance deterrence. What would one want to protect with Limited Strategic Defense and what are the strategic consequences of *mutual* Soviet and American limited defense deployments? Would limited defenses reduce the likelihood of nuclear conflict? Would such defense deployments lower the risks of accidental nuclear war? Finally, I will examine SDI 3, the Politburo's nightmare of major U. S. defenses leading to American nuclear superiority. Why are Soviet leaders so concerned about U.S. defense efforts?

One final introductory point should be emphasized: limited defense options will remain an important issue in the long term regardless of what happens with respect to strategic arms control in the near future. Whether or not defensive technology developments, beyond component testing and laboratory research, are constrained in arms control agreements in exchange for offensive reductions, decisions about limited defense will continue to hover on the immediate horizon. Not only will some limited defense options, permitted within the constraints of the ABM Treaty, continue to exist, but any evaluation of the advantages of continuing defense constraints must begin with an assessment of the effects of initial limited deployments. It is therefore critical that the gap between rhetoric and reality in the Star Wars debate be closed, and that the strategic consequences of limited defense deployments receive detailed scrutiny.

SDI 1: The President's Dream of Perfect Defense

Despite continued public statements from the White House about U.S. SDI deployments unilaterally eliminating the danger of nuclear war, there is a widespread consensus among strategic experts that the U.S. development of perfect population defenses is *exceedingly* remote for the foreseeable future. This view is by no means limited to dovish critics of the Reagan Administration's defense programs, although they have certainly been the most vocal in attacking visionary notions of Star Wars technology. In fact, the major defense and foreign policy officials of recent Republican and Democratic administrations all maintain that foreseeable U.S. defensive technology simply cannot eliminate the nuclear threat of a determined Soviet adversary. Consider the following statements:

> There is no serious likelihood of removing the nuclear threat from our cities in our lifetime—or in the lifetime of our children.[6]
>
> —James R. Schlesinger, U.S. Secretary of Defense, 1973–1975

For defense of populations against a responsive threat, they [the prospects for ballistic missile defense] look poor through the year 2010 and beyond.[7]
—Harold Brown, U.S. Secretary of Defense, 1977–1981

A foolproof defense of civilian population—which seemed implied by that speech [the March 1983 SDI announcement]—is a mirage; even a 90 percent effective defense would still let enough weapons through to destroy an unacceptable portion of our population.[8]
—Henry Kissinger, U.S. Secretary of State, 1973–1977

Although SDI spokesmen still indulge in exuberant rhetorical excess on occasion,[9] in more sober moments even such a Star Wars advocate as former Secretary of Defense Caspar Weinberger, who vigorously fought against any Congressional cuts of the program, has acknowledged that the prospect of perfect defense is simply not on the horizon. "We *hope* that strategic defense will eventually render nuclear missiles obsolete," he argued in 1986, adding, "That is our *long range vision.*" Yet he also acknowledged that *"for the foreseeable future,* however, nuclear weapons will be the inescapable backdrop of U.S.–Soviet relations."[10] Similarly, the June 1985 White House statement on SDI admitted that "for the foreseeable future, offensive nuclear forces and the prospect of nuclear retaliation will remain the key element of deterrence."[11]

This new consensus of both SDI supporters and opponents—that for the foreseeable future, U.S. strategic defenses alone cannot render "nuclear weapons impotent and obsolete"—is based on a combination of four basic facts about defense against ballistic missile attacks.

1. *Near-perfect leakage rates would be necessary to provide complete population protection.* Proponents of SDI are correct to note that, historically, most offensive military developments, considered "absolute weapons" at the time, were eventually countered by effective defensive systems.

Yet one of the fundamental changes that thermonuclear weapons have made in strategy is that their high explosive yield radically reduces the number of weapons necessary to inflict high levels of damage to urban-industrial targets. During World War II, for example, the British on their best day successfully destroyed 100 out of 104 German V-1 conventionally armed rockets fired at London.[12] Had these rockets been armed with thermonuclear warheads, however, London would have been destroyed. Given the destructive power of thermonuclear forces, less-than-perfect defenses might possibly "limit damage" or reduce "collateral damage" from some countermilitary attacks, but they cannot prevent massive societal damage in the event of an all-out nuclear exchange.

2. *The defensive technologies about which we know the most are the technologies least likely to provide full population protection.* Considerable progress has been made in research on defensive technologies under the SDI program during the past five years, but significant uncertainty still exists concerning the feasibility of the most exotic technologies. There is general agreement that limited capabilities, based on nonnuclear ground-based interceptors, are technologically feasible and that some limited kinetic-energy weapons in space will likely be possible before the turn of the century. The technologies that could provide for more highly effective layered strategic defense—such as neutral particle beam weapons; chemical, eximer, or free-electron lasers; or the nuclear-explosive-driven "x-ray" laser—are still quite uncertain. Research on such technologies is continuing under the SDI program, and will likely continue under any arms control regime. But there is general expert agreement that it is simply too early in the research phase to determine the technological feasibility of the most interesting potential defensive systems.[13]

3. *Offensive countermeasures must be taken into account.* The effectiveness of future U. S. strategic defenses

must be measured not against current Soviet nuclear offensive capabilities but against probable future Soviet capabilities including, but not limited to, offensive countermeasures against our defenses. Soviet writings on SDI and military development programs have displayed a great deal of interest in the full range of active and passive offensive countermeasures against potential U.S. defensive systems. Potential countermeasure programs include technical "fixes" to offensive systems such as the development of quick-burn missile boosters or ablative coating of missiles to prevent boostphase intercept; operational changes such as camouflaging missile launches with smoke screens or launching ICBMs on different azimuths or directions; antisatellite weapons and other forms of defense suppression; efforts to overwhelm potential defenses by warhead proliferation; the building of "dummy" missile boosters and various midcourse or terminal penetration aids; and increased emphasis on nuclear delivery systems not susceptible to ballistic missile defense.[14]

Moreover, many of the potential technological breakthroughs that could be useful in strategic defense may also enhance offensive countermeasure efforts. It is obviously impossible to know the precise mixture of countermeasures that will eventually be developed against a future U.S. strategic defense system, the technological structure of which is currently so uncertain. Nor is it possible to assess accurately the cost-effectiveness at the margin of each offensive countermeasure. (Soviet claims that offensive countermeasures will be significantly less expensive are obviously self-serving, but not necessarily untrue.) Yet the majority of expert opinion believes that an aggressive Soviet countermeasure program, while not necessarily negating the strategic or political usefulness of limited U.S. strategic defense, would eliminate the prospect of perfect population protection. As Richard DeLauer, the Reagan Administration's Under Secretary of Defense for Research and Engineering, acknowledged in 1983, "With unconstrained [offensive] proliferation, no defensive system can work."[15]

4. *Means of nuclear weapons delivery, other than ballistic missiles, exist.* Even if highly effective U.S. defenses against ballistic missiles could be developed, tested, and deployed, equally effective defenses against all other means of delivering nuclear weapons would be necessary to meet the ultimate Reagan objective of "rendering these nuclear weapons impotent and obsolete." To twist the commonly used metaphor, not only would there need to be an American "Astrodome" defense, but all the doors and windows to the country would also need to be closed. The Soviet Union currently has, according to Defense Department estimates, over three hundred Bear, Bison, and Blackjack strategic bombers capable of launching cruise missiles or dropping gravity bombs against targets in the continental United States.[16] U.S. air defense capabilities in the late 1950s and early 1960s were significant, but were allowed to wither as the Soviets placed greater emphasis on their ICBM and SLBM offenses. The Soviets are also expected to deploy large numbers of advanced long-range SLCMs (sea-launched cruise missiles) with nuclear warheads in the near future; the SS-N-21 has already been tested and the SS-NX-24 is expected to be operational before long.[17] American strategic defenses would have to cope with both of these air-breathing threats and, although many SDI programs (such as system acquisition and tracking and kill assessment) will be useful in air defense, a comprehensive program for potential deployment of such air defenses has neither been as thoroughly analyzed nor as generously funded as has the ballistic missile defense program.

Continued Research

Although these basic considerations have led the vast majority of technical and strategic experts to believe that development of near-perfect population defenses is unlikely to be possible for the remainder of this century, it has not led to a consensus against continuing the SDI research program. Indeed, most critics of SDI would agree that it is critical to continue a vigorous research program to provide an improved understanding of the potential technologies, to ensure that the Soviet Union is not alone in exploring advanced strategic defense systems, and to deter and prepare possible reactions to any Soviet breakout from the ABM Treaty's constraints. Still, despite the progress in SDI programs since 1984, there is currently no reason to revise the principal judgment of the Office of Technology Assessment's (OTA) initial report, *Directed Energy Missile Defense in Space*:

> The prospect that emerging "Star Wars" technologies, when further developed, will provide a perfect or near-perfect defense system, literally removing from the hands of the Soviet Union the ability to do socially mortal damage to the United States with nuclear weapons, is so remote that it should not serve as the basis of public expectation or national policy about ballistic missile defense.[18]

SDI 2: The Pentagon's Hope for Limited Defense

At the same time as there is a widespread belief among experts that perfect strategic defenses are not technically feasible, there is an equally strong consensus that limited defenses—strategic defenses with a level of effectiveness well below that necessary to protect the entire U.S. population—are possible. Indeed, the Soviet Union for over ten years has had a small-scale, operational anti-ballistic missile system around Moscow, and the U.S. technologies for a variety of ground-based interceptor rocket systems currently exist. The disagreements among strategists concerning such limited U.S. defenses are not over whether such capabilities are possible. The debate is over whether Limited Strategic Defense is desirable.

Is the deployment of limited defense capabilities in the

U.S. national interest? In order to examine this critical issue, it is necessary to define the strategic purpose of such defenses. What would we be seeking to protect and why? The following section will critically assess the various purposes that proponents of limited defenses have argued will be served by U.S. deployment.

Fundamentals of Limited Defense

Four general principles should be kept in mind when discussing limited defenses. First, it is highly misleading to analyze the strategic effect of U.S. strategic defense improvements alone, while ignoring likely Soviet reactions. All too often, as will be seen, arguments in favor of U.S. limited defenses simply demonstrate that, all other things being equal, the United States is better off with some strategic defenses than without them. That is undoubtedly true. It is also quite irrelevant, for other things are rarely equal in the real world. Meaningful analyses must weigh the effect of U.S. defenses against potential Soviet offensive countermeasures and reactive defensive deployments.

Second, the U.S. strategic purpose in deploying limited defense—the targets we are seeking to protect and the kinds of attacks we are attempting to defeat—will severely affect the appropriate cost-effectiveness criteria used in assessing the advisability of deployment. This is true for two basic reasons. First, there may be an asymmetry of interests between American defensive goals and Soviet offensive missions. As Ashton Carter has noted, "A defense that defends a target set we care more about protecting than the Soviet Union cares about attacking need not be as cost-effective at the margin as one that defends a target set the Soviet Union is determined to threaten."[19] In addition, limited defense deployments may seek to protect the United States against very specific limited Soviet offensive options. For example, it might be valuable to use limited defenses to prevent the prospect of a successful "decapitation" strike against U.S. command centers by Soviet submarines based off the Atlantic and Pacific coasts even though the targets defended could eventually be destroyed by equally effective, but far more distant, Soviet ICBM forces. In addition, if the purpose of U.S. limited defenses is to protect against an accidental launch of a small number of Soviet missiles, competitive cost-effectiveness criteria may not be relevant.

The third principle of sound analysis about limited defenses is that they must be assessed in the context of genuine U.S. military strategies. All too often, both critics and proponents of strategic defense lapse into calculations based upon the false assumption that U.S. (or Soviet) targeting policy is to destroy a certain percentage of the adversary's population.[20] But since neither the Soviet Union nor the United States measures its offensive deterrent effectiveness by such MAD criteria, meaningful assessments of the impact of limited defenses on "strategic stability" should not either.

Fourth, other means of protecting limited target sets must not be ignored. The attractiveness of utilizing active defenses to provide protection to a missile silo, a command and control aircraft, or even a population center, must be measured against "passive" defense measures such as increased hardening of military targets, increased mobility, or civil defenses. Such "passive" measures may provide better alternatives or a useful complement to limited strategic defense efforts.

The specific arguments for and against limited strategic defense can now be examined, taking these general considerations into account. What purposes might be served by limited U.S. strategic defense deployments? Proponents have suggested seven objectives for Limited Strategic Defense.

Prevention of Unauthorized or Accidental Ballistic Missile Attacks

Defending against accidental or unauthorized attacks has been a recurring theme in the debate ever since Robert

McNamara justified the proposed Sentinel ABM system in 1967, partly on the grounds that it would add protection against an accidental missile launch. Reagan Administration spokesmen have often used the issue to support SDI, although, as was the case with McNamara, it is clearly a secondary argument.[21] In January 1980 Democratic senator Sam Nunn also called for serious consideration of a limited antimissile shield, "the Accidental Launch Protection System"(ALPS).[22] The prospect of such a limited defense system raises two fundamental issues: What kinds of defenses can protect the United States from what kinds of accidental or unauthorized launches? And how critical is the danger of such nuclear missile accidents?

It should first be noted that an ABM Treaty–compliant system (that is, one hundred ground-based interceptors at one site in Grand Forks, North Dakota, in accordance with the ABM Treaty) would protect the United States against the effects of some, but by no means all, possible "accidental" nuclear missile attacks. At one extreme is the possibility of a launch of a large proportion of the Soviet ICBM force due to a false warning that a U.S. attack is underway. A one hundred-interceptor system would clearly be irrelevant in this "accidental" war scenario. At the other extreme is the unauthorized or accidental launch of a *single* ICBM or an SLBM from a Soviet submarine on an Arctic patrol. A treaty-compliant system could clearly protect against this danger. The utility of such a limited defense system to protect against the action of a deranged Soviet submarine captain or an otherwise accidental launch of a "boatload" of SLBMs, depends primarily upon the class of Soviet submarine in question. The older Yankee-class SSBNs (nuclear ballistic missile submarines) carry twelve to sixteen SS-N-6 or SS-N-17 missiles on board (each with only one or two warheads), and the early Delta-class SSBNs (Delta I and II) also each carry twelve to sixteen single-warhead missiles.[23] While a treaty-compliant system would protect against launches of the arsenal of these submarines, a more extensive defensive system would be required to protect against more modern Soviet submarines, the Delta III and IV classes, or the Typhoon SSBNs, which can each carry between sixteen and twenty MIRVed missiles totaling between 112 and 200 nuclear warheads per submarine.[24] Similarly, a treaty-compliant U.S. defense system might be effective against an accidental launch of up to a hundred single-warhead ICBMs, but if a technical failure in the Soviet command system or a group of deranged officers in Launch Control Centers (LCCs) produced a launch of over ten of the ten-warhead SS-18 missiles, the U.S. system would be overwhelmed.

In addition, utilizing present technology, a single-site ABM Treaty–compliant system at Grand Forks would not be effective against an accidental or unauthorized launch of a "boatload" of missiles from any Soviet submarine based off either of the U.S. coasts. The currently available exoatmospheric interceptor missiles—Lockheed's ERIS systems—require more time to track and destroy a missile than would be available in the case of closely based Soviet submarines.[25] Thus, protection from such a threat would require a modification of the ABM Treaty to permit interceptors to be deployed at coastal sites and not just at the single North Dakota ABM site.

Insufficient information exists to predict accurately the likelihood of the various types of accidental or unauthorized Soviet launch scenarios. It is widely believed, however, that the Soviet Union maintains extremely tight command and control, and very strict safety procedures, over its long-range nuclear forces. Such Soviet measures reportedly include PAL (permissive action link)-type locking devices on all ICBM forces and perhaps even on Soviet submarine SLBM forces, an accident prevention measure that the U.S. has never implemented.[26] The probability of a purely accidental or unauthorized launch of Soviet nuclear forces in peacetime is, therefore, widely considered to be extremely low. Serious technical failures in the Soviet space program, however, should serve as a reminder of the danger of mistaken orders produced by faulty command and control systems. In September 1988, for example, an incorrectly formatted radio message was accidentally sent to the Soviet Mars space probe, which caused it to self-destruct.[27] The prospect of similar mistakes causing an accidental missile launch is very remote, but it cannot be ruled out entirely.

The strategic ballistic missile forces of the other nuclear powers—France, Great Britain, and China—might be more susceptible to accidental or unauthorized launch, since their safety procedures reportedly are less tight than are those of the two superpowers. Yet, even in the event that there was a French, British, or Chinese accidental or unauthorized launch, *it is highly unlikely that the United States would be the victim* since the strategic forces of these countries are exclusively or primarily aimed at the Soviet Union.[28] (The Soviet government apparently recognizes this situation, since it has claimed that a purpose of the Moscow ABM system is precisely to protect against "third-party" attacks.) The threat of French, British, or Chinese accidental missile launches provides little support, therefore, for U.S. defense deployments.

Given the tight Soviet nuclear command and control system, and the fact that the other nuclear ballistic missile powers are all friends or allies of the United States, protection against unauthorized or accidental launches does not appear to be a high enough priority that it would *alone* warrant the expense of a U.S. limited defense program. (Estimates have ranged from $4.5 billion for the treaty-compliant system to over $15 billion for a six-site defensive system.)[29] If defenses are deployed on other strategic grounds, accident protection would be an important additional benefit. Most proponents of limited defenses appear to agree with this assessment.

Defense against Deliberate Attacks by Third Countries or Terrorists

A related argument, which also recalls the 1960s ABM debate, is that strategic defenses of limited effectiveness should be deployed to protect the United States from *delib-*

erate nuclear attacks launched by nations or groups other than the Soviet Union.[30] This rationale—with respect to either "third-party nations" or terrorist organizations—is not compelling *in the immediate term*. Again, consider first that the nations other than the superpowers that currently possess both nuclear weapons and long-range ballistic missiles—China, France, and Great Britain—are either formally allied or cooperating actively with the United States against Soviet military expansion. *Mutual* and *symmetrical* limited capabilities to defend against such third-party nuclear forces would, therefore, benefit the Soviet Union more than the United States. Currently, in the event of a conventional war against NATO, Soviet leaders must consider the possibility that their counterparts in Washington, Paris, *or* London (or Beijing, if China is attacked as well) might make the difficult decision to initiate the use of strategic nuclear forces. Deterrence of Soviet conventional aggression is strengthened, therefore, by the cumulative probability that at least one of these powers will use nuclear weapons first, even if others might back away at the brink.[31]

While it would be more clearly in the U.S. interest to have defenses against potential threats from such states as Khomeni's Iran or Qaddafi's Libya, the likelihood of such states developing or otherwise procuring *both* nuclear weapons and long-range ballistic missiles in the near future is significantly less than the probability of their acquiring nuclear weapons alone. In the event that such U.S. adversaries do in the near future acquire nuclear weapons, means of delivery other than ballistic missiles—aircraft, surface ships, or even smuggled "suitcase" bombs—would likely be the primary threat. This is also the case with respect to potential nuclear terrorism. The limited ballistic missile defenses currently envisioned as the first step in the SDI deployments would be largely irrelevant, therefore, to these serious, if unlikely, third-party threats and provide little support for a crash program of such deployments.

In the longer term, however, the ballistic missile threat from developing states is likely to become far more serious. Indian and Brazilian space launchers, for example, could in the future be converted into nuclear weapons delivery vehicles without difficult modification. Other developing states, including Pakistan, Iran, and Iraq, are actively pursuing a medium-range ballistic missile production capability, which could eventually be expanded to include longer-range ICBMs. Moreover, numerous Third World powers—including Iran, Iraq, Syria, and North Korea—have highly potent *chemical* weapons in their arsenal, and could therefore pose a threat to the United States if they acquired ICBMs even without getting *nuclear* warheads.[32]

U.S. maintenance of an ability to deploy limited defenses against such possible threats is therefore a critical *long-term* national security objective. This objective requires continued research into defense technology and eventual readiness to deploy highly limited defenses quickly if necessary. It does not, however, require immediate deployments.

Protection of U.S. ICBMs

The possibility of providing active defense for the U.S. ICBM force is by no means a new issue. Such defenses— utilizing endo- and exoatmospheric interceptor missiles— have been *technically* feasible since the 1970s, when the U.S. government unilaterally deactivated what it considered an excessively costly Safeguard ABM system. Renewed interest in ICBM defense has emerged recently, however, because greater hardening of ICBM silos and potential ICBM mobility increase the effectiveness of possible limited defenses and because near-perfect defense capability is not necessary when protecting ICBMs. Since the purpose of such capabilities would be to defend our deterrent, U.S. defenses that permitted some Soviet warheads to arrive on target would still be strategically significant if they nevertheless enabled sufficient ICBM retaliatory strikes to take place.

The continued debate about such ICBM defenses is not therefore primarily over technical feasibility. It is about the need for survivable U.S. ICBM forces and the expected costs of active defense deployments when compared with alternative means of decreasing ICBM vulnerability. The traditional arguments in favor of maintaining a U.S. ICBM force remain compelling: ICBMs provide the most effective prompt hard-target destruction capabilities, retain the highest assurance of tight command and control, and provide a hedge against future breakthroughs in Soviet air defense or anti-submarine warfare. In addition, as was emphasized in the Scowcroft Commission report, ICBMs that are vulnerable to Soviet counterforce attacks nevertheless retain some deterrent utility for two reasons. First, their existence lends a measure of survivability to U.S. alert bomber forces: precursor attacks by less accurate Soviet SLBM forces off the U.S. coasts against American bomber bases would permit subsequent ICBM retaliation, while initial launch of accurate but more distant Soviet ICBMs would permit successful launch of the bomber force based on tactical warning. Second, a conservative Soviet planner could not entirely rule out the possibility that ICBMs would be launched on warning or under attack.[33]

Critics of the Reagan Administration argued that the Scowcroft Commission "closed the window of vulnerability" and that, therefore, increased ICBM survivability is no longer necessary.[34] This view is inaccurate, however, since the Commission presented its support for fixed-based MX ICBMs specifically as an interim stopgap measure. When future Soviet SLBMs acquire sufficient accuracy to threaten U.S. silo-based ICBMs, the need for improved survivability will become even more critical. Moreover, even if the future U.S. strategic requirement for prompt hard-target kill capability is restricted, along the lines presented in chapter 2, the need for some survivable ICBMs will remain, for limited options and to provide a hedge against Soviet anti-submarine warfare improvements.

It is not yet clear, however, whether active defenses can contribute to cost-effective U.S. ICBM survivability enhancement. In the near term, ICBM mobility would appear to provide more effective and less expensive protection against a Soviet disarming first-strike than simply adding active defenses to U.S. fixed-silo ICBM forces. The *political* feasibility of the various mobility schemes for the MX and the small ICBM (Midgetman) remains in question, however, and without effective arms control limitations unrestricted proliferation of Soviet warheads could provide barrage attack potential against all but the most widespread mobile ICBM configuration.[35] Great interest exists, therefore, in determining whether future limited defense deployments *coupled* with mobile or deceptively based ICBM systems could provide longer-term cost-effective survivability. Because such defenses could be utilized in a *preferential* manner, that is, to destroy only the Soviet warheads attacking genuine U.S. ICBM targets, significant leverage might exist.

It is very premature at this time, however, to make a near-term ICBM defense deployment decision given currently available defense technology and the Soviets' ability to proliferate warheads on their largest missiles. Moreover, if the Soviet Union was able to "match" limited U.S. defense deployments of ICBMs with similar defenses of its own, the net effect on the strategic balance would be minimal. Indeed, completely reciprocal, but low-level, ICBM defenses would appear to favor the Soviet Union given its current advantage in ICBM warhead strength and initial deployment of mobile missiles.

In the longer term, however, the critical factors determining the attractiveness of such deployments—the costs and effectiveness of future U.S. defense technologies, the feasibility of mobility plans, and the size and structure of the Soviet ICBM force—may change. U.S. SDI research should, therefore, continue to examine the relevant technologies, coupling potential preferential defense with alternative ICBM basing-modes, to provide better information for a future determination on whether ICBM defense is economically cost-effective, militarily useful, and politically feasible.

Deterrence of Soviet Limited Nuclear Attacks during a
Conventional War

Another frequently used argument for limited defense deployments is their potential effect in deterring a Soviet limited nuclear attack during a NATO–Warsaw Pact conventional war in Europe. The Hoffman report, "Ballistic Missile Defenses and U.S. National Security," provided the most explicit presentation of the rationale for deploying ballistic missile defenses for U.S. ports and conventional reinforcement bases. Ability to destroy such U.S. targets with a *limited* attack makes such Soviet escalation more likely, according to the Hoffman study and the subsequent work of its authors:

> While the risk of provoking large-scale U.S. response to nuclear attacks on CONUS [continental United States] might be unacceptable to the Soviets, they might also feel that—given the stakes, the risks of escalation if conflict in Europe is prolonged, and the strength of their deterrent to U.S. initiation of a large-scale nuclear exchange—the *relative* risks might be acceptable if the attack size were small enough and their confidence of success sufficiently high. Without defenses, very small numbers of ballistic missiles could in fact achieve high confidence in such an attack. However, an intermediate ballistic missile defense deployment of moderate capabilities could force the Soviets to increase their attack size radically. This would reduce or eliminate the Soviets' confidence that they could achieve their attack objectives while controlling the risks of a large scale nuclear exchange.[36]

There are, however, two strong counterarguments against this line of reasoning. First, a limited ballistic missile defense that merely forced the Soviets to increase the number of missiles used in a "small-scale" attack against U.S. ports would not necessarily make such attacks more risky and therefore less likely. Given the enormous size of the Soviet arsenal, high military confidence in the attack's effect could be easily maintained by simply adding more warheads to the limited option. Yet since the U.S. reaction to such a strike would likely be determined less by the number of missiles launched than by the number of U.S. targets destroyed, the larger attack in a world of limited defense would not likely appear to be more escalatory than would a smaller attack today.[37]

Second, it should be remembered that NATO traditionally has relied upon the threat of limited nuclear escalation to a much greater degree than have the Soviet Union and the Warsaw Pact. To the degree that the Hoffman report's analysis on limited nuclear options is correct, the development of *symmetrical* limited defenses by both superpowers would likely benefit the Soviet Union more than the United States. Only *unilateral* U.S. deployment of effective Limited Strategic Defense, a highly implausible event, would avoid this dilemma.

Protection of U.S. Command and Control

Another common argument for U.S. limited ballistic missile defense deployments is to protect U.S. nuclear command and control capabilities. Despite considerable progress made in hardening and adding redundancy to U.S. command and control, one of the most significant dangers of nuclear war remains the possibility that in a deep crisis or conventional war a precursor nuclear "decapitation" strike, perhaps by Soviet closely based submarines, against central U.S. command and control targets, might appear to be the least disastrous military option available to the Soviet leadership. (See chapter 4 for further analysis of this scenario.) Although it is unlikely that such an attack could prevent U.S. retaliation completely—given alternative

communications means and the possibility of predelega-
tion of command authority under such extreme circumstances—Soviet military planners might expect that such
an attack under many circumstances would blunt American retaliation, reducing it to a less coordinated counter-
strike and thereby limiting damage to the USSR.

Ballistic missile defenses of moderate effectiveness might
significantly reduce the danger of a preemptive decapitation strike, either from Soviet submarines or initial ICBM
warheads. The major criticism of the Hoffman report's
argument about deterring limited attacks against U.S.
ports—the ease with which the Soviets could overwhelm
the limited defense by simply utilizing larger numbers of
warheads—does not apply as clearly to this scenario. It is
important to note, however, that a treaty-compliant U.S.
defense system, using currently available interceptors,
would not be sufficient to protect against a Soviet decapitation threat by submarines based off the American coasts.
Although the small number of Yankee-class submarines
that normally have been kept off the U.S. East and West
coasts throughout the 1970s and 1980s carry only approximately 100 to 150 total warheads, in April 1988 Presidential
Science Adviser William Graham acknowledged that the
launch of such missiles would not be picked up by early
warning radar in sufficient time to permit tracking and destruction of the SLBM warheads by ERIS interceptors in
Grand Forks.[38] Moreover, a Soviet decision to move the
newer Delta- or Typhoon-class submarines close to the
U.S. coasts would overwhelm a one-hundred-interceptor
treaty-compliant system. A treaty-modified system, with
both more interceptors and sites near the coasts, would
therefore be required to protect against this potential decapitation threat.

Insufficient information exists in the open literature
about the U.S. nuclear command and control system, and
U.S. anti-submarine warfare (ASW) capabilities, to provide an assessment of the level of effectiveness required
for such a limited defensive system. Two considerations,

however, should be taken into account. First, it is unlikely that Soviet military authorities could be confident of their ability to maintain a large SSBN force off U.S. coasts during a conventional war, the scenario under which a preemptive decapitation strike option would appear most possible. U.S. ASW forces might not be able to track and destroy *all* Soviet submarines near American coasts, but the Soviet Navy could not easily maintain forces sufficient to overwhelm a moderate-sized U.S. interceptor force. Second, if U.S. defenses could be used preferentially, they might be especially useful in protecting critical U.S. mobile command systems—such as the National Emergency Airborne Command Post, SAC's Looking Glass Command Post, and the U.S. Navy's TACAMO aircraft—from the threat of an SLBM barrage attack.

Finally, it should be noted that *symmetrical, but limited*, Soviet and American ballistic missile defenses protecting critical command and control facilities would not decrease the effectiveness of the U.S. retaliatory deterrent even under the countervailing strategy. Because most Soviet leadership targets need not be struck promptly under the doctrine outlined in chapter 2, limited Soviet active defense of its central command structure against *initial* missile strikes would not be unduly alarming. Indeed, such a defense already exists around Moscow.

An Increase in Soviet "Attack Uncertainty"

An increasingly common rationale for Limited Strategic Defense deployments, one that is strongly influenced by the countervailing doctrine's emphasis on denying Soviet war aims, is to increase the Soviet military's nuclear "attack uncertainty." The Hoffman report, for example, concluded that "defenses of intermediate levels of capability can make critically important contributions to our national security objectives. . . . *In particular, they can reinforce or help maintain deterrence by denying the Soviets confidence in their ability to achieve the strategic objectives of their contemplated attacks as they assess a decision to go to war.*"[39]

This line of analysis is based on an important insight: the Soviet General Staff's "military-technical" estimates of its ability to achieve its wartime objectives with a first strike—objectives that are today measured by specific high levels of nuclear damage expectancy against *the full set* of U.S. targets—could significantly influence political and military decisions to initiate large-scale nuclear war. Today, given the absence of U.S. strategic defenses and the high accuracy of the large Soviet ICBM force, the technical calculations leading to high confidence in an attack against all U.S. fixed-site targets are not excessively complex. As Hoffman has noted:

> A Soviet attack planner may adopt similar approaches as those used by a bridge-building engineer for controlling uncertainties. For such matters as missile accuracy, launch reliability, and estimates of the hardness of U.S. protective structures, he or she can make conservative assumptions based on empirical distributions drawn from test data or engineering estimates. The central element that distinguishes bridge building from war is absent: an active and unpredictable opponent.[40]

If, however, even highly imperfect U.S. ballistic missile defenses could be used in a *preferential manner*—that is, to concentrate defensive efforts against the specific warheads aimed at critical U.S. military targets—Soviet military planners could not easily retain the same high confidence in destroying the full set of U.S. targets by striking first. Such U.S. preferential defenses would "change the rules of the game for Soviet war planners," according to Paul Kozemchak of the Hoffman report study team, because "they would not be able to predict which targets were defended, nor would they be able to predict which of their missiles would reach their target." Under such conditions, "Soviet war plans would be scrambled, and the number of weapons the Soviets would require to accomplish their wartime objectives would be drastically increased."[41]

What this argument ignores, however, is the possibility that Soviet offensive war planning *objectives* would also be dramatically altered by the deployment of improved Soviet ballistic missile defenses in response to U.S. limited defense deployments. Current Soviet war plans apparently call for very high damage expectancies against *all* U.S. nuclear force targets, for example, because every U.S. ballistic missile not destroyed by Soviet offensive preemption could potentially retaliate against the Soviet homeland.[42] These strict offensive war-planning criteria could be greatly loosened, however, if Soviet ballistic missile defenses could destroy a more significant percentage of the U.S. retaliatory force. Indeed, *symmetrical* defenses of limited effectiveness in the U.S. and the USSR might *increase* the Soviet military's confidence in its ability to limit damage through an offensive first strike coupled with preferential defense of priority leadership, military, and industrial assets.

In short, the current focus on reducing Soviet *attack confidence* is far too narrow. A more reasonable, but far more difficult, objective would be to reduce overall Soviet nuclear *campaign confidence* (a product of the expected Soviet offensive and defensive capability). Given current Soviet advantages in both offensive prompt hard-target destruction capability and passive defensive measures, Soviet overall nuclear campaign confidence could be reduced if, but only if, U.S. ballistic missile defenses were significantly more effective than Soviet defenses. In the longer term, if exotic technologies for missile defense prove feasible, such an asymmetry may emerge favoring the United States. For the rest of this century, however, this is not likely to be the case.

Damage Limitation

The final rationale for U.S. limited defense deployments is to limit damage to civilian populations in the event of nuclear war. The critical uncertainty here is *not* whether limited U.S. defenses could protect U.S. urban areas from a massive Soviet nuclear attack deliberately designed to destroy them. They would not. It should not be forgotten that Soviet military writings, though rarely displaying an interest in producing the level of direct high-population fatalities seen in American concepts of Assured Destruction, do emphasize the need to destroy critical enemy military-industrial targets in the event of large-scale war.[43] The debate is instead over the degree to which limited defenses would reduce the *collateral damage* to urban areas resulting from a Soviet *limited* nuclear attack designed to destroy U.S. military targets. "When we understand that the problem of protecting civilians is primarily the problem of dealing with collateral damage," Fred Hoffman has argued, "it becomes clear that we do not need leakproof defenses to achieve useful results." "He concludes that the more effective the defenses, the greater the protection."[44]

Two strong counterarguments, however, exist. First, it should be noted that collateral damage resulting from a Soviet nuclear attack against military targets only, would be the product of the number of *warheads* that penetrate to the general target area and *not* the number of *missiles* initially launched in the attack. Therefore, if the U.S. defenses were so limited that the Soviets could simply overwhelm them by increasing the size of the attack, as was discussed above with respect to the NATO reinforcement scenario, then civilian collateral damage would not be reduced. Only in the event that U.S. defenses were very effective, sufficiently robust to prevent a large number of military targets from being struck at all, would collateral damage be significantly decreased in the event of a limited Soviet countermilitary strike.

Second, one should note that *civil defense*, not active ballistic missile defense, has long been the most cost-effective way of limiting collateral damage to the U.S. civilian population in the event of limited nuclear war. This is likely to remain the case for a long time to come. It is not clear, of course, that the political support for even modest civil defense spending—which has been lacking since the early 1960s—will increase sufficiently in the future to permit adequate funding. It is also not clear, however, whether political support for limited ballistic missile defense can be sustained, especially if near-term damage limitation objectives are emphasized as the public becomes more aware of the infeasibility of perfect Star Wars defense.

SDI 3: THE POLITBURO'S NIGHTMARE OF U.S. STRATEGIC SUPERIORITY

If President Reagan's goal of perfect protection of the U.S. population is technically infeasible and if the prospects for realization of the Pentagon's hope for limited U.S. defenses that enhance deterrence are still uncertain, a key question is obvious. Why are the Soviets so worried about SDI? Why have they so vigorously opposed the program in public propaganda forums as well as in serious arms control negotiations?

Although any answer must remain highly speculative— as is so often the case with analysis of Soviet military policy—the recent statements of the Soviet leadership and the recent history of Soviet military policy suggest that there are four related reasons for Moscow's strong opposition to SDI. The first is the *potential economic costs* involved in the Soviet effort to respond to U.S. strategic defenses. Soviet government spokesmen have clearly attempted to downplay the potential costs. General Secretary Gorbachev has consistently maintained that Soviet offensive countermeasures can be built far more cheaply than U.S. defenses, and the February 1986 report of the Committee of Soviet Scientists for Peace, Against the Nuclear Threat, "The Large-Scale Anti-Missile System and International Security," concluded that "in any combination counteraction measures invariably prove at least several times less expensive than large-scale ABM systems with space-based echelons."[45] Yet numerous other statements display the genuine Soviet concern over costs of the potential countermeasures. Such costs would likely be enormous because the probable Soviet response to SDI would emphasize both offensive and defensive systems: the need to respond to the technological advances involved in SDI—as well as the Soviets' experience in continuing ballistic missile, civil defense, and air defense programs despite their high costs—strongly suggests that the Soviet Union would eventually adopt both defensive "emulating" and an offensive "offsetting" strategy to counter any U.S. defense deployments.[46] The visceral Soviet fear of U.S. technology, as well as the determination to respond to U.S. defenses, was perhaps best seen in an editor of *Pravda*'s remark in 1985 that "if necessary we will eat only once a day" to counter SDI.[47] Although the history of the Soviet regime has shown that it can certainly discipline its population to make major economic sacrifices if necessary, in the current era of economic and political restructuring, it would obviously prefer to get the United States to abandon SDI unilaterally. The vigorous Soviet campaign against the program should be seen at least partly in that light.

The second major reason for Soviet opposition to SDI appears to be the program's potential for providing *major technological spin-offs*, benefiting the West in other military and industrial arenas. Not only would an arms race with the United States in defensive space-based systems be terribly costly, but it would mean competing in an area that greatly favors the West. The Soviet experience in technological competition with the United States can only confirm its fears that the United States can successfully harness its economic and scientific strengths to produce what once appeared impossible: witness, for example, the U.S. reconnaissance satellite program and the Apollo space program. The recent keen interest within the Soviet military in the uses of advanced technology in warfare—microcircuitry, directed energy systems, and genetic engineering—would further heighten General Staff concerns about potential SDI spin-offs.[48]

The third major cause for the Soviet opposition to SDI is

its *potential enhancement of U.S. offensive military capabilities.* The initial Soviet denunciations of the program emphasized the direct offensive capabilities of "space-strike weapons" in attacking the Soviet homeland. While such considerations are by no means entirely trivial, Soviet public emphasis on direct offensive uses of space-based rockets and laser systems also served the useful propaganda purpose of focusing public attention away from Soviet ground-based interceptors and civil defenses and onto potential U.S. "Star Wars" technology. What is apparently the most serious fear of Soviet leadership—that imperfect U.S. defenses coupled with the MX, D5, and stealth bomber programs could restore a U.S. first-strike nuclear superiority—was emphasized by Premier Yuri Andropov within days after President Reagan's March 1983 speech:

> In fact, the strategic offensive forces of the United States will continue to be developed and upgraded at full tilt and along quite a definite line at that, namely that of acquiring a nuclear first strike capability. Under these conditions, the intention to secure itself the possibility of destroying, with the help of the ABM defenses, the corresponding strategic systems of the other side, that is of rendering it unable to deal a retaliatory strike, is a bid to disarm the Soviet Union in the face of the U.S. nuclear threat.[49]

In late 1987, Marshal Sergei F. Akhromeyev, Chief of the Soviet General Staff, was quite direct in explaining his opposition to U.S. defenses:

> [The USSR is] deeply convinced that creating a space-based ABM defense to cover the territory of the United States would radically step up the military threat toward the Soviet Union. . . . At the same time the United States would have in its hands the strategic forces capable of delivering a strike against Soviet territory. That is, the United States would have a nuclear sword and a space-based shield.[50]

Although President Reagan was careful, in his original March 1983 speech, to warn that defenses "if paired with offensive systems . . . can be viewed as fostering an aggressive policy," other advocates of SDI have been less cautious.[51] For example, Colin Gray's argument that U.S. defenses are needed to restore "the diplomatic utility of our offensive forces" would likely appear as a quest for strategic superiority from Moscow's perspective.[52] Although Soviet spokesmen have clearly exploited such arguments for propaganda benefits, especially in Europe, it would be a mistake to treat this concern as disingenuous. Soviet political and military leaders have consistently displayed keen interest, both in their writings and in their positions in the arms control negotiations, in inhibiting any U.S. technological development that represents even a small chance of moving the United States back toward the superiority it held in the 1950s and early 1960s.

A final reason for Soviet opposition to even a limited U.S. defense system is not its offensive potential, but rather precisely its *defensive potential*. The Soviet Union has, through great effort and considerable investment, developed an offensive ICBM force capable of destroying the U.S. land-based force in a first strike. Regardless of whether one believes that the Soviets have acquired this capability to provide themselves with a genuine preemptive capability in a crisis or simply to inhibit the U.S. threat to initiate limited nuclear use in the event of a conventional war in Europe, it is clearly against Soviet interests, as the Soviets perceive them, to have the United States deploy limited defenses that might increase U.S. ICBM or command and control survivability. Furthermore, the Soviets have invested considerably in their own strategic defenses, including air defense against U.S. bombers, significant leadership protection through civil defense sheltering, the Moscow ABM system, and a suspected limited air defense capability against U.S. SLBMs.[53] Again, regardless of one's assessment of Soviet motives in building up such defenses, it can be seen that improved U.S. defenses would decrease the ability of Soviet defenses to limit damage in the event of a Soviet preemptive attack in a nuclear war. It is thus not surprising that Soviet spokesmen have opposed any form of U.S. strategic defense, whether it promises to be highly effective or relatively ineffective. Even if limited defenses are deployed in such a manner as not to threaten a disarming first strike when coupled with U.S. offensive modernization, the current Soviet advantages in prompt counterforce capability might be seriously diminished.

ARMS CONTROL AND LIMITED DEFENSE DEPLOYMENTS

There has been a conspicuous and curious contrast between the quality of the public debate in the 1980s concerning offensive modernization and that concerning potential deployment of strategic defenses. The debate on the MX missile and the Midgetman missile has included detailed analyses of potential basing-modes and studies of possible Soviet countermeasure programs, as well as extensive examinations of the specific purposes to be served by U.S. deployments. Moreover, the offensive forces debate has usually focused on the Soviet-American strategic *balance* and how various weapons systems on both sides can influence the current balance. In contrast, the SDI debate has too often deteriorated into conflicting assertions about prospects for technological breakthroughs in the distant future. Inadequate attention has been paid to the serious issues concerning near-term deployment options for limited defenses. The emerging early analyses of Limited Strategic Defense have, unfortunately, often been vague and unfocused. This is in part due to necessity. It is simply not yet clear what technologies will be most effective, what their relative costs will be, and what kinds of Soviet countermeasures are feasible. But the emerging debate has also reflected basic conceptual flaws. Insufficient analysis has been devoted to the potential Soviet offensive and *defensive* responses; yet certainly the *balance* of future Soviet and American defenses will be as important as are offensive force comparisons today. Most important, inadequate thought has been given to the question of the purposes of limited defense deployments. What are we seeking to defend and why?

The Purposes of Limited Defense Deployments

The analysis presented in this chapter suggests that a large number of common arguments for rapid deployment of limited U.S. strategic defenses based on currently available technology are fundamentally flawed. Arguments for U.S. limited defense deployments to deter Soviet limited nuclear attacks in a conventional war, or to limit civilian collateral damage from such attacks, ignore Soviet *offensive* countermeasures and the option of simply increasing the size of the attack to compensate for U.S. defenses. The argument that U.S. limited defense deployments would enhance deterrence by reducing the Soviet military's confidence in its attack plans ignores the likely effects of Soviet *defensive* countermeasures. Reciprocal deployments of limited defenses would not necessarily favor the United States, however, especially in the near term.

Indeed, a crash effort to deploy currently available ground-based systems would entail abandonment of the ABM Treaty and its beneficial limitations on *Soviet* defense deployments. A Soviet and American race to deploy "first-generation" limited defenses, however, is likely to weaken deterrence and benefit the Soviet Union more than the United States for three basic reasons. First, the Soviet Union has a great deal more experience in these systems and, most important, a hot production line for ground-based ABM systems. In the immediate term, therefore, the Soviet Union is much better positioned to deploy limited defenses, increasing its damage limitation capability, especially in the event that it strikes first in a crisis or conventional war. Second, as has been discussed, *mutual* limited defenses capable of destroying only moderate-sized missile attacks would disproportionately benefit the Soviet Union because of the current structure of the global alliance system. Because all nonsuperpower strategic nuclear missile arsenals belong to adversaries of the Soviet Union—France, Great Britain, and China—moderate-sized defensive systems might reduce deterrence of Soviet aggression on the Eurasian land mass. The third reason for avoiding a mutual deployment race with current defense technologies is that symmetrical levels of land-based missile defenses—which is what is likely *at best* in the immediate term—might well also favor the Soviet Union, given its current advantages in offensive prompt hard-target destruction capability, its passive defenses for leadership protection, and its currently deployed mobile ICBM forces. Simply placing an equal layer of moderately effective strategic defenses onto the current force structure, even if it enabled more U.S. ICBMs to survive a Soviet first strike, would simultaneously reduce the effectiveness of U.S. retaliation against the very targets the U.S. government maintains the Soviet leadership values the most: itself, its military power and political control apparatus, and its industrial capability to wage war.

One of the other arguments reviewed provided some *conditional* support for extremely limited defense deployments. *If* potential adversaries in the developing world appear to be close to producing their own long-range ballistic missiles, *then* the need for protection from third-party threats would become significantly stronger. This argument provides support for a robust SDI research program, but not for a rapid near-term deployment.

The two most important purposes that could be served by U.S. deployments of limited defenses are protection of U.S. command and control and reduction of the danger of an accidental or unauthorized ballistic missile attack. A slightly modified ABM Treaty, perhaps permitting a total of up to two hundred interceptors at three sites, could significantly reduce the risk of a decapitation strike against U.S. command and control centers, especially the critical mobile airborne commmand posts. Such a decapitation strike would only be plausible in the event that a desperate Soviet leadership believed that war was virtually inevitable and that such a command and control strike provided the best remaining hope of limiting damage to the Soviet homeland. The increased uncertainty provided by limited defenses might further dissuade even a desperate opponent from striking first. A U.S. defense system capable of destroying approximately two hundred missile warheads would also provide the extra benefit of protection against a number of improbable, though not impossible, accidental or unauthorized launch scenarios. Although such a system would be overwhelmed by a massive coordinated Soviet attack—whether launched under conditions of false warning or in a premeditated fashion—it would protect against single ICBM and SLBM launches or the accidental launch of the entire arsenal of even the most modern Soviet strategic submarine.

Serious military and technical research is clearly called for to determine whether such defenses are feasible and whether Soviet countermeasures could and would be designed to overcome them. Serious political negotiations, with both the Soviets and U.S. allies, would also be required on this issue. Because a major Soviet penetration aids program might severely limit the effectiveness of U.S. defenses, negotiations with the Soviets would be required to reduce the danger that they would interpret low-level deployment as a precursor to nationwide area defenses. (Although ground-based endo- and exoatmospheric defenses could be incorporated into a modified ABM Treaty regime without severe difficulties, extensive work and negotiations would be required to determine whether verifiable limitations could be decided upon for even limited space-based defensive systems.) Negotiations with allies would also be necessary to ensure that NATO members did not perceive the mutual Soviet and American developments in this area as a threat to their security. Specifically, the limited defense capabilities eventually decided upon would have to remain below the levels of the British or French nuclear arsenals to minimize the negative impact on NATO strategy.

Strategic Options and Negotiations

Although only low-level defense deployments, under such conditions, appear to be in U.S. near-term interests, this need not be the case in the longer term. Any one of three developments could produce conditions calling for more extensive defense deployments. First, U.S. technological breakthroughs may occur. If future research permits the development of militarily effective space-based defenses that are survivable and cost-effective compared with Soviet offensive countermeasures, and superior to Soviet defensive responses, then an extensive deployment decision would be sound. A vigorous SDI program—emphasizing basic research on advanced technologies—should both permit this long-term possibility and ensure that the Soviet Union is not alone in pursuing advanced strategic defenses. Second, U.S. defense deployments would undoubtedly be part of the U.S. response *if* the Soviets break out of the ABM Treaty in a militarily significant way. Last, if Soviet offensive deployments continue unabated, U.S. fixed and potentially mobile ICBMs, bombers, and submarines in port could someday be vulnerable to a Soviet first strike. Unrestricted Soviet development of highly accurate SLBMs, coupled with continued increases in Soviet ICBM effectiveness and warhead numbers, could conceivably produce a more effective preemptive Soviet nuclear attack option. Absent restraint or effective arms control, such a development would produce enormous pressures for U.S. defense deployments. In short, it is important to keep in mind that the decision to deploy a large-scale ballistic missile defense is not ours alone to make. Soviet defensive activities, as well as unrestricted offensive modernization, could force our hand.

A very difficult set of objectives in U.S. arms control negotiations is therefore in order. The possibility of near-term deployments of ABM Treaty–compliant, or slightly modified, defensive systems should continue to be discussed in the negotiations. Long-term research prospects should be protected and, at the same time, Soviet offensive and potential defensive threats should be constrained. This is clearly not an easy task. But I suspect that the more vigorously the United States pursues defense research efforts, the more likely that the Soviets will find it in their interests to restrict their offensive and defensive forces in exchange for U.S. concessions. If the Soviet leadership becomes so concerned about the longer-term prospects of U.S. defenses that it is willing to reduce significantly the current and future Soviet "damage limitation" capability— for example, reducing the ICBM force to the level below that needed to destroy U.S. ICBMs and placing tight restrictions on Soviet air defense and ballistic missile defense improvements—in exchange for U.S. assurances not to abandon the current, or a slightly modified, ABM Treaty for a set period of time, then both nations' interests may well coincide.

One final warning is in order. In order to reach useful agreements over the past decade, American administrations have had to strike a delicate balance between displaying sufficient resolve to build up strategic forces when necessary and maintaining adequate flexibility to accept arms control compromises when necessary. Leaning too far in either direction proved unproductive. The Carter Administration learned this lesson the hard way. It was widely criticized in its first years in office for pursuing arms control with excessive enthusiasm and arms programs with insufficient vigor, but it developed a more balanced approach by 1979 and was able to reach the SALT II agreement. The Reagan Administration was, in some ways, the mirror image. It was widely criticized in the first term for displaying excessive zeal for weapons modernization and insufficient desire for arms control. The Reagan Administration, too, learned the need for a more balanced approach in the second term and met with considerable success.

It would be very unfortunate if the current Administration repeated the mistakes of either of its predecessors. It is also unnecessary. As Bismark once noted: "Only a fool learns from his mistakes; a wise man learns from the mistakes of others."

CHAPTER FOUR

Accidental War and Operational Arms Control

IN ORDER to maximize deterrence of deliberate aggression, the United States and the Soviet Union each maintain over ten thousand strategic nuclear weapons—on land-based ICBMs, aboard submarines, and on long-range bomber aircraft—aimed at their adversaries. These massive nuclear arsenals threaten destruction beyond historical precedent, and large numbers of the weapons on each side are kept at very high levels of alert, ready to be launched at a moment's notice. Given these harsh facts of the modern nuclear age, it is not surprising that most individuals believe that a deliberate, premeditated decision to initiate a nuclear exchange is far less likely than some form of an "accidental" nuclear war—a war started through an unauthorized use or an accidental detonation of a nuclear weapon, a nuclear strike ordered in response to a false warning of an imminent nuclear attack, or inadvertent escalation caused by uncontrolled military operations.

The prevention of an accidental nuclear war is every bit as important a national objective as is deterrence of Soviet aggression. It should be recalled, however, that the "usability paradox" has produced and will continue to produce many tensions and trade-offs between efforts to maintain strong deterrence and steps to reduce the danger of accidental war. This chapter will, therefore, first review the steps that the U.S. government has taken in the past to reduce the risks of accidental nuclear war while maintaining robust deterrent capabilities. It will then examine a number of recent proposals to decrease such dangers even further. Although many of the proposals are related, in the sense that their effects would overlap, they can nonetheless be divided into five different categories: (1) improved communications capabilities between the United States and the Soviet Union; (2) policies to reduce the risk that a false warning of attack could produce a mistaken "retaliatory" launch; (3) proposals to tighten even further the control of U.S. nuclear weapons by placing electromagnetic locking devices on nuclear weapons aboard U.S. Navy vessels; (4) changes in U.S. military procedures designed to enhance the safe management of nuclear alerts in a severe crisis; and (5) possible U.S. efforts to help the Soviet Union improve its warning systems and command and control over its nuclear forces.

Not all proposals to reduce the risks of accidental war—however well intentioned—are wise; some may be counterproductive or unnecessary, and some may unduly reduce the strength of deterrence. Yet this analysis will also identify a number of unilateral actions and bilateral "operational" arms control agreements (agreements that constrain military operations, not arsenals) that could dampen the risks of accidental war *without* compromising the effectiveness of the U.S. nuclear deterrent. Considerable progress has been made since the 1960s in reducing the risks of accidental war. Considerable scope for further progress, however, still exists.

PAST EFFORTS TO PREVENT ACCIDENTAL WAR

A sharp contrast exists between the American public's perception of the likelihood of a nuclear war beginning through a tragic accident in peacetime and the views of most national security experts. Public fears, fueled by such films as *Dr. Strangelove, Fail-Safe,* and *War Games,* focus on the possibility of a crazy military commander, failed communications, or a faulty computer starting a nuclear war when no one expects it. The widely shared consensus among both civilian experts[1] and professional military leaders,[2] however, is that the danger of such an event under normal peacetime conditions—a "purely" accidental war or an "accidental war out of the azure"—is as remote as is the proverbial bolt-from-the-blue surprise attack.

This is not the case because the problem of accidental war is a trivial one. On the contrary, the reason a peacetime accidental launch or unauthorized attack is so remote is precisely because government officials have recognized the seriousness of the accidental war problem and have, over many years, developed a complex set of technical systems and military procedures to reduce such risks. It would be useful, therefore, to examine the major improvements in accident prevention that have been implemented over the past twenty-five years.

Unauthorized Use and PALs

The danger of an unauthorized use of a U.S. nuclear weapon by a deranged military officer was virtually non-existent during the early years of the atomic age for the simple reason that under the Truman Administration, U.S. atomic weapons were kept under the custody of the Atomic Energy Commission, to be turned over to the Strategic Air Command and other military forces only by direct presidential order in a crisis or war.[3] President Eisenhower's decisions in the early 1950s to build a large arsenal of tactical nuclear weapons and to release complete atomic weapons to the control of U.S. military units abroad or at sea, however, began the movement toward widely dispersed nuclear capability. By 1961, when the Kennedy Administration entered office, approximately twenty thousand nuclear weapons were under the direct control of U.S. and allied military units abroad and in the United States.[4] Although these weapons were designed so as not to detonate by accident, there were insufficiently strict safeguards preventing unauthorized use.

The most critical innovation in this area in the early 1960s was the development of PALs (permissive action links), mechanical locking devices that permitted activation of the weapon only upon insertion of specially controlled codes, or "keys." In December 1960, participants in a congressional tour of NATO military bases had been deeply disturbed by a fundamental lack of precaution against unauthorized use of nuclear weapons. At NATO bases in Turkey and Germany, for example, they saw foreign pilots sitting in the cockpits of the QRA (Quick Reaction Alert) bombers, which were loaded with "live" atomic weapons, with no more than a single armed U.S. sentry standing on the runway to prevent unauthorized activities.[5] Responding to such concerns in June 1962, President Kennedy signed National Security Action Memorandum 160, ordering PAL locks to be placed on all nuclear weapons in Europe, and U.S. government officials publicly described the new locking devices, and other U.S. command and control procedures, in a deliberate effort to encourage the Soviet Union to develop similar safety precautions.[6] Although full details are not available, it is widely believed that the Soviet Union eventually followed the United States by placing external control devices on its nuclear forces.[7]

Since the 1962 PAL decision, the original simple four-digit locking devices have been greatly improved (including the development of a limited-try capability that renders the weapon unusable if incorrect codes are repeatedly inserted) and have been placed on all Air Force and Army nuclear weapons deployed outside the United States. During the 1970s, similar locking control devices were also placed on the Strategic Air Command's bombers and ICBM forces.[8] PALs have not, however, been placed on the U.S. Navy's nuclear weapons. Instead, a complex system of procedural "checks and balances" was developed to maintain control over sea-based nuclear weapons. A recent official description of submarine missile launching procedures, for example, suggests that a minimum of seven naval officers, with the knowledge of the entire crew, must work together to launch an SLBM.[9] Finally, there is the "two-man rule" for command and control of

nuclear weapons: at least two individuals are to be involved in every sensitive action—from loading the weapons to verifying orders to execute the forces—taken with
U.S. nuclear weapons. Such a mixture of technical and
procedural innovations has, it is widely believed, virtually
eliminated the risk of a peacetime unauthorized launch of
a U.S. nuclear weapon by an insane American military officer.

False-Warning Dangers

A similar mixture of technological and organizational improvements has significantly reduced the danger of a false
warning of a nuclear attack leading to an accidental war in
peacetime. When the Soviets tested their first ICBM in August 1957, the United States had no reliable missile warning system and no procedures for rapid and safe launching
of the Strategic Air Command's bomber force under attack. In the event that warning of a Soviet missile attack
existed, SAC might not receive orders to launch the bombers in time; yet, in the event that U.S. bombers were successfully launched into the air, they would have proceeded to attack the Soviet Union in the absence of further
instructions. Under such procedures, therefore, if the
bombers were launched on *false warning* and if a "return
home" message did not get through for whatever reason,
an accidental nuclear war would have begun.

The Air Force responded to the emerging Soviet ICBM
threat in the late 1950s by building the BMEWS (Ballistic
Missile Early Warning System) radars and developing PCL
(positive control launch), or "fail-safe" procedures,
whereby bombers could be launched into the air upon
warning of attack, but would return to base *unless* they received further orders. Equally important, with the new
PCL procedures in place in March 1958, authority was
given to SAC to launch the bombers immediately upon
warning of attack.[10] The early BMEWS system was unreli-
able, however, and in October 1960 the moon was picked

up by the radar beams, indicating to SAC that "a number of high-flying objects" were heading for the United States. According to SAC's Commander in Chief (CINCSAC), Gen. Thomas Power, his "first impulse was to launch the ground-alert force as a precautionary measure," but after consultation with his staff and NORAD headquarters he decided that "the BMEWS system was still too unproven to warrant action in response to signals which, to all indications, had to be caused by something other than enemy missiles."[11] A similar incident occurred in November 1961 when an equipment breakdown at the Thule Greenland BMEWS cut off all its communications with SAC Headquarters. Fearing the initiation of war, Power ordered bomber crews to race to their planes and ready them for takeoff. Immediately, however, communications from SAC's new "backup" warning system at Thule—a SAC plane on airborne alert that flew over the BMEWS station precisely to provide a redundant source of warning—reported that the air base had not been attacked, and the preparations for bomber launch were terminated.[12]

Although SAC's PCL "fail-safe" bomber authority has remained in effect throughout the 1970s and 1980s, the recallable bombers (and of course the nonrecallable nuclear missiles) have never been launched in response to tactical warning. Since 1961 great improvements in both the technical reliability of individual warning devices and the overall redundancy of the U.S. warning system have taken place. Improved PAVE PAWS radars were built in the late 1970s to provide better warning and attack assessment against Soviet offshore submarines, a significant BMEWS radar upgrade program began in the mid-1980s, and a satellite warning system has been operational since 1971.[13] These capabilities have provided the United States not only with redundancy in warning systems but also—since one is based on radar and the other on infrared sensors—with "dual phenomenology" to substantiate warning. Moreover, in the 1980s the United States began deploying a sophisticated nuclear detection system aboard new satellites providing a much more effective third type of warning and attack assessment information—data confirming whether initial nuclear weapons have detonated on U.S. territory.[14] Finally, a requirement for human evaluation of warning data prior to any alerting measures or retaliatory action has been in effect throughout the past two decades and continues to exist today.

The Problem of Predelegation

Perhaps the most severe example of the usability paradox can be seen in the deep tension that is inherent in the two critical purposes of the U.S. strategic command and control system. The first purpose of the system is to ensure that the weapons in the U.S. arsenal would actually be launched *if* the National Command Authority ordered a nuclear strike. Without such a demonstrable capability, deterrence through the threat of nuclear retaliation would appear to be an incredible and ineffective bluff. The second purpose of the command and control system, however, is to ensure that American nuclear weapons are never used *unless* proper authorities order such an attack. Without this capability to control the arsenal, the risk of an accidental or unauthorized use of nuclear weapons would be unacceptably high.

It would be quite simple to design a command and control system that would virtually guarantee that *only one* of these two central objectives was met. At one extreme, it would be possible to have secure electronic safety locking devices placed on all U.S. nuclear weapons, and have them controlled by a single coded "key" stored in the black bag that is kept near the President at all times. Such a completely centralized command system—a "super PAL," if you will—would eliminate the risk of an unauthorized nuclear launch, but it would also guarantee that a single nuclear detonation in Washington would successfully "decapitate" the U.S. arsenal and undermine deterrence by eliminating the threat of nuclear retaliation. At the other extreme, it would be possible to give every Minuteman missile launch-control officer, every B-52 crew, and every U.S. SSBN commander the ability and authority to launch, by himself, the nuclear forces under his command. Such a remarkably decentralized command system would eliminate the risk of complete "decapitation," but would simultaneously increase the danger of nuclear accidents or actions taken by panicked or psychotic military officers.

The precise details of how successive presidents have chosen to balance these competing requirements is among the government's most highly classified secrets. It would be wildly imprudent for Soviet leaders to assume, however, that destroying Washington in an initial nuclear attack would ensure that retaliation would be eliminated. (It would be equally imprudent for U.S. leaders to assume that destroying Moscow in a "decapitating" attack would eliminate the risk of retaliation.)

The limited amount of unclassified information available on this subject can be briefly summarized. In 1956 and 1957, President Eisenhower delegated some authority to senior U.S. military commanders to use the nuclear weapons under their control. Commanders of the Air Defense Command and Atlantic Command were apparently authorized to use defensive nuclear air-to-air and surface-to-air missiles immediately in the event of a Soviet attack, and predelegated authority was given to senior military officers for an offensive nuclear response in extreme emergency conditions.[15] Although Eisenhower's specific orders on this matter remain classified, declassified 1957 Air Force documents suggest that the JCS agreed that "authority to order retaliatory attack may be exercised by CINCSAC if time or circumstances would not permit a decision by the President."[16] In July 1961, President Kennedy was explicitly warned, moreover, that the Eisenhower policy had created "a situation today in which a subordinate commander faced with a substantial Russian military action could start the thermonuclear holocaust on his own initiative if he could not reach you [by failure of communication at either end of the line]."[17]

Despite the greatly improved and redundant communication capabilities developed over the past decades, the possibility of a Soviet nuclear surprise attack that would destroy Washington and the President in a matter of minutes continues to exist. Although the details of current policy in this area are kept highly classified, it is known that the President retains the authority to delegate any of his responsibilities to other officials in the event that he is incapacitated.[18] Whether recent presidents have had enough confidence in the mechanical and organizational inhibitions to unauthorized use to predelegate authority to senior military commanders in the field in the event of a "decapitation" attack is not known. Secretary of Defense Harold Brown, writing in 1983, broadly hinted, however, that this might be the case:

> Submarine-launched missiles could wipe out Washington with no more than ten minutes warning, perhaps less. It is inappropriate to go into the details of the arrangements that have been made for such contingencies and to suggest to the Soviets how to get around those arrangements. But one criterion for such arrangements ought properly to be that such a decapitating attack should have the effect of making the response an all-out unrestrained one.[19]

ACCIDENTS IN CRISES

The technological systems and organizational procedures developed over the past thirty years have made the likelihood of a purely accidental war in *peacetime* highly remote. In a serious *crisis*, however, especially if strategic nuclear forces on both sides were alerted, the danger of accidental war or inadvertent escalation would be greatly increased. Not only could psychological stress affect political and military decision makers, but at higher states of alert readiness, some of the complex mechanical and organizational inhibitions to nuclear use could be significantly loosened. In addition, in a crisis the *likelihood* of a false warning of imminent attack could increase. Alerting actions might produce an accidental detonation, for example, or one side's preparations for potential retaliation could be interpreted by its adversary as the start of an offensive first strike. Moreover, the *effect* of false warnings could be more grave in a crisis, when military commanders and political leaders anticipate an attack and would be more likely to interpret ambiguous information in the worst light. Finally, the possibility of rapid, reciprocal increases in potentially dangerous military alerting activities—each side reacting to the other's actions—would also be heightened in a severe crisis.[20]

The point is best made by briefly examining a set of partially hypothetical scenarios. No system to prevent accidents is perfect; incidents of some sort are bound to happen. What if some of the rare accidents that have occurred in peacetime had instead happened in the middle of a serious crisis?

In January 1961, a B-52 carrying two hydrogen bombs crashed near Goldsboro, North Carolina. Although no nuclear blast occurred, official Department of Defense reports state that four of the six special safety devices on one of the weapons were triggered.[21] Yet even if one of these bombs had exploded, it is extremely unlikely that authorities would have ordered a nuclear strike on the basis of what would have appeared to be a tragic peacetime accident. Secretary of Defense Robert McNamara was nevertheless sufficiently alarmed by the Goldsboro incident to have warned President Kennedy to be highly suspicious of any peacetime emergency reports from SAC Headquarters stating that Soviet nuclear weapons had already struck the United States.[22]

More recently, in June 1980, a faulty computer chip in the NORAD warning system resulted in SAC being informed that a number of Soviet SLBMs had been launched against the United States.[23] Preliminary preparations for a

U.S. nuclear response were initiated—SAC pilots were ordered to start the engines of the alert B-52 bomber force and the Pacific Command's Airborne Command Post took off—while on-duty officers in the command centers, the Pentagon, and SAC and NORAD headquarters quickly reviewed all warning indicators.[24] These command centers, utilizing redundant warning capabilities, rapidly recognized that the attack warning was due to a technical glitch in the system, and was not a genuine Soviet nuclear attack. Higher political authorities were notified accordingly and the preliminary alert measures were terminated.

Imagine, however, that either of these incidents had occurred in the middle of a severe superpower crisis. If NORAD warning systems reported that a small number of Soviet SLBMs had been launched against the United States during a crisis, what would political authorities be told and how would they react? If a B-52 bomber crashed while landing at a SAC base during an emergency airborne alert during a crisis (the practice of routine peacetime airborne alert was ended in the late 1960s) and one of the weapons on board detonated, would this be reported to higher authorities as an accident or the first confirmed indication of a Soviet nuclear attack? How would authorities react? Worse yet, imagine that both of these kinds of accidents occurred simultaneously in a crisis.

The Cuban Crisis Revisited

The reliability of nuclear weapons' safety devices and tactical warning systems has improved significantly since the 1960s and, in this sense, crisis military operations today may appear to be less dangerous. Yet if one takes into account the existence on both sides of highly alerted strategic nuclear forces and modern rapid-response warning systems, a different assessment emerges. Indeed, advanced intelligence systems and modern capabilities to launch ICBMs on warning may have offset some of the crisis safety improvements developed during the past decades.

The potential for accidental war can be dramatically highlighted by considering a repetition today of three of the most serious close calls that occurred during the 1962 Cuban Missile Crisis. The first major problem developed in the Air Force missile alert procedures implemented in the crisis. When the United States placed SAC on a high-level alert during the crisis, B-47 bombers were dispersed to civilian and military airfields, additional B-52 bombers were placed on airborne alert, and SAC missiles were readied for launch. These alerting activities had been well-planned and practiced in advance, and were executed without major accident problems. At the same time that SAC put its forces on alert, however, an Emergency Combat Capability plan involving the Air Force Systems Command went into effect, automatically turning over test missile sites to SAC. At Vandenberg Air Force Base, the major testing site, nine ICBM test and training facilities were secretly loaded with nuclear warheads and placed on alert.[25] One of the Vandenberg test ICBM facilities was not readied with nuclear warheads, however, and this ICBM was launched on a test flight, without further specific crisis orders from the Pentagon, at 4:00 A.M. on October 26 in the middle of the crisis.[26] There was no known Soviet reaction to this ICBM launch, and, indeed, given the lack of Soviet satellite intelligence at the time, it is possible that Moscow officials did not learn of the test flight until well after the event. A similar poorly timed U.S. ICBM test launch during a crisis today would be picked up immediately by Soviet warning systems and possibly misinterpreted as the initial launch of an attack.

A second highly dangerous event took place in Moscow. On October 22, after Kennedy announced the implementation of the blockade of Cuba, Col. Oleg Penkovsky—a Soviet military intelligence officer whom the KGB had correctly suspected was serving as a spy for the West—was immediately arrested in his Moscow apartment. Penkovsky had been given a special telephone number and a set of coded signals to use in case of emergencies—for example, if he was about to be arrested or if he received information that a Soviet attack was imminent. For reasons that remain unclear, at the moment of his arrest Penkovsky reportedly used the emergency telephone message system to contact the CIA, *and signaled that a Soviet attack was imminent.* Fortunately, his Western intelligence handlers— against the background of Penkovsky's previous unstable behavior and their understanding of the tense crisis situation—decided to suppress the information and did not even report the message to CIA headquarters.[27] Under modern conditions, if Soviet nuclear forces were being placed on a higher state of readiness, different Western intelligence officials given similar information in a severe crisis might react differently and not fully discredit such a dangerous warning.

The third, and perhaps most grave, incident took place in the Arctic. On October 27, at the height of the crisis, a U-2 pilot, on a North Pole air-sampling mission to detect possible radioactivity from Soviet nuclear tests, became lost when the aurora borealis prevented him from properly using celestial navigation. Within hours the reconnaissance plane accidentally strayed into Soviet airspace over the Chukotski Peninsula, and Soviet fighter aircraft were scrambled to attack the U-2.[28] In response, American fighter interceptors in Alaska, with nuclear weapons aboard, were launched from their bases in an attempt to rescue the lost pilot. Fortunately, the Soviet and American interceptors did not come into contact with one another, and the U-2 safely found its way back to Alaska. The danger of inadvertent escalation in a confrontation between Soviet and American interceptors, however, was severe.[29] There was also a serious danger that the Soviet government might misinterpret the U-2 penetration. President Kennedy was concerned, when he learned of the incident, that the Soviets might believe that this was a last-minute "pre-SIOP reconnaissance" mission, just prior to an

American nuclear attack.[30] In fact, Premier Khrushchev did issue an immediate protest to President Kennedy:

> The question is, Mr. President: How should we regard this? What is this, a provocation? One of your planes violates our frontier during this anxious time we are both experiencing, when everything has been put into combat readiness. Is it not a fact that an intruding American plane could be easily taken for a nuclear bomber, which might push us to a fateful step?[31]

It was very fortunate that this U-2 incident occurred at a time during which, despite Khrushchev's claims to the contrary, Soviet strategic nuclear forces had *not*, in fact, been placed on a high-alert status.[32] Had a group of *Soviet* military aircraft accidentally penetrated North American airspace in the crisis—with SAC on DEFCON (defense condition) 2 and fighter interceptor forces fully loaded with nuclear air-to-air missiles in Alaska and the northern United States—the danger of an accidental war would have been much greater. Indeed, there is some declassified evidence suggesting that the United States might even have launched a nuclear attack in response to such a false warning: in a 1961 top secret military exercise, the full SIOP was ordered to be launched in response to reports that a large-scale aircraft penetration of the DEWline radars had just occurred.[33]

Tensions and Trade-offs

If, in a future crisis, the forces of both superpowers are placed on a high state of alert, the risk of a rapid response to any of these kinds of potential false warnings of attack cannot be entirely discounted. Indeed, if one considers the possible interlocking, or "tight coupling," of each superpower's warning and response systems, each reacting rapidly to actions by the other, the dangers could be compounded. Senior military and political leaders on either side might react strongly if their intelligence agencies reported that unidentified aircraft had entered their airspace, that an ICBM launch had been detected, or that well-placed agents in the adversary's capital had reported that war was imminent. What if the SAC commander, acting fully within his authority, then launched his bomber force under the PCL procedures? Soviet intelligence might learn of such a launch immediately and might interpret this bomber launch as further evidence that an American nuclear attack was imminent. What would Soviet central authorities be told by their military intelligence officers and how would they react? If they ordered ICBMs to be placed on the highest alert state possible, preparing to launch on further warning, U.S. intelligence might only know that critical Soviet ICBM communications nets were being utilized. How would such Soviet actions be interpreted? How would U.S. leaders react?

The likelihood of such events should not be exaggerated. They are remote. But the likelihood of a deliberate Soviet decision to launch a nuclear attack against the United States is also remote. The prevention of accidental nuclear war and deterrence of deliberate attack should not be considered in isolation from one another. Difficult assessments, trade-offs between accidental war prevention and the maintenance of secure deterrence, must often be made. What will be the effect of accident measures on the credibility of U.S. military commitments to allies, on the flexibility of U.S. retaliatory options, or on the ability to implement U.S. military plans? Can confidence-building measures lead to misplaced complacency or provide significant opportunities for Soviet deception? The following examination of accidental war prevention measures, therefore, assesses both the potential benefits and the potential risks of adopting such proposals.

IMPROVED COMMUNICATIONS CAPABILITIES

The first set of initiatives to reduce the risks of accidental war involves improving communications capabilities between the U.S. and Soviet governments.

The Hot Line

The need for special superpower communications links became evident during the Cuban Missile Crisis in October 1962. Throughout the crisis, President Kennedy and Premier Khrushchev could certainly communicate with one another, but the process was neither rapid nor entirely reliable. For example, perhaps the most important diplomatic message of the negotiations—Robert Kennedy's warning to Soviet ambassador Anatoly Dobrynin that the United States would attack the Cuban missile sites if the Soviets did not agree by the next day to remove them— was delivered orally to the Soviet ambassador on the evening of October 27. The scope for miscommunication was significant: there were no written instructions for what Robert Kennedy was supposed to say, and Dobrynin presumably had to write his own report of the conversation to send back to Moscow.[34] The time required for such a message to be sent from the President to the Premier was also quite lengthy: Dobrynin had to go to the Justice Department from the Russian Embassy, and then back again, before even beginning to relay the information to Moscow.[35]

In the wake of the crisis, Kennedy and Khrushchev agreed to establish a Direct Communications Link (DCL)— commonly known as the "hot line," or in the Pentagon as the "Molink" (Moscow link)—and less than two months after the agreement, the DCL was activated. It provided a capability to exchange printed messages, in a secure code, at sixty-six words a minute. In September 1971, the superpowers agreed to upgrade the hot line from the original wire telegraph circuit (with a backup radio telegraph circuit) to a dual satellite circuit. Six years later (the delay was necessary to overcome considerable technical problems and build satellite earth stations), the upgraded hot line became operational, with the wire circuit kept as a backup in case both U.S. and Soviet satellites should malfunction.[36]

Public information on actual use of the hot line in crises is limited, since only the President is authorized to release such information. It appears, however, that the DCL has been utilized quite sparingly since 1963: only two cases of hotline use—by both superpowers during the Middle East War of 1967 and by the Soviets during the 1973 Middle East War—have been officially acknowledged. In addition, officially unconfirmed reports have stated that the hot line was used during the 1971 Indo-Pakistani War, after the Turkish invasion of Cyprus in 1974, after the 1979 Soviet invasion of Afghanistan, and during the Polish civil disturbances in the mid-1980s. Despite such relatively infrequent DCL use, a direct and secure communications link has been considered beneficial by both governments.

In response to congressional pressures in late 1982, the Department of Defense evaluated proposals for further improvements in crisis communications.[37] Subsequently, in July 1984, the United States and the Soviet Union agreed to upgrade the hot line further, to include facsimile transmission capabilities. The now operational facsimile capability improves the crisis communications ability between heads of state in four ways. First, maps, pictures, charts, and plans can be sent over rapid and secure channels. Such a capability could be important, for example, in establishing a cease-fire line, or exchanging detailed schedules and plans for a mutual "dealerting" of military forces. Second, three times as much printed information can be transmitted over the same period of time, which could prove important if lengthy communications were required in a crisis. Third, by eliminating the need for keyboarding during message transmission, the risk of an operator error is reduced. Finally, graphic transmissions would permit improved authentication of messages by signature.

Further improvements to the Washington-Moscow DCL are not likely, however, in the near future. In both the original 1963 negotiations and the 1983 Defense Department report to Congress on Direct Communications Links, direct voice and video conference capabilities were specifically rejected. Such communications lack the precision of written messages, are more subject to misinterpretation, and might encourage rash or instantaneous responses rather than more deeply considered replies. These reasons for limiting the hot line to printed messages remain persuasive.

A proposal to add "hot-line" capability to alternate national command centers, such as the U.S. National Emergency Airborne Command Post (NEACP), however, does deserve serious consideration. Today, if the hot-line terminals in either capital were destroyed in a limited nuclear attack, or by an accidental, an unauthorized, or even a terrorist act in a crisis, rapid and secure communications between the heads of state would not be possible. The major objection to such a proposal is that a hot-line to NEACP might compromise the plane's location and thereby undermine deterrence.[38] If technical means can be developed that would permit secure communications between alternate and mobile command posts, without compromising the location and survivability of such command facilities, an "alternate emergency hot line" would prove a useful addition to current Soviet-American communications links.

Nuclear Risk Reduction Centers

In November 1983, a bipartisan study group cochaired by Senators Sam Nunn and John Warner recommended the establishment of "nuclear risk reduction centers" in Moscow and Washington. The proposed centers, possibly jointly manned by political and military officers from both countries, were to serve a number of purposes: to discuss procedures to be followed in the event of accidental or terrorist use of a nuclear weapon; to exchange information on nuclear proliferation problems; to clarify potentially provocative military activities in a crisis; and to "establish a dialogue about nuclear doctrine, forces, and activities."[39]

Pentagon officials, however, opposed the idea of jointly manned centers, or involvement of such centers in super-power crisis management activities, on four grounds: U.S. intelligence might be compromised; Soviet disinformation might be spread more easily; such centers would likely be bypassed in a serious crisis; and multiple sources of information and communication between the U.S. and the USSR might actually increase, rather than reduce, confusion and miscommunication in crises. A 1983 Pentagon report did, however, support the establishment of a Joint Military Communications Link, a "warm line" to permit easier exchanges of information between the two governments below the head-of-state level. Following the November 1985 Reagan-Gorbachev summit agreement to examine the various nuclear risk reduction concepts, high-level negotiations began in earnest, and in September 1987 an agreement was signed. The Moscow and Washington Nuclear Risk Reduction Centers will be staffed by political and military officers *from the host country only* and will be used primarily to exchange information (such as the notification of missile tests discussed below) as required by existing arms control agreements.[40]

The eventual role for these nuclear risk centers will depend, obviously, on how future Soviet and American political authorities decide to utilize them. Their potential usefulness should neither be exaggerated nor disparaged. As a provider of a dedicated lower-level communications line between the capitals in peacetime, they will likely foster more efficient and timely exchanges of arms control information. The Nuclear Risk Reduction Centers are not, however, likely to play a significant role during severe superpower crises because urgent communications in such dangerous periods will likely be limited to the heads of state using the hot line. The centers might nevertheless play a useful role in helping to implement any negotiated terms or agreements after the resolution of a crisis. For example, if it became clear that technical uncertainties emerged concerning the details of a cease-fire agreement or standoff zone, lower-level communications channels might prove very useful in resolving unintended ambiguities.

REDUCING FALSE-WARNING DANGERS

After the false-warning incidents in 1979 and 1980, improvements in the U.S. warning and surveillance systems were a high priority in the Reagan Administration's defense modernization programs, both to guard against false alarms and to ensure accurate warning of a genuine nuclear attack. The specific human procedural mistakes and computer chip failures that produced the momentary false alarms in one element of the warning system were rapidly fixed. A repetition of the specific operational error that produced the 1979 false alarm—putting a NORAD training tape of a Soviet attack into the real warning system—was eliminated by the construction of a completely off site training and test facility. In addition, the computer processors in which the 1980 chip malfunction occurred were rebuilt, and a software message-checking system was added to the system.[41]

Fixing these specific problems should not, however, breed a sense of complacency. Given the complexity of the technology and organizations that make up the U.S. warning system, further sources of error are likely to emerge.[42] Continued improvements in warning reliability should therefore continue to be a high priority. Two other initiatives—one in the arms control arena and the other a change in U.S. nuclear force employment policy—have also been proposed as a way of further reducing the false-warning danger.

Missile Launch and Exercise Notification

During the 1970s, the United States and the Soviet Union agreed to provide advance notification of a number of categories of ballistic missile test launches. Under the 1971

Accident Measures Agreement, each superpower is required to notify the other of planned ICBM launches beyond its national territory in the direction of the other party. The 1972 Incidents at Sea Agreement requires both sides to issue NOTAMs (Notices to Airmen and Mariners) announcing projected impact areas for missile launches that impact in international waters. The 1979 SALT II Treaty required advance notification of any *multiple* ICBM launches or a single ICBM launch that extends beyond the signatory's national territory. In 1983 the Defense Department reported that the United States had provided detailed notification to the USSR of such launches since 1979, while the Soviets provided less detailed, but still treaty-compliant, notifications.[43] Such testing notifications continued under the Reagan Administration despite the termination of other elements of the SALT II regime.

In the mid-1980s, Reagan Administration arms control negotiators proposed broadening this confidence-building measure to include advance notification of the test launch of one or more ICBMs or SLBMs. U.S. and Soviet arms negotiators also reportedly discussed advance notifications of major operational exercises involving nuclear forces, such as mass launches of nuclear-capable aircraft and large-scale dispersal of nuclear ballistic submarines from port.[44] Such a broader advance notification regime was designed to reduce even further the risk that test launches or nuclear exercises would be mistaken for an attack. (For example, it was reported that in 1982 the Soviet Union simultaneously launched two SS-11s, an SS-20, an SLBM, two anti-ballistic missiles, and an antisatellite weapon, alarming American warning officers.)[45]

A limited agreement was finally reached at the 1988 Moscow Summit. Although exercises and dispersal activities were not covered, both President Reagan and Secretary Gorbachev agreed to provide advance notification of all ballistic missile test launches. Such notifications are expected to contribute to improved verification of current or future arms control agreements, by enabling each side to mobilize proper intelligence assets to monitor such tests more thoroughly, as well as reduce the risk of a test launch being misperceived as an attack. A dangerous repetition of the unannounced test missile launch during the Cuban Missile Crisis has therefore been made less likely.

A further broadening of the advance notification regime to include all launches or dispersals of bombers or submarines does not, however, appear to be in the U.S. interest. The survivability of the alert bomber force—and to a lesser extent of the nonalert bombers and submarines in port—depends critically on its capability to be "flushed" or dispersed *rapidly* in a crisis or upon warning of an imminent attack. Adding a lengthy notification process would impair that important crisis response capability. Indeed, it could be counterproductive to the goal of reducing the danger of accidental war. For example, if the SAC commander or Washington authorities believed it was necessary, in a rapidly unfolding crisis, to disperse the alert bomber force, or even launch it under positive control or "fail-safe" procedures upon receipt of ambiguous warning of a Soviet attack, they would likely be compelled to break the advance notification agreement. This could add to the provocative nature of the U.S. military activities and, therefore, the existence of an agreement might actually *increase* Soviet perceptions that such defensive measures were actually the initiation of a U.S. nuclear attack. In short, it would be imprudent to accept restrictions on U.S. military operations that the United States was not fully prepared to abide by even in a severe crisis.

A No-Immediate-Retaliation Policy?

The trade-offs that can exist between reducing the risk of accidental war and the maintenance of robust deterrence are also starkly evident in recent proposals for adoption of a "no-immediate-second-use" policy. The debate over such proposals revolves around the following question: *When* should the United States *plan to retaliate*, or at least

have the *capability to retaliate*, in response to a Soviet attack? At one extreme, Bruce Blair has recently proposed
that the United States eventually adopt a policy of not re-
taliating in response to a Soviet nuclear attack until at least
twenty-four hours have passed, in order to ensure that the
"attack" is neither a false warning nor an accident, and to
give the National Command Authority increased time to
decide upon the appropriate response. "Authority to conduct offensive operations would be withheld for at least
twenty-four hours," according to Blair's proposal, "and
military units would be programmed to operate accordingly."[46]

Such a lengthy delayed retaliation policy, might, however, seriously undermine deterrence. It is not difficult to
speculate on the improved effectiveness of an offensive
war plan designed by the Soviet General Staff to take advantage of a twenty-four-hour "no-immediate-second-
strike" policy: ICBM and SLBM forces could be launched
in prolonged waves and reloaded and reconstituted with
impunity; follow-on ICBMs could be easily retargeted and
launched to compensate for any ICBM launch failures;
bomber forces or cruise missiles would have more than
enough time to reach their U.S. targets; reconnaissance information on the results of initial attacks could produce
improved retargeting or even bomber "search and destroy" missions against U.S. forces and command and
control; and barrage attack options against U.S. submarines would be more attractive with the larger Soviet reserve and reloaded ICBM force. For a Soviet military planner interested in limiting damage to the USSR in the event
of a nuclear war, a twenty-four-hour delay in U.S. retaliation would provide significant opportunities. (The same
would be true for SAC planners if the Soviets adopted
such a delayed-response policy.) Indeed, given current or
any realistically achievable U.S. command and control system and strategic forces, a twenty-four-hour-delay policy
would bring us uncomfortably close to a "no-second-use"
policy.

This does not mean that the United States should adopt the other extreme, a firm policy of launching vulnerable forces on receipt of tactical warning of Soviet attack (tactical warning here refers to satellite warning and radar confirmation).[47] A more prudent position would be to maintain the capability and plans to "launch under attack"— that is, after confirmed detonations of a number of Soviet nuclear weapons on U.S. soil but before the entire Soviet attack plan was completed[48]—with the NCA making the final decision concerning appropriate response. If, at the height of a severe crisis or conventional war, for example, Soviet ICBMs and submarines off U.S. coasts were launched simultaneously against the United States, the SLBM warheads would strike their targets (presumably nonhardened command and control targets and bomber bases) approximately twelve to twenty minutes before Soviet ICBM warheads arrived to destroy hardened targets (such as the U.S. ICBM silos) (see fig. 4-1). Under such conditions, as Walter Slocombe has argued, "It might be

FIGURE 4-1
U.S. Launch Under Attack (LUA) Timeline

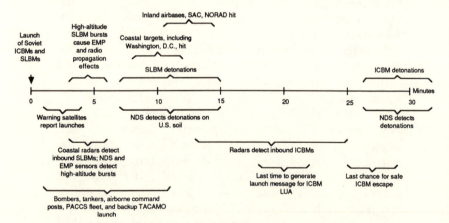

Source: Ashton B. Carter, "Assuring Command System Vulnerability," in Ashton B. Carter, John D. Steinbruner, and Charles A. Zraket, *Managing Nuclear Operations* (Washington, D.C.: Brookings, 1987), p. 580.

appropriate to fire U.S. ICBMs at Soviet nuclear targets before the incoming attack destroyed them."[49]

Any decision to execute such a prompt retaliation "in kind" against remaining Soviet ICBMs, like *any* decision to use nuclear weapons, would require that agonizing appraisals about the possible purposes of the Soviet nuclear attack and the purposes of the American response be made by the National Command Authority. Whether the NCA would, in the limited time available, actually make the momentous decision to launch U.S. forces is by no means certain. Two points about Launch Under Attack (LUA), however, should be emphasized. First, it would be highly imprudent for the United States to rely, that is, to base its entire deterrent strategy, on such a risky and uncertain option.[50] Not only are there grave technical and psychological uncertainties concerning whether the United States could and would retaliate so promptly, but under other plausible attack scenarios—such as a simultaneous Soviet ICBM and SLBM laydown—a U.S. Launch Under Attack option would be virtually impossible. Acquisition of more survivable command and control capabilities and nuclear forces, as well as improved capabilities to retarget surviving missiles after an attack,[51] should therefore remain a high priority in U.S. strategic modernization programs to reduce pressures for prompt launch. Second, the demonstrable *capability* to launch under attack would enhance deterrence by adding an element of grave uncertainty to any Soviet preemptive attack plans.

Secretary of Defense Harold Brown has best expressed the resulting policy:

> I think launch under attack is something that is important to have as an option. . . . I don't think [however] that that is a credible sole strategy. . . . The Soviets should not be able to count, and I think aren't able to count, on our not doing it, but we surely should not count on being able to.[52]

Brown concludes, "That is uncomfortable, but that is the way it is. And I think that contributes to deterrence."[53]

Increasing Warning Time

Another set of proposals is designed to reduce the risk of accidental war by lengthening, or at least not diminishing further, the amount of warning time available to central decision makers in the event of a nuclear attack. Such proposals have the unusual, but very attractive, feature of decreasing both the danger of accidental war (by allowing more time for confirmation of attack to take place in case of false warning) and deliberate attack (by decreasing the likelihood that a potential aggressor would believe that precursor attacks against command and control centers could successfully surprise an adversary). The nuclear weapons that pose the most severe threat of a rapid surprise "decapitation" strike, as well as attacks against coastal bomber bases, are the SLBMs in submarines closely based off the coasts of the adversary. In addition, the possibility of low-observable cruise missile surprise attacks against command and control targets from either submarines offshore or long-range bomber aircraft is emerging as a serious problem. Although both air-launched cruise missiles (ALCMs) and sea-launched cruise missiles (SLCMs) move too slowly to be utilized as a massive first strike against ICBMs, decision makers on both sides might well be concerned that a very small number of cruise missiles could escape detection.[54] The importance of this problem will be increased with the future development of stealthy and supersonic cruise missiles. A number of arms control proposals address these specific systems.

An SLBM Depressed Trajectory Ban

Although Soviet submarines were occasionally tracked in the western Atlantic in the 1960s, the Soviet Union first established regular patrols of strategic submarines off the coasts of the United States around 1970. Currently, SLBMs launched from these submarines could destroy Washington in approximately ten minutes and also threaten rapid attacks on Strategic Air Command bomber bases, especially those nearer the U.S. coasts.[55] A Soviet and American agreement to ban the testing of ballistic missiles in a severely depressed trajectory mode would not increase the warning time available to decision makers, but it would prevent the potential flight times of SLBMs from becoming even shorter. (A recent estimate was that a Soviet SS-N-6 SLBM fired in a depressed trajectory mode could strike a target at a range of 1,500 kilometers in six to seven minutes rather than in the estimated eleven minutes required under a normal minimum energy trajectory launch.)[56]

Because reentry vehicles would be subject to unpredictable, and potentially destabilizing, amounts of heat and pressure if entering the atmosphere on a depressed trajectory, extensive testing of such launches would be required for either side to have confidence in such operations. Currently, there are no public reports of either the Soviet Union or the United States having *repeatedly* tested severely depressed trajectory missile launches, suggesting that a significant opportunity for a complete ban on such operations exists.[57] Serious verification problems would still need to be resolved in negotiations; there may be difficulties, for example, in distinguishing between "failures" of permitted test launches and successful depressed trajectory testing. (The improved verification capability provided by the 1988 missile test notification agreement may prove helpful here.) In addition, it would be important to ensure that certain essential American missile testing procedures—such as subjecting reentry vehicles to greater than expected heating by launching flights on trajectories that are slightly less than the nominal apogees for a given range—were not unduly inhibited. Serious technical work and preliminary negotiations on the possibility of a depressed trajectory ban appear in order to determine whether such impediments to a mutually beneficial agreement can be resolved.[58]

Standoff Zones

A related confidence-building measure is the proposal for a standoff zone for all nuclear ballistic missile submarines (SSBNs) off each other's coasts. The length of the additional warning time provided to command authorities and alert bomber forces would depend upon the parameters of the zone. If the zone was extensive enough, bombers and command and control aircraft on coastal bases could have much higher confidence than exists today in receiving warning of an SLBM attack in sufficient time to take off and fly a safe distance from their runways.

The U.S. government has never seriously pursued SSBN standoff zones in arms control negotiations, believing such an agreement would not be in the U.S. interest for a mixture of four reasons. First, U.S. acceptance of an SSBN standoff zone away from Soviet coasts could impede other important U.S. Navy missions. Indeed, because the Soviet Union, like the United States, has great difficulties differentiating an SSBN from an SSN (attack submarine), any NATO mission requiring forward deployment of SSNs would be restricted: a thousand-kilometer submarine standoff zone would, for example, prevent forward U.S. anti-submarine warfare (ASW) activities and SSN support for U.S. surface-ship presence or amphibious landings in Norway, both of which are considered critical elements of current U.S. maritime strategy, as well as possible submarine intelligence missions; a two-thousand-kilometer zone would force the United States to withdrawal from its base at Holy Loch, Scotland, and would not permit a tight anti-submarine barrier to be established along the Greenland–Iceland–United Kingdom (GIUK) gap. The second set of potential problems with SSBN standoff zones concerns verification and compliance. Because a single submarine covertly entering the zone would threaten many military and command and control targets, U.S. monitoring capabilities would have to be extremely effective to provide adequate confidence. Futhermore, the efforts necessary to convince the public or Congress that sufficient verification was possible or that a violation had occurred might compromise U.S. intelligence and ASW capabilities.[59]

In addition, there is at least some possibility that an effective unilateral U.S. "maritime exclusion zone" could be established in a severe crisis or conventional war. In a very serious crisis, the United States could declare that any unfriendly submarines found, perhaps after a brief "grace" period, within a certain distance from U.S. coasts would be subject to conventional attack. At a minimum, military and political prudence would suggest that the successors to the National Command Authority be evacuated to secure locations in such a crisis. If a crisis led to a major conventional war, such ASW attacks would be a high priority. The British Navy maintained such a maritime exclusion zone, with respect to its fleet, during the Falklands War, and the U.S. Navy may have some capability to enforce a one-sided SSBN standoff unilaterally.[60] The severe risks of escalation inherent in following such a policy in a serious crisis would have to be weighed against the extreme risks of allowing SSBNs to patrol off U.S. coasts under conditions in which a "decapitating" or damaging limiting attack might be considered a serious option in Moscow.

The fourth problem with submarine standoff zones is that they might prove counterproductive in a crisis. It is certainly possible, in a crisis, that a submarine could inadvertently stray within the zone or that false underwater contacts could be received. If such "false warnings" occurred, senior officials would likely react more vigorously than they would have without the standoff zone agreement.

Similar problems and trade-offs exist with respect to proposals to negotiate standoff zones for other kinds of military forces. With respect to strategic bombers, a standoff zone sufficiently large to reduce Moscow's fears of air-launched cruise missile carriers coming close to the Soviet Union, might well restrict the Strategic Air Command's important conventional mission in the event of war in Europe or the Persian Gulf. Similarly, Soviet proposals for aircraft carrier standoff zones could greatly inhibit U.S. carrier support for allied wartime missions. Although serious analyses of the advantages and disadvantages of such standoff zones should continue, it appears likely that the best solution from the U.S. perspective would be plans for unilateral actions to limit dangerous Soviet military operations in crisis or war, coupled with prudent unilateral restraints placed on U.S. force activities as necessary.

PALs for the Navy

Since June 1962, when the initial decision to place devices on U.S. nuclear weapons in Europe was made, the use of electronic coded locking devices has spread throughout most of the U.S. nuclear arsenal. Today, all deployed land-based U.S. nuclear forces have some sort of mechanical locking device, installed in either the warhead itself or its control facility, to ensure that the weapon is not used in an unauthorized manner. With the exception of nuclear depth charges stored ashore in peacetime, however, the U.S. Navy has never placed mechanical locking devices on its nuclear weapons. The existence of thousands of nuclear weapons at sea—SLBMs (submarine-launched ballistic missiles), SLCMs (sea-launched cruise missiles), gravity bombs on carrier aircraft, and shipboard surface-to-air and surface-to-surface missiles—has led a number of strategic analysts to suggest that a major program of PALs for the Navy should be implemented.[61]

The Navy has long maintained, however, that PAL-type devices are not necessary for effective protection against unauthorized use. The complex nuclear command and control procedures that are currently in place, requiring simultaneous action on the part of numerous officers to launch a weapon, are considered sufficient. Moreover, it is often argued that the important deterrent role of the SSBNs, and their relatively vulnerable communications links, requires that the *capability* to launch forces be maintained on board; putting PALs on the SLBM force would heighten the danger of nuclear decapitation if the Soviet Union believed it could sever communications links in a nuclear first strike and the submarines would never retaliate.

Which of these arguments is more compelling? It is impossible to assess the trade-off between maintaining deterrence and preventing accidents at sea in full detail without complete information on naval command and control systems and procedures. Sufficient information exists, however, to make the following recommendation for a change in policy. Although the arguments against placing mechanical locking devices on the strategic submarines are strong, the arguments against putting PALs on Navy surface ships and dual-capable aircraft are far less compelling. A program to add more effective mechanical locking devices for those forces appears warranted.

Two key points favor maintaining the current system for U.S. Navy submarines, but not other naval forces. First, the critical decapitation argument—that the inevitable Soviet uncertainty about what U.S. Naval commanders would do with the missiles under their command if all communications were cut off in a nuclear attack significantly reduces the risk of such an attack—applies primarily to the submarines.[62] Second, it should be kept in mind that the purpose of PALs is not just to reduce the risk of unauthorized use by insane or mistaken U.S. military officers, but also to reduce the danger of a terrorist, an adversary, or a third party gaining control of "usable" U.S. weapons. Submarines pose a negligible risk in this regard. Even if the strict U.S. Navy procedures do adequately protect against U.S. officers using weapons in an unauthorized fashion, however, they are unlikely to protect fully against other parties taking over surface vessels and their on-board weapons. Although the risk of such an event is less than that of terrorists or others seizing U.S. land-based weapons, after such incidents as the *Pueblo* or *Ma-*

yaquez takeovers it should not be dismissed. A program placing locking devices on U.S. Navy nuclear weapons on surface ships would eliminate this danger, without raising the risk of successful decapitation.

CONTROLLING NUCLEAR ALERTS

An awareness of the degree to which the danger of inadvertent escalation or accidental war would increase if both the Soviet Union and United States alerted strategic nuclear forces in a crisis has led some leading strategic analysts to recommend that the United States refrain from ordering nuclear alerts in crises. Senior American political and military leaders certainly should not take a decision to alert forces lightly. Soviet and American strategic nuclear forces have never simultaneously been placed on a high state of readiness in a crisis, and the potential for dangerous interactions, misinterpretations of intent, or false warning of attack might precipitously rise in a full crisis alert.[63]

Despite these dangers, a blanket U.S. "no-nuclear-alerts policy" would be inadvisable on both political and military grounds. Politically, a U.S. refusal to alert nuclear forces in some severe crisis conditions might send a misleading political signal to the Soviet Union. For example, if Soviet or Warsaw Pact conventional forces were threatening to attack U.S. or allied forces in the Persian Gulf or Europe, complete U.S. failure to generate strategic forces might tempt the Moscow leadership to continue escalating the crisis in the belief that American inaction reflected a willingness to back down. Given past American crisis behavior, Moscow decision makers might also plausibly believe that U.S. reluctance to respond reciprocally to any Soviet nuclear alerting pressures implicitly signals U.S. intent not to challenge Soviet conventional incursions.[64]

The military rationale for alerting U.S. nuclear forces in a number of severe superpower crisis scenarios is also strong, a point that is often overlooked. This is often due to a serious misunderstanding: even knowledgeable analysts in the West have argued that the United States keeps its strategic forces on a higher state of alert readiness than does the Soviet Union.[65] This was certainly true throughout the 1950s and 1960s, but it is no longer the case today.

A proper comparison of strategic alert levels is complex since each side has chosen to emphasize different kinds of forces in its nuclear arsenal. The Soviet ICBM force holds over 60 percent of the USSR's strategic warheads and dwarfs its submarine-based force and small bomber force. The U.S. arsenal, in contrast, is more evenly balanced, with a larger percentage of warheads in both the submarines and bombers than the ICBMs. Although the United States keeps approximately one-third of its strategic bombers on day-to-day alert, while the Soviets do not, and two-thirds of U.S. submarines are kept at sea, compared with only approximately 25 percent of the Soviet submarines, the structure of the Soviet arsenal makes such comparisons misleading.[66] Indeed, a careful examination of each power's nuclear arsenal reveals that the Soviets actually maintain a slightly higher state of *overall* strategic force readiness, as measured by the nuclear warheads available for immediate attack (see Fig. 4-2).

This change in alert status is due to two basic developments in Soviet strategic forces in the late 1970s and 1980s. First, Soviet ICBM alert readiness levels were raised until they became roughly comparable to the high U.S. ICBM alert rates.[67] Virtually all the ICBMs on both sides are now kept at full alert, ready to be launched in a matter of minutes upon receipt of authentic orders. Yet given the massive numbers of Soviet ICBM warheads available, this portion of the Soviet alert nuclear force, *by itself*, equals or surpasses (depending on how one defines U.S. SSBN alert levels) the *overall* U.S. alert warhead numbers. Second, while the United States continues to keep a larger percentage of its SSBNs at sea, this is not a proper measure of alert status. The United States keeps only approximately one-third of its submarines on station and on full alert;

FIGURE 4-2
The Nuclear Balance and Alert Forces, 1987

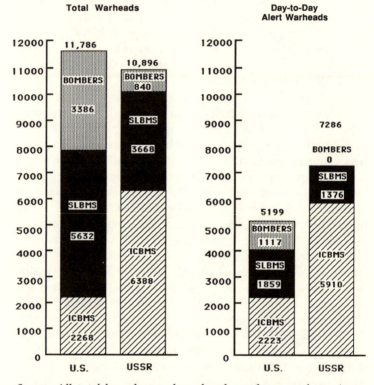

Source: All total launcher and warhead numbers are from *Arms Control Today*, vol. 17, no. 18, October 1987, pp. 10–11.

one-third are *not* on full alert while in transit or in sea training, and one-third are in port.[68] The Soviet Navy must also maintain submarines in transit and on training missions, and probably has roughly the same percentage of its submarines, at sea, on alert. It is important to note, however, that because recent classes of Soviet SSBNs have sufficient range to reach American targets *from port*, the percentage of the submarines at sea is no longer an accurate measure of Soviet SLBM alert levels. The Defense Intelligence Agency reported in 1981 that "certain submarines and combatant units at their home bases are probably on a high state of readiness,"[69] and the U.S. Navy estimates that 25 percent of Soviet SSBNs *in port* are at a high alert status *there*, capable of launching their missiles immediately.[70]

The significance of these alert levels depends upon one's views of the requirements of deterrence, as discussed in chapter 2. If one believes that Assured Destruction capabilities are all that is required for deterrence, then a U.S. alert of strategic forces is not necessary on purely military grounds. Under day-to-day alert, U.S. alert submarines carry a sufficient number of warheads to destroy, if targeted to perform that mission, a large portion of Soviet urban-industrial society. To the degree, however, that the Soviet military's behavior in a crisis would be influenced by its perception of the nuclear "correlation of forces"—and by its ability to achieve very specific military objectives in war—then an American decision to alert forces might prove to be important. Placing the remaining two-thirds of the U.S. bomber force on alert, for example, would not only reduce the bombers' vulnerability to a Soviet attack but would also enable the United States to target Soviet ICBM and leadership shelters more effectively. Indeed, from the perspective of the countervailing doctrine, one particularly worrisome crisis scenario would develop if the Soviet Union alerted only its air defense forces and implemented its civil defense and leadership-protection plans, on grounds that these were purely "self-defense" measures, while refraining from "provocative offensive measures" such as sending submarines to sea or alerting bombers. In such a scenario, U.S. refusal to alert nuclear forces might undercut the strength of the U.S. deterrent under current U.S. military doctrine.

The dangers would be especially acute if the United States failed to raise the alert level of its *command and control system* for strategic forces in a crisis. If the U.S. command system (including airborne and ground-mobile command posts) was brought to a higher alert status, the likelihood of a successful Soviet decapitation or damage-limiting attack would be greatly reduced. If, however, U.S. nuclear command and control was kept at a routine readiness level, even the more optimistic analyses available in the open literature suggest that American retaliation might be significantly blunted by a Soviet decapitation attack.[71] Thus, at a minimum, U.S. alert activities in a severe crisis should include raising the readiness of the command system in as sustainable a manner as possible.

Managing Alert Activities

If a nuclear alert is ever deemed necessary in a crisis, however, it will be essential that central authorities carefully control military activities in order to reduce the risks of inadvertent escalation or mistaken warning of attack. Four unilateral U.S. actions could be very important in this regard. First, U.S. alert plans should be designed so as to make alert activities appear nonprovocative, when possible, to the Soviet Union. As the previous example of a Soviet "defensive" alert suggested, the meaning of most alert actions would be highly ambiguous, but some potentially provocative actions might be identified and restricted. For example, it is not obvious that Soviet intelligence could tell the difference between a *dispersal* of U.S. bombers to alternate bases (to decrease their vulnerability to Soviet attack) and an actual *launch* of the bomber force. A thorough reexamination of bomber dispersal procedures with this question in mind would be useful. It might also be wise, under a number of crisis scenarios, to consider plans to alert U.S. nuclear forces and supporting command and control in a *gradual* and *sequential* manner, rather than in a rapid, full force generation. Such an alerting option might reduce the risk that the Soviets would perceive U.S. activities as the start of offensive operations, as well as enhance the sustainability of the U.S. alert posture in a prolonged crisis. This crisis management initiative would, it is important to note, require much greater centralized political or military control over alerting activities than currently exists. Under current rules, senior military commanders have complete authority to alert the forces under their control.[72] A high-level review of such authorization is therefore also necessary if the danger of misperceptions caused by nuclear alerting activities is to be significantly reduced.

Second, U.S. *reconnaissance activities* in crises require close scrutiny at senior levels. In previous nuclear crises, there were a number of potentially dangerous reconnaissance activities undertaken by military commanders or intelligence agencies that would not have been approved if higher authorities had been fully aware of them, for fear that the actions might be provocative.[73] Although it is not clear that all potentially provocative missions should be called off in future crises (some may still be necessary for critical intelligence purposes), it is clear that it is the central decision makers who should determine whether, and when, such missions go forward. It is unlikely, however, that senior officials today have either adequate familiarity with the full details of such crisis activities or the specialized staff with the necessary information to enable them to make prompt and proper judgments on these complex issues in a rapidly escalating crisis.

Third, senior political and military authorities should carefully review SAC's operational plans to implement an airborne alert posture in a severe crisis. Bomber dispersal, increased alert status on runways, and CINCSAC's authority to launch the bombers on tactical warning under the positive control launch procedure, can effectively protect the bomber force from a Soviet first strike today. In addition, it should be noted that airborne bomber alerts are by no means completely unprovocative. There is always some small chance, as occurred at least once in the late 1950s, that one or more U.S. bombers on airborne alert or following "fail-safe procedures" might inadvertently penetrate the Soviet early warning net.[74] Given the Soviets' sensitivity to bombers flying off their coasts (as evidenced by their START CBM proposal to ban such activities) and the increased danger of a nuclear weapons accident occurring in the United States during landing or aerial refueling, a serious review of these military operations might suggest that the limited benefits of airborne alert are no longer worth the risks. At a minimum, current airborne alert procedures should be reviewed by senior political and military authorities to reduce the danger of unanticipated and undesirable operations occurring in a crisis.

Finally, the U.S. military alert system should be revised to exclude the use of any new or less than fully tested weapons systems or operational procedures. In the past, many of the most serious crisis management problems developed precisely when new weapons systems were introduced or novel military operations were implemented in a crisis. The command and control problems caused by placing fully armed SAC missiles into the Vandenberg testing facilities and other less than fully prepared silos during the Cuban crisis, for example, were severe: adequate safety procedures were not implemented, and the potential danger caused by the test missile launch was not anticipated.[75] The Alaskan U-2 incident was also the result of new, untested military operations being implemented in a crisis. This particular North Pole reconnaissance mission had only been attempted twice before the October 27 mission, and no one, in the heat of the crisis, anticipated the navigational problems that caused the plane to stray into Soviet airspace.[76] Similar safety problems are likely to emerge in future crises and can be minimized if emergency capability plans and alert procedures eliminate the use of new and untested systems and procedures.

These recommendations would have modest, but useful, effects in making nuclear crises less dangerous. They would not make nuclear alerts a safe crisis signaling device or tool of diplomatic coercion; the uncertainties are far too grave to treat alerts as anything other than extraordinary and dangerous operations. Yet, since alerts may be deemed necessary in a crisis, despite the dangers involved, it is prudent to make them as nonprovocative, sustainable, and as little prone to accident as possible.

COOPERATION WITH THE SOVIETS?

The risk of accidental nuclear war is a mutual problem, and there is every reason to believe that the Soviet Union considers the dangers at least as seriously as does the United States. American defense experts do not generally consider improvements in Soviet military command and control capabilities to be in the interests of the United States, yet with respect to preventing accidental war, there may be instances in which this is the case. In such cases, Washington authorities may want to cooperate with Soviet officials in joint improvements of nuclear command and control procedures. Such actions would not be entirely unprecedented: the publicity that the United States gave to its initial steps to reduce the risks of accidents in the early 1960s (open discussion of the PALs program and "two-man rule" procedures) was due, in part, to a desire to encourage similar Soviet actions.[77] In addition, in May 1970 Ambassador Gerard Smith presented Soviet SALT negotiators with a carefully prepared official statement on U.S. command procedures and technical devices to prevent accidental or unauthorized nuclear use. The Soviet delegation, however, refused Smith's offer for more detailed discussions of such accident prevention measures to take place on a reciprocal basis.[78]

There are many plausible, even likely, Soviet command and control failures that might become known to Western intelligence agencies. In April 1988, Soviet authorities revealed that a low-level civil defense alert had been started by accident,[79] and it is highly likely that other more serious Soviet "accidental" alert actions have been caused by false warnings of attack, similar to the 1979 and 1980 NORAD false alarms in the United States. There have also been reports that on at least one occasion Soviet air defense forces incorrectly identified a U.S. RC-135 reconnaissance aircraft flying near the Soviet coastline on an intelligence gathering mission as a B-52 bomber about to penetrate the Soviet border.[80] Similar problems in Soviet warning identification and implementation of proper command procedures may well become known to Western observers of Soviet military exercises.

It would be very much in U.S. interests to ensure that such Soviet military mistakes did not occur in a real world crisis. Should the U.S. government inform the Soviet government of its knowledge of such an incident?[81] The Soviet political leadership itself might not always learn the details of such military activities, especially if lower-level Soviet military officials sought to cover up their mistakes. Should American officials offer to provide technical information or assistance to reduce the risks of accidental war? Clearly, no general answer can be given. But on a case-by-case basis, taking full account of the danger of compromising U.S. intelligence sources, the United States should consider providing limited assistance to the Soviet leadership to improve its command and control system.

At a minimum, we should be willing to inform Soviet officials about how we have fixed our problems in this area. For example, it would be helpful to share the details of the U.S. construction of an off-site training facility for warning-system operators to eliminate the possibility of a repeat of the 1979 false-warning incident. Certainly, if we are thinking about sharing sensitive SDI information and technology in the future, we should think more about sharing intelligence and command and control information that could help prevent accidental war today. This may be a useful subject to be discussed at military-to-military talks or at future U.S. Secretary of Defense and Soviet Defense Minister meetings.

MODEST AND ACHIEVABLE STEPS

The unilateral initiatives and bilateral operational arms control agreements proposed in this chapter will not restructure the superpower nuclear arsenals. They will not require major changes in either side's deterrence requirements or targeting objectives. Nor will they result in a radical decrease in the likelihood of nuclear war. But they can make a small contribution to reducing the risk of war and, given the monumental stakes involved, even small improvements are very important.

Indeed, it is precisely the limited nature of these unilateral steps and bilateral confidence-building measures that makes them easier to negotiate, agree upon, and implement than major arms control agreements affecting the superpower arsenals. It would, therefore, be wise to have negotiations concerning accidental war prevention held separately from ongoing structural arms control negotiations. Although domestic political support for such operational arms control measures might be more difficult to gather, domestic political and bureaucratic opposition might be more difficult to arouse as well. Thus, perhaps the greatest obstacle to progress in this area is indifference: there is a widespread belief among strategic analysts that the risk of accidental war is already extremely remote. This is only true, however, in peacetime, and it would be a tragic mistake if we waited until the outbreak of a superpower crisis—during which the need for the initiatives discussed here would be much more apparent, but the likelihood of achieving them more remote—to take the steps toward reducing the danger of accidental war that could be taken now.

CHAPTER FIVE

A Delicate Balancing Act

THERE ARE many paths by which a nuclear war could begin, and a prudent American strategy must, therefore, strike a balance between a number of competing national security objectives. If our only goal was to deter deliberate and premeditated Soviet aggression against the United States and our allies, we could build an awesome nuclear arsenal primed to destroy the Soviet leadership, population, and military power in an instant retaliation to any attack. Such a force, however, raises legitimate concerns about potential provocation in a crisis and the danger of accidental response to a false warning of attack. If our sole problem was to avoid provoking a mistaken preemptive Soviet nuclear strike in a crisis, we could build only countercity nuclear capabilities and scrupulously avoid taking any potentially threatening alerting measures in a confrontation. Such a policy, however, might tempt deliberate aggression in a severe crisis and reduce the credibility of our commitment to retaliate in response to attacks against our allies or limited attacks against the United States. If the only problem we faced was that of accidental nuclear war, we could place PAL locks on all the weapons and centralize authority for any military alert activities in the hands of the President. Such a policy, however, would raise both the risk of paralysis in a crisis and the danger of "decapitation" in a nuclear war.

In reality, the problem we face is precisely that we seek to prevent *all* potential paths to a nuclear war, and we do not know how to reduce the risks of one danger without increasing the risks of another. This book has sought to examine the difficulty with which senior American political and military leaders have coped with the "usability paradox" inherent in the nature of nuclear deterrence. To a significant degree, the architects of U.S. nuclear doctrine, and the designers of the military organizations prepared to implement that doctrine if necessary, have been successful with their uneasy compromises and delicate balancing act in keeping U.S. nuclear weapons "usable, but not too usable." None of the potential scenarios for a nuclear war are likely; all of them remain possible. The continued risk of nuclear war is not due to a lack of intelligence, good intentions, or resolve among our political and military decision makers. It is the result of the continued coexistence of nuclear weapons and international rivalries and the inevitable tensions caused by conflicting strategies designed to reduce the contrasting dangers of aggression, provocation, and accidental war.

The U.S. government has found no permanent solution to the dilemmas of nuclear deterrence in the past, and I see no prospect for eliminating the problems in the future. I do believe, however, that there is significant scope for improvement of U.S. national security if our nuclear doctrine and arms control policies are carefully crafted to reduce the tensions between conflicting U.S. strategic objectives. The analysis of a more restricted second-strike counterforce doctrine in chapter 2, therefore, suggested ways in which the powerful deterrent of the current countervailing strategy can be maintained without heightening the risk of provocation and mistaken Soviet preemption in a crisis. A counterforce doctrine and force posture designed to threaten Soviet leadership targets and reserve military forces in a retaliatory strike, but not pose an increased danger of a major disarming U.S. first strike, could significantly lessen the tension between robust deterrence and crisis stability. The examination of limited strategic defense options in chapter 3 focused on potential opportunities to utilize highly restricted defenses to reduce the twin dangers of decapitation and accidental war, without producing mutual fears of an all-out "Star Wars" arms race or movement toward first-strike superiority. Finally, the examination of operational arms control measures in chapter 4 identified a number of unilateral changes in our military procedures, as well as formal agreements with the Soviet Union, that might reduce the risk of accidental war without reducing the strength of the U.S. nuclear deterrent: placing PAL-type locks on the nuclear weapons aboard U.S. Navy surface ships, improving our strategic nuclear alert procedures to make them less provocative and less likely to produce accidents, a mutual ban on testing of depressed trajectory missiles, and an increase in our willingness to share nuclear safety information with the Soviet Union.

I am under no illusion that even such moderate changes in U.S. nuclear doctrine, force structure, and arms control policy will be easy to implement. The history of U.S. nuclear weapons policy, after all, has fully demonstrated the tenacious strength of the many political, technological, and institutional impediments to change. Even when senior officials have been able to build sufficient support for a change in policy guidance, the actual effects on doctrine and operations have always been incremental and usually not exactly as anticipated. Constructive change has, nonetheless, taken place over time, and it has often been encouraged by elements of public support and usually enhanced by the direct involvement of senior U.S. political and military authorities.

Sustainable Deterrence?

In a democracy, national security policy requires at least a modicum of public support if it is to be sustainable over the long run. In the 1960s and 1970s, the pursuit of arms control agreements provided what Joseph Nye has appropriately called "the glue that held a centrist position together." A political consensus in favor of prudent nuclear force modernization, coupled with mutual superpower restraint, was supported as long as the public believed serious arms control efforts were also underway.[1] The Reagan

Administration's initial opposition to arms control, however, produced significant popular opposition to its strategic modernization programs in 1981 and 1982. The nuclear freeze initiative won in forty-one of the forty-six electoral contests in which it appeared in 1982, and 205 city councils, forty-three county governments, and eleven state legislatures also passed freeze resolutions that year.[2] Although strategic factors also played some role in the initial policy, Reagan's March 1983 speech announcing the new Star Wars objective of making "nuclear weapons impotent and obsolete," was also a deliberate political effort to steal the moral high ground away from the freeze movement. Indeed, the SDI announcement itself was hastily tacked onto a speech that was designed to raise political support for defense budget increases and was soon widely utilized in public forums by Administration spokesmen as evidence that Reagan's policy of rapid force modernization aimed at a higher goal than "mere" nuclear deterrence.[3] Although the political strategy did appear to work for a short time, public and congressional support for the SDI program waned in the second Reagan Administration as the impracticality of the President's vision of perfect defense gradually became more widely appreciated. What had originally been a political glue for public consensus behind the Reagan Administration's defense programs gradually appeared more as a political solvent, both a symbol and a cause of the nation's growing disunity over nuclear weapons policy.

Deep Cuts and Operational Arms Control

Although there is current widespread public support for arms control agreements emphasizing deep reductions in strategic weaponry, there is a worrisome possibility that the concept of "deep cuts" might become the Star Wars of the 1990s—a politically attractive and idealistic objective that could produce excessive public disillusion with nuclear deterrence when the extreme version of the concept is eventually exposed as being strategically infeasible. It is important to stress that this point is *not* an argument against all reductions in the current superpower arsenals; indeed, START agreement reductions, from approximately twelve thousand strategic weapons on each side to somewhere between six thousand and nine thousand each, are not in my view destabilizing and, as was argued in chapter 2, could help reduce the continuing vulnerability of U.S. land-based missiles by encouraging the development and deployment of a U.S. mobile ICBM force. The danger here is that truly radical reductions, of the sort envisioned by much of the U.S. public as being the eventual objective of the START enterprise, would eventually create significant sources of nuclear instability.

There are two basic reasons for this. First, the enormous size of each portion of the strategic triad of land-based ICBMs, SLBMs on submarines, and bomber-delivered weapons is a source of both unnecessary overkill and needed redundancy in weapons systems. The widely recognized virtue of redundancy in strategic systems is that it provides a hedge against the potential technological breakthroughs of an adversary that could threaten all retaliatory forces and thereby produce an incentive to go to war. In any future "deep cuts" agreement, it will be necessary to avoid throwing out the baby of strategic redundancy with the bathwater of overkill. Political pressure for rapid, ill-conceived agreements, however, could easily produce movement in the wrong direction. For example, President Reagan's impulsive embrace, in the final hours of the 1986 Reykjavik Summit, of an agreement to abolish all ballistic missiles within ten years, was extremely unwise since it would have permitted the concentration of Soviet defense efforts into a buildup of surface-to-air missiles and fighter interceptors. Similarly, any deep reductions that radically reduce the size of the U.S. SSBN force would raise the dangerous prospect of major anti-submarine-warfare breakthroughs. At some future point, continuing deep cuts would produce precisely such instabilities.

The second source of potential instability is the existence

of the nuclear forces of third parties. At some point, well before achievement of the general public's vision of reductions below the level that would threaten its destruction, the arsenals of current nuclear powers such as France, Britain, and China would become significant. And, if reductions are made to truly minimum levels, even potential nuclear proliferators could be dangerous. In short, the new "deep cuts" ideal produces the same fundamental problem that plagued old schemes for the abolition of nuclear weapons: at low levels of forces, minor increments of weaponry by any power could produce a usable strategic superiority and thereby increase the likelihood of war.[4]

Basing public support for the maintenance of strong deterrent forces on the promise of continuing deep reductions through arms control agreements raises these serious concerns. Still, the need for some kind of motivating force behind public support for maintenance of nuclear deterrence force remains strong. The development of a visible alternative symbol of genuine reductions in the danger of nuclear war is, therefore, an additional reason to support major progress in the operational arms control measures that are feasible in the coming years. Historically, operational arms control measures—such as the hot line or the Nuclear Risk Reduction Centers—engendered much less public attention than have the SALT-type agreements limiting the size and character of the nuclear arsenals themselves. The potential for public support for such agreements has never really been tested, however, and rapid progress and visible signs of increased Soviet and American cooperation in resolving nuclear safety problems or crisis management issues might prove to be a highly beneficial glue for a future political consensus behind prudent U.S. nuclear deterrent improvements.

Ethics and Targeting Policy

The need for public consensus behind security policy in a democracy also provides an extra incentive for movement toward a second-strike counterforce doctrine. A U.S. targeting policy that threatens Soviet leadership shelters and military forces directly, and deliberately attempts to minimize Soviet general population casualties, would provide a more moral, and thus a more sustainable, basis for deterrence over the long term. It would, as I argued in chapter 2, make little strategic sense to attack the Soviet leadership in response to conventional aggression or a limited nuclear attack, since that would provide great incentives for full-scale Soviet retaliatory attacks on U.S. population centers. In response to a full Soviet nuclear strike, however, the grisly retribution of nuclear retaliation would surely be more appropriately leveled upon the individuals responsible for the war than on the general Soviet population.

There will continue to be grave limits to the discrimination possible in a nuclear war. Although current developments in missile accuracy and advanced conventional and nuclear munitions hold great promise for significant reductions in the collateral damage caused by many potential retaliatory strikes, some targets might continue to require high-yield weapons. Certainly, given the accuracy and yield of the present generation of U.S. nuclear weapons, the collocation of populated areas and many military and leadership targets, and the inevitable "fog of war," millions of innocent Soviet citizens would be killed in any massive U.S. retaliatory strike.

This fact, however, should be treated as a reminder of the inevitable horror of nuclear war. It should not become an excuse to maximize it.

DETAILS AND LEADERSHIP

There is a common adage—"The devil is in the details"—that reminds us that it is much easier to devise abstract solutions to our problems than to work out the difficult operational details that can make them a reality. This is clearly the case in the complex world of nuclear strategy. The history of the evolution of U.S. nuclear doctrine, as well as the study of actual U.S. military operations in crises, provides ample testimony to the frustrations senior U.S. political and military authorities have confronted in their efforts to control military organizations. There is little reason, therefore, to believe that the recommended changes in U.S. military doctrine and in actual operational plans and procedures discussed in this book will be adequately implemented unless senior authorities more fully understand the difficulties involved and thoroughly exert control over the details of the plans and operations for which they are ultimately responsible.

Although the changes in U.S. nuclear targeting doctrine that have taken place since the 1950s certainly followed the general guidance passed on by senior officials, many of the details of the resulting plans were often unanticipated and inadequately understood. Thus, under Robert McNamara's "no-cities" doctrine in the 1960s, the President could have ostensibly withheld initial attacks against Soviet urban-industrial targets, but the counterforce option was so large that, as James Schlesinger later admitted, "it would be *impossible* to ascertain whether the purpose of a strategic strike was limited or not."[5] Yet, while Schlesinger was able to create more meaningful limited nuclear options to increase the possibility of escalation control in the 1970s, the NSDM-242 guidance on "counter-recovery" also unexpectedly led to major increases in the targeting of Soviet industry.

It is critical that future U.S. nuclear doctrine be kept under much tighter political control. While major improvements in civilian oversight over nuclear planning were made in the 1980s—for example, the civilian responsibility for reviewing targeting doctrine has now been institutionalized and assigned to the Assistant Secretary of Defense for International Security Policy—the recurrence of gaps between political guidance and operational reality can only be avoided by thorough and sustained involvement of senior officials. The operational details of U.S. nuclear doctrine under the countervailing strategy, and the further refinements I have described, raise extraordinarily sensitive and sobering questions: How are counterleadership "withholds" to be designed? How can limited counterforce capabilities and actual options be identified as such? How can noncombatant casualties best be minimized? Such questions can only be properly answered by senior authorities with full information and thorough preparation.

Past efforts to manage U.S. military operations in crises have highlighted similar gaps between the theory of central civilian control and the reality of the inevitably decentralized nature of operations in a huge, global military machine. For example, in May 1960 Secretary of Defense Thomas Gates accidentally ordered a worldwide DEFCON 3 alert when he issued vague operational orders intended merely as a communications readiness test.[6] Although the central political authorities of the Kennedy Administration devoted considerable attention to managing U.S. Navy and Air Force operations during the Cuban Missile Crisis, many potentially dangerous incidents—such as the Vandenberg test ICBM launch and the Alaskan U-2 incident discussed in chapter 4—escaped their control. More recently, when President Reagan was shot in March 1980, initial military alert activities were apparently ordered by Secretary of Defense Weinberger, without full understanding of what that entailed, during the confusion and crisis in Washington.[7] It is critical that all U.S. military operations in a crisis be kept under tighter control. The proposed arms control measures and unilateral changes in military procedures could reduce the risk of accidents in future confrontations, but future political authorities must make concerted efforts to learn about such military operations in peacetime to be better prepared to manage them in a crisis.

American civilian and military authorities must work together more effectively for constructive change to take place in this arena. There is an understandable, but unfortunate, tendency for professional military officers to interpret the political guidance they are given in a parochial manner, serving their service perspective and what *they* believe to be the national interest, without full understanding of the political and strategic objectives sought by higher authorities. At the same time, however, there can be a tendency for higher authorities to issue guidance for ambitious changes in nuclear policy and even operational orders in crises without fully understanding the difficulties of implementation. Not all potentially useful changes in doctrine or crisis military activities are technically feasible, and it is the duty of military subordinates to point this out.

There is great need for improvement here among both civilians and soldiers. Although it is the responsibility of the professional military to educate civilian authorities on questions of nuclear strategy and operations, there are severe impediments on both sides to thorough training and adequate civilian involvement in these sensitive matters. The professional military's deep resentment over what it views as the "micromanagement" excesses of the McNamara Pentagon and the Vietnam War, has produced strong reservations against exposing civilian authorities to what is seen as excessive detail concerning operational plans. The widespread fear that deep civilian involvement in the details of nuclear planning will produce harmful interference in military operations is not entirely unjustified. But it is misguided. Civilian authorities *will* become involved in military planning and operational activities in crises, when the pressing need is more obvious. The operational details of planning nuclear options, managing nuclear alerts, or controlling crisis interactions are far too complex, however, to be adequately understood and changed under the pressure of a crisis. The dilemmas here can be made less dangerous only if military and political authorities work together well ahead of time to minimize potential misunderstandings.

The strongest impediment to better civilian control over nuclear strategy and military operations, however, is found in civilian political leaders themselves. There are simply too many other pressing issues on the agendas of senior civilian authorities to make understanding the details of nuclear strategy a high priority. There are always meetings to attend in the Pentagon, speeches to give to the public, and budgets to build on Capitol Hill. Given the unpleasantness of the whole subject of nuclear weapons, and the sincere hope that the United States will never have to consider actually using the plans and crisis procedures that have been constructed, there is a tendency among most U.S. political officials to place issues of nuclear strategy on the back burner. But because the military strategies we adopt, and the plans and procedures we are prepared to implement in crises, can have a strong influence on the likelihood of war, this temptation must be resisted. It is on the back burner, away from the scrutiny of senior political and military leaders, that the devil in the details becomes most dangerous.

Notes

INTRODUCTION
The Usability Paradox

1. James Reston, "Dawn of Atomic Era Perplexes Washington," *New York Times*, August 12, 1945, p. 6.

2. The Jeffries Committee report, September 1944, quoted in Lawrence Freedman, *The Evolution of Nuclear Strategy* (New York: St. Martins, 1981), p. 41.

3. See Albert Carnesale, Paul Doty, Stanley Hoffmann, Samuel P. Huntington, Joseph S. Nye, Jr., and Scott D. Sagan, *Living with Nuclear Weapons* (Cambridge, MA: Harvard University Press, 1983), pp. 34–35.

4. Military doctrine has been well defined by Barry Posen as the "subcomponent of grand strategy that deals explicitly with military means. Two questions are important: *What* means shall be employed? and *How* shall they be employed?" Nuclear doctrine is more complex given the twin goals of U.S. strategy and the resulting usability paradox. I have therefore included the *means* by which the U.S. reduces the risk of accidental war in my study of U.S. doctrine. See Barry R. Posen, *The Sources of Military Doctrine* (Ithaca: Cornell University Press, 1984), p. 13.

5. The most significant scholarly work on the development of U.S. nuclear strategy and targeting policy has been that of David Alan Rosenberg and Desmond Ball. Their most important work appears in Desmond Ball and Jeffrey Richelson (eds.), *Strategic Nuclear Targeting* (Ithaca: Cornell University Press, 1986). The seminal works on U.S. nuclear command and control and the problems of accidental war are Bruce G. Blair, *Strategic Command and Control* (Washington, D.C.: Brookings, 1985); Paul Bracken, *The Command and Control of Nuclear Forces* (New Haven: Yale University Press, 1983); and Ashton B. Carter, John D. Steinbruner, and Charles A. Zraket (eds.), *Managing Nuclear Operations* (Washington, D.C.: Brookings, 1987).

6. The best studies of the evolution of complex theories about nuclear deterrence are Lawrence Freedman, *The Evolution of Nuclear Strategy* (London: MacMillan, 1981); Robert Jervis, "Deter-

rence Theory Revisited," *World Politics*, vol. 31, no. 2, January 1979, pp. 289–324; and Patrick Morgan, *Deterrence: A Conceptual Analysis* (Beverly Hills: Sage Publications, 1977). For important examples of the U.S. weapons programs case-study literature see Desmond Ball, *Politics and Force Levels: The Strategic Missile Program of the Kennedy Administration* (Berkeley and Los Angeles: University of California Press, 1980); and Ted Greenwood, *Making the MIRV: A Study of Defense Decision Making* (Cambridge, MA: Ballinger, 1975).

CHAPTER ONE
The Evolution of U.S. Nuclear Doctrine

1. This layman's myth about MAD was most commonly found in the statements of both dovish and hawkish critics of U.S. defense policy in the late 1970s. In 1979, for example, Rep. Ronald Dellums objected to Pentagon plans to shift to "a primary military target mode" instead of aiming at "populations and industrial bases which has been our historical targeting approach," and Sen. Malcolm Wallop wrote that "over the past fifteen years, at least four American presidents, and their leading defense advisers, have built weapons and cast strategic plans well nigh exclusively for the purpose of inflicting damage upon the enemy's society." Ronald Dellums, quoted in Aaron L. Friedberg, "A History of the U.S. Strategic 'Doctrine'—1945 to 1980," *Journal of Strategic Studies*, vol. 3, no. 3, December 1980, p. 66 n. 1; and Malcolm Wallop, "Opportunities and Imperatives of Ballistic Missile Defense," *Strategic Review*, vol. 7, no. 4, Fall 1979, p. 13. The myth still continues, however, even in the writings of otherwise well informed authors. For example, Leon Wieseltier has noted that "recent studies of American targeting policy deduce from the declassified documentation that, *with the exception of the short-lived and bureaucratically inspired adaptation of the doctrine of mutual assured destruction by the McNamara Pentagon . . . it has never been the American intention to strike first against cities.*" Leon Wieseltier, "When Deterrence Fails," *Foreign Affairs*, vol. 63, no. 4, Spring 1985, p. 832 (emphasis added).

2. Harold Brown, *Department of Defense Annual Report for FY 1981*, p. 66.

3. In their effort to debunk the layman's myth about MAD,

many knowledgeable experts strayed too far in the opposite direction. For example, Albert Wohlstetter has written: "MAD was not declaratory policy before the mid-1960s. And it has never been operational policy." In addition he maintains that "McNamara said we would use a MAD *capability* for deterrence without seriously intending to assure the destruction of noncombatants." Albert Wohlstetter, "Bishops, Statesmen, and Other Strategists on the Bombing of Innocents," *Commentary*, vol. 80, no. 12, June 1983, pp. 19 and 26. In a similar exaggeration of the lack of importance of MAD on U.S. targeting doctrine, Colin Gray has argued that "assured destruction has falsely been assumed to enjoy a widespread following among civilian strategists, and even more falsely has been assumed to have been influential in the design of the United States SIOP." Colin S. Gray, *Strategic Studies and Public Policy* (Lexington: University Press of Kentucky, 1982), p. 148.

4. See Desmond Ball, *Politics and Force Levels: The Strategic Missile Program of the Kennedy Administration* (Berkeley and Los Angeles: University of California Press, 1980), pp. 203–11; Alton Frye, *A Responsible Congress: The Politics of National Security* (New York: McGraw-Hill, 1975), pp. 66–70; and Ted Greenwood, *Making the MIRV: A Study of Defense Decision Making* (Cambridge, MA: Ballinger, 1975), pp. 70–71. For other examples see Albert Wohlstetter, "The Political and Military Aims of Offensive and Defensive Innovation," in Fred S. Hoffman, Albert Wohlstetter, and David S. Yost (eds.), *Swords and Shields: NATO, the USSR, and New Choices for Long-Range Offense and Defense* (Lexington, MA: Lexington Books, 1987), pp. 18–20.

5. *Appendix 1 to the Draft Memorandum for the President, Recommended Long Range Nuclear Delivery Forces, 1963–1967*, September 23, 1961 (henceforth DPM-61), Office of the Secretary of Defense, Freedom of Information Act (henceforth, OSD-FOI), pp. 4 and 6.

6. Donald Rumsfeld, *Department of Defense Annual Report for FY 1978*, p. 68.

7. Caspar Weinberger, *Department of Defense Annual Report for FY 1987*, p. 75.

8. Alexander de Seversky, "Atomic Bomb Hysteria," *Reader's Digest*, February 1946, pp. 121 and 124.

9. *The National Defense Program—Unification of Strategy*, 81st Congress, 1st session, p. 170, quoted in Robert Frank Futrell,

Ideas, Concepts, Doctrine: A History of Basic Thinking in the United States Air Force, 1907–1964 (Maxwell AFB, AL: Air University, 1971), p. 122.

10. Curtis LeMay letter to Carl Spaatz (ca. July 28, 1947), quoted in David Alan Rosenberg, "American Atomic Strategy and the Hydrogen Bomb Decision," *Journal of American History*, vol. 66, June 1979, p. 67 (emphasis removed).

11. *The Atomic Energy Years, 1945–1950*, vol. 2 of *The Journals of David E. Lilienthal* (New York: Harper and Row, 1964), p. 391.

12. Rosenberg, "American Atomic Strategy and the Hydrogen Bomb Decision," pp. 68–69. "Halfmoon" was approved by the JCS only for "planning purposes" and not as the "primary" short-range war plan after Admiral Leahy questioned the wisdom of placing sole reliance on atomic weapons when authorization to use them was not guaranteed. Kenneth W. Condit, *The History of the Joint Chiefs of Staff, The Joint Chiefs of Staff and National Policy 1947–1949*, vol. 2 (Wilmington, DE: Michael Glazier Inc., 1979), pp. 288–89.

13. On the impact of the Berlin Crisis on U.S. nuclear planning see Samuel R. Williamson, Jr. (with the collaboration of Steven L. Rearden), *The View from Above: High Level Decisions and the Soviet-American Strategic Arms Competition, 1945–1950*, October 1975 (declassified with deletions), OSD-FOI, pp. 88–130.

14. Steven L. Rearden, *The Formative Years, 1947–1950*, vol. 1 of *History of the Office of The Secretary of Defense* (Washington, D.C.: GPO, 1984), p. 292. On the atomic "signal" see Richard K. Betts, *Nuclear Blackmail and Nuclear Balance* (Washington, D.C.: Brookings, 1987), pp. 23–31; and Gregg Herken, *The Winning Weapon: The Atomic Bomb in the Cold War, 1945–1950* (New York: Knopf, 1981), pp. 257–60.

15. Rearden, *The Formative Years*, p. 293; and J. C. Hopkins and Sheldon A. Goldberg, *The Development of the Strategic Air Command, 1946–1986* (Headquarters SAC, Offutt AFB, NE), p. 14.

16. Williamson, *The View from Above*, pp. 105–6.

17. Thomas H. Etzold and John Lewis Gaddis (eds.), *Containment: Documents on American Policy and Strategy, 1945–1950* (New York: Columbia University Press, 1978), p. 343.

18. Ibid., p. 343.

19. Walter Millis (ed.), *The Forrestal Diaries* (New York: Viking, 1951), p. 458.

20. Ibid., p. 487; and Robert H. Ferrell (ed.), *Off the Record: The*

Private Papers of Harry S. Truman (New York: Harper and Row, 1980), pp. 148–49.

21. LeMay diary, January 23, 1951, quoted in David Alan Rosenberg, "The Origins of Overkill: Nuclear Weapons and American Strategy, 1945–1960," *International Security*, vol. 7, no. 4, Spring 1983, p. 18 (emphasis added).

22. The paragraph is based on JCS 1952/1, "Evaluation of Current Strategic Offensive Plans," December 21, 1948, reprinted in Etzold and Gaddis, *Containment*, pp. 357–62.

23. Rosenberg, "The Origins of Overkill," pp. 14–15. By December 1, 1948, fifty B-29s and B-50s were ready. Williamson, *View from Above*, p. 118.

24. Walter S. Poole, *The History of the Joint Chiefs of Staff, The Joint Chiefs of Staff and National Policy, 1950–1952*, vol. 4 (Historical Division, Joint Secretariat, JCS), p. 169.

25. The Harmon Committee report in Etzold and Gaddis, *Containment*, p. 362. Also see Rosenberg, "American Atomic Strategy," pp. 71–75.

26. NSC-20/4, in Etzold and Gaddis, *Containment*, p. 207.

27. Rosenberg, "The Origins of Overkill," p. 23; and Thomas B. Cochran, William M. Arkin, and Milton M. Hoenig, *U.S. Nuclear Forces and Capabilities*, vol. 1 of *Nuclear Weapons Databook* (Cambridge, MA: Ballinger, 1984), p. 15.

28. JCS 2081/1, February 13, 1950, Report by the Joint Intelligence Committee, "Implications of Soviet Possession of Atomic Weapons," p. 12, Geographic File, 350.09 USSR, CCS 472.6 USSR (11-8-49), 5.2, Records of the Joint Chiefs of Staff 1954–1956, National Archives (emphasis added). The JCS had anticipated this problem as early as 1945. See Rosenberg, "Origins of Overkill," p. 17.

29. NSC-68, in Etzold and Gaddis, *Containment*, pp. 417 and 431. For an important examination of the continued interest in preventive war inside the U.S. government, see Marc Trachtenberg, " 'A Wasting Asset'?: American Strategy and the Shifting Nuclear Balance, 1949–54," *International Security*, forthcoming 1989.

30. Etzold and Gaddis, *Containment*, p. 432 (emphasis added).

31. David Alan Rosenberg, "A Smoking Radiating Ruin at the End of Two Hours: Documents on American Plans for Nuclear War with the Soviet Union, 1954–1955," *International Security*, vol. 6, no. 3, Winter 1981–1982, p. 9.

32. *Department of Air Force Appropriations for 1956*, U.S. House of Representatives, 84th Congress, 1st session, pp. 1542–43, quoted in Futrell, *Ideas, Concepts, Doctrine*, p. 216.

33. *Air Force*, February 1955, p. 29, quoted in Futrell, *Ideas, Concepts, Doctrine*, p. 216.

34. Richard H. Kohn and Joseph P. Harahan (eds.), "U.S. Strategic Airpower, 1948–1952: Excerpts from an Interview with Generals Curtis E. LeMay, Leon W. Johnson, David A. Burchinal, and Jack J. Catton," *International Security*, vol. 12, no. 4, Spring 1988, p. 86.

35. Ridgway memorandum for the record, May 17, 1954, quoted in Rosenberg, "The Origins of Overkill," p. 34.

36. Ibid.

37. NSC-5440/1, December 28, 1954, quoted in Rosenberg, "The Origins of Overkill," p. 34. Also see Trachtenberg, " 'A Wasting Asset.' "

38. A. J. Goodpaster Memorandum of Conference with the President, Ann Whitman Files, Ann Whitman Papers, box 3, Eisenhower Library, quoted in Robert A. Wampler, "The Die is Cast: The United States and NATO Nuclear Planning, 1951–1954" (unpublished paper, Harvard University, 1987), pp. 1–2.

39. NSC-5515, "Study of Possible Hostile Soviet Actions," March 21, 1955, Declassified Documents Reference Collection, Carrolton Press, 1986, No. 002158, p. 4. (Henceforth DDRC, followed by year and number.)

40. Goodpaster and Burke memorandums, quoted in Rosenberg, "Origins of Overkill," p. 42.

41. Appointments, November 9, 1957, November 1957 folder 2, Ann C. Whitman Diary, box 9, Whitman Files, Eisenhower Library, quoted in Rosenberg, "The Origins of Overkill," p. 47.

42. Goodpaster memorandum, August 19, 1960, DDRC, 1987, No. 001139.

43. Portions of the speech are reprinted in Robert J. Art and Kenneth N. Waltz, *The Use of Force* (Lanham, MD: University Press of America, 1983), p. 144.

44. Hagerty Diary, December 13, 1954, quoted in John Lewis Gaddis, *Strategies of Containment* (New York: Oxford University Press, 1982), p. 150.

45. The paragraph is based on the declassified "Briefing of WSEG Report No. 12," reprinted in Rosenberg, "A Smoking Radiating Ruin," pp. 30–37.

46. Ibid., p. 33.

47. Ibid., p. 27.

48. *Department of Defense Appropriations for 1960*, Hearings before the Subcommittee of the Committee on Appropriations, U.S. House of Representatives, 86th Congress, 1st session, part 1, p. 929.

49. Between 1958 and 1960, JCS exercises with "over 200 time over target (TOT) conflicts highlighted the degree of conflict in existing execution plans." *History of the Joint Strategic Target Planning Staff: Background and Preparation of SIOP-62*, History and Research Division, Headquarters SAC (partially declassified and released by Joint Secretariat, OJCS, April 1980), p. 4.

50. Transcript, Admiral Burke's conversation with Captain Aurand, November 25, 1960, Transcripts and Phone Conversations (NSTL), Burke Papers, Naval Historical Center, Washington, D.C., quoted in Rosenberg, "Origins of Overkill," p. 6.

51. The briefing is presented in Scott D. Sagan, "SIOP-62: The Nuclear War Plan Briefing to President Kennedy," *International Security*, vol. 12, no. 1, Summer 1987, pp. 22–51. All information in the paragraph is from that document with one exception: that North Korea and North Vietnam were targeted is demonstrated in CINCPAC Operation Plan No. 1-61, Pacific Command General War Plan, appendix 1 to annex B, SIOP Operations, p. B-I-7, CCS 3146 (January 26, 1961) sec. 1, Records of the Joint Chiefs of Staff, 1961, National Archives.

52. Sagan, "SIOP-62: The Nuclear War Plan Briefing to President Kennedy," pp. 50–51.

53. Ibid., p. 51.

54. Ibid., pp. 44 and 51.

55. Covering note on Henry Kissinger's memo on Berlin, July 7, 1961, Germany-Berlin-General, July 7, 1961, box 31, National Security Files (NSF), John F. Kennedy Library (JFKL), Boston.

56. W. W. Rostow, *The Diffusion of Power* (New York: Macmillan, 1972), pp. 172–73.

57. DPM-61, p. 4.

58. DPM-61, p. 4.

59. DPM-61, pp. 12 and 14.

60. Proposed Outline for Presentation of SIOP-63 to the President, CCS 3105, Joint Planning, March 8, 1961 (3), box 30, Records of the Joint Chiefs of Staff, 1961, National Archives; and Sa-

gan, "SIOP-62: The Nuclear War Plan Briefing to President Kennedy," pp. 38–39.

61. James R. Schlesinger testimony, *U.S.-U.S.S.R. Strategic Policies*, Hearings before the Subcommittee on Arms Control, International Law, and Organization of the Committee on Foreign Relations, U.S. Senate, 93d Congress, 2d session, March 4, 1974, p. 9; and Henry S. Rowen, "Formulating Strategic Doctrine," *Commission on the Organization of the Government for the Conduct of Foreign Policy*, June 1975, vol. 4, appendix K, p. 227.

62. Statement of Secretary of Defense Robert S. McNamara before the Senate Armed Services Committee, FY 1963–1967 Defense Program and 1963 Defense Budget, January 19, 1962, p. 15, OSD-FOI, National Security Archives, Washington, D.C.

63. Robert McNamara, Ann Arbor speech, June 16, 1962, reprinted in Art and Waltz (eds.), *The Use of Force*, p. 149.

64. The quotation is from the review of McNamara's December 1963 proposed nuclear forces signed by the Chairman, Joint Chiefs of Staff; the Chief of Staff, U.S. Army; the Chief of Naval Operations; and the Commandant of the Marine Corps (but not the Air Force Chief of Staff, who supported a full first-strike capability). They add that SIOP options should be planned "dividing our effort between urban/industrial and military targets according to the circumstances of preemption or retaliation." *Draft Memorandum for the President, Recommended FY 1965–FY 1969 Strategic Retaliatory Forces*, December 6, 1963 (henceforth DPM-63), p. I-3, OSD-FOI.

65. *Draft Memorandum for the President, Recommended FY 1964–FY 1968 Strategic Retaliatory Forces*, November 21, 1962 (henceforth DPM-62), p. 8, OSD-FOI.

66. The speech is reprinted in Robert F. Kennedy, *Thirteen Days* (reprint, New York: W. W. Norton, 1971), p. 156. Also see "White House Tapes and Minutes of the Cuban Missile Crisis," *International Security*, vol. 10, no. 1, Summer 1985, p. 193.

67. For details see Stephen M. Meyer, "Soviet Nuclear Operations," in Ashton B. Carter, John D. Steinbruner, and Charles A. Zraket (eds.), *Managing Nuclear Operations* (Washington, D.C.: Brookings, 1987), pp. 487–89.

68. Statement of Secretary of Defense Robert S. McNamara before the House Subcommittee on Defense Appropriations, FY 1964–1968 Defense Program and 1964 Defense Budget, February 6, 1963, p. 50, National Security Archives, Washington, D.C.

McNamara noted in the 1963 Draft Presidential Memorandum that the Soviet long-range bomber "capability for intercontinental attack remains limited, even though the Soviets have given considerable emphasis to arctic staging exercises and to aerial refueling practice in an effort to overcome range deficiencies of their bomber force." DPM-63, p. I-9.

69. DPM-63, p. I-35. McNamara also told Stewart Alsop in an interview published in December 1962 that if the Soviets acquired a sure second-strike capability through hardening their missiles, "you might have a more stable 'balance of terror.' " Stewart Alsop, "McNamara Thinks about the Unthinkable," *Saturday Evening Post*, December 1, 1962, p. 18.

70. *Executive Sessions of the Senate Foreign Relations Committee* (Historical Series), vol. 14, 87th Congress, 2d session, 1962, p. 149. Made public April 1986.

71. DPM-63, p. I-5.

72. Ibid., p. I-20.

73. The 1963 Draft Presidential Memorandum defined Assured Destruction criteria as "Soviet government and military controls plus a large percentage of their population and economy (e.g. 30% of their population, 50% of their industrial capacity and 150 of their cities)." In his FY 1966 budget statement, McNamara gave figures of 25 to 30 percent of the Soviet population and about 66 percent of its industrial capacity. In the FY 1968 budget statement the Assured Destruction criteria were lowered to 20 to 25 percent of the population and 50 to 66 percent of Soviet industrial capacity. See DPM-63, p. I-5; Statement of Secretary of Defense Robert S. McNamara before the House Armed Services Committee, FY 1966–1970 Defense Program and 1966 Defense Budget, February 18, 1965, p. 39, National Security Archives, Washington, D.C.; and Statement of Secretary of Defense Robert S. McNamara before a Joint Session of the Senate Armed Services Committee and the Senate Subcommittee on Department of Defense Appropriations, FY 1968–1972 Defense Program and 1968 Defense Budget, January 23, 1967, p. 39, National Security Archives. For a discussion of how these estimates were developed, see Alain Enthoven and K. Wayne Smith, *How Much is Enough?* (New York: Harper and Row, 1971), p. 207.

74. DPM-63, p. I-5.

75. DPM-62, p. 13. DPM-63 does not include this statement,

but the target list and U.S. assignment of weapons are based on the same guidance assumptions.

76. DPM-63, pp. I-16, I-17, and I-37. These estimates used "expected" U.S. operational factors and "medium" projected Soviet forces. Additional fallout estimates ranged from 25 to 35 million, to 70 to 80 million, depending on assumptions about Soviet civil defense.

77. *Draft Memorandum for the President, Strategic Offensive and Defensive Forces*, January 15, 1968 (henceforth DPM-68), p. 9, OSD-FOI.

78. Robert S. McNamara, interview with author, July 9, 1987. Also see Rowen, "Formulating Strategic Doctrine," p. 232; and *Status of U.S. Strategic Power*, Hearings before the Preparedness Subcommittee of the Committee on Armed Services, U.S. Senate, 90th Congress, 2d session, part 1, p. 138. According to Henry Kissinger, "When I entered office, former Defense Secretary Robert McNamara told me that he had tried for seven years to give the President more options. He had finally given up, he said, in the face of bureaucratic opposition and decided to improvise." Kissinger, *White House Years* (Boston: Little, Brown, 1979), p. 217.

79. Alsop, "McNamara Thinks about the Unthinkable," p. 18.

80. DPM-68, p. 19.

81. *Draft Presidential Memorandum on Strategic Offensive and Defensive Forces*, January 9, 1969, p. 2, OSD-FOI.

82. Remarks by Secretary McNamara, NATO Ministerial Meeting, May 5, 1962, Restricted Session, pp. 12–13, OSD-FOI. The best studies of Flexible Response are David Schwartz, *NATO's Nuclear Dilemmas* (Washington, D.C.: Brookings, 1983); and Jane E. Stromseth, *The Origins of Flexible Response* (New York: St. Martins, 1988).

83. *Draft Memorandum for the President, The Role of Tactical Nuclear Forces in NATO Strategy*, January 15, 1965, p. 37, OSD-FOI.

84. Robert S. McNamara, "The Military Role of Nuclear Weapons: Perceptions and Misperceptions," *Foreign Affairs*, vol. 62, no. 1, Fall 1983, p. 79.

85. Kissinger, *White House Years*, p. 216.

86. Richard M. Nixon, *U.S. Foreign Policy for the 1970s*, "A Report to Congress," quoted in Rowen, "Formulating Strategic Doctrine," p. 219.

87. As the January 1968 Draft Presidential Memorandum put

it: "If war started with less than an all-out attack, we would want to carry out plans for the controlled and deliberate use of our nuclear power to get the best possible outcome. The lack of such nuclear war plans is one of the main weaknesses of our posture today." DPM-68, p. 6.

88. *U.S. News and World Report*, April 12, 1965, p. 52.

89. Kissinger, *White House Years*, p. 203.

90. *U.S.-U.S.S.R. Strategic Policies*, p. 9 (emphasis added).

91. See Herbert Scoville, "Flexible Madness," *Foreign Policy*, no. 14, Spring 1974. The most balanced appraisal is Lynn E. Davis, *Limited Nuclear Options: Deterrence and the New American Doctrine*, Adelphi Paper 121 (London: IISS, 1975–1976).

92. BBC Radio 4, "Analysis," October 24, 1974, quoted in Davis, *Limited Nuclear Options*, p. 5 n. 17, and p. 6 n. 18.

93. James R. Schlesinger, *Department of Defense Annual Report for FY 1975*, p. 41.

94. Ibid., pp. 35–38.

95. Donald H. Rumsfeld, *Department of Defense Annual Report for FY 1978*, p. 68.

96. *Department of Defense Appropriations for Fiscal Year 1978*, Hearings before the Committee on Appropriations, U.S. House of Representatives, 95th Congress, 1st session, part 2, p. 212.

97. Testimony of Maj. Gen. Kelly H. Burke, *Department of Defense Appropriations for 1980*, Hearings before a Subcommittee of the Committee on Appropriations, U.S. House of Representatives, 96th Congress, 1st session, part 3, p. 167. Also see testimony of Dr. William Perry and Adm. Frank McMullen, *Hearings on Military Posture and HR 1872*, Committee on Armed Services, U.S. House of Representatives, book 1, part 3, pp. 11–16; and testimony of Vice Adm. Kenneth M. Carr, Department of Defense, *DOD Authorization for Appropriations for FY 1982*, Hearings before the Committee on Armed Services, U.S. Senate, 97th Congress, 1st session, part 7, p. 3797. There were apparently different definitions of the "counter-recovery" mission during this period, with different emphases given to political, economic, and military assets contributing to recovery.

98. Priority here refers to *assurance* of eventual destruction, not *time urgency*. See Rowen, "Formulating Strategic Doctrine," p. 220.

99. The actual SIOP guidance documents have not been declassified. This statement is based on *Draft Memorandum for the*

President, Recommended FY 1967–71 Strategic Offensive and Defensive Forces, November 1, 1965, p. 11, OSD-FOI.

100. See the discussion in Desmond Ball, "The Development of the SIOP, 1960–1983," p. 74, and Michael Kennedy and Kevin N. Lewis, "On Keeping Them Down; or, Why Do Recovery Models Recover So Fast?" pp. 194–208, both in Desmond Ball and Jeffrey Richelson (eds.), *Strategic Nuclear Targeting* (Ithaca: Cornell University Press, 1986).

101. *Hearings on Military Posture and HR 1872,* p. 11.

102. Leon Sloss and Marc Dean Millot, "U.S. Nuclear Strategy in Evolution," *Strategic Review,* vol. 12, no. 1, Winter 1984, p. 24. For other descriptions of the development and implementation of the countervailing strategy see Walter Slocombe, "The Countervailing Strategy," *International Security,* vol. 5, no. 4, Spring 1981, pp. 18–27; and the Department of Defense annual reports of the period. The best overall critique is Robert Jervis, *The Illogic of American Nuclear Strategy* (Ithaca: Cornell University Press, 1984).

103. *Nuclear War Strategy,* Hearing before the Committee on Foreign Relations, U.S. Senate, 96th Congress, 2d session, September 16, 1980, p. 10 (emphasis added).

104. Harold Brown, Naval War College Speech, August 20, 1980, Office of Assistant Secretary of Defense (Public Affairs), news release, p. 6.

105. Ibid., p. 8. In congressional testimony, Brown quoted Marshall Ogarkov's statement that "the war could also be protracted" and that "in this case the Soviet Union and the fraternal Socialist states" have "objective possibilities for achieving victory." But in a written response to congressional questions, Brown also acknowledged that "our understanding of Soviet concepts of the role and possible results of nuclear war is uncertain. . . . This is partly because our evidence is ambiguous and our analysis clouded by great ambiguity, partly no doubt because even in the totalitarian Soviet state different observers address these inherently uncertain issues from different perspectives." *Nuclear War Strategy,* pp. 9 and 38.

106. Rosenberg, "Smoking Radiating Ruin," pp. 31–32; and DPM-63, p. I-5.

107. *Nuclear War Strategy,* p. 26.

108. Harold Brown, *Department of Defense Annual Report for FY 1981,* p. 78. This intelligence shortfall in the 1980s was due in part

to the emphasis intelligence agencies gave in the 1970s to providing information on the Soviet economy and industrial civil defense in order to support the "counter-recovery" doctrine.

109. Lawrence K. Gershwin, *Soviet Strategic Force Developments*, Joint Hearing before the Subcommittee on Strategic Theater Nuclear Forces of the Committee on Armed Services and the Subcommittee on Defense of the Committee on Appropriations, U.S. Senate, 99th Congress, 1st session, June 26, 1985, p. 17.

110. Department of Defense, *Soviet Military Power 1987*, p. 52.

111. See the testimony of Gen. Richard Ellis (CINCSAC), in *DOD Authorization for Appropriations for FY 1982*, part 7, Strategic and Theater Nuclear Forces, p. 3816.

112. According to Harold Brown, PD-59 provided "guidance for the continuing evolution of U.S. planning, targeting, and system acquisition." Brown, *Department of Defense Annual Report for FY 1982*, p. 39. According to Caspar Weinberger, nuclear policy guidance "clarifies and emphasizes the direct link between nuclear weapon deterrence strategy and acquisition strategy; i.e. our objectives and national security requirements if we fail to deter in a conflict will directly determine our systems acquisition and weapons requirements in peacetime." *U.S. Strategic Doctrine*, Hearings before the Committee on Foreign Relations, U.S. Senate, 97th Congress, 2d session, December 14, 1982, p. 100.

113. According to Walter Slocombe, Deputy Under Secretary of Defense for Policy Planning when PD-59 was drafted, "Nothing in the countervailing concept offers the United States the prospect of eliminating Soviet ability to respond effectively to an American attack. Even with the fruition of our full force modernization program, the United States will not have a capability to threaten the overall Soviet deterrent." Slocombe, "The Countervailing Strategy," p. 26.

114. See *Soviet Military Power 1987*, p. 18.

115. *Nuclear War Strategy*, p. 30.

116. Brown, *Department of Defense Annual Report for FY 1982*, p. 40; Caspar Weinberger, *Department of Defense Annual Report for FY 1987*, p. 75.

117. Sloss and Millot, "U.S. Nuclear Strategy in Evolution," p. 24.

118. Gen. Larry Welch, Strategy and Arms Control Seminar, Harvard University, March 4, 1987.

119. Caspar Weinberger, *Department of Defense Annual Report for FY 1987*, pp. 74–75.

120. This is the essential argument of the "cult of the offensive" theorists. See Stephen Van Evera, "The Cult of the Offensive and the Origins of the First World War," and Jack Snyder, "Civil Military Relations and the Cult of the Offensive, 1914 and 1984," both in Steven E. Miller (ed.), *Military Strategy and the Origins of the First World War* (Princeton: Princeton University Press, 1985), pp. 58–107 and 108–46. The most recent elaboration of this argument is in Charles-Philippe David, *Debating Counterforce* (Boulder, CO: Westview Press, 1987), pp. 209–14. For a critical assessment see Scott D. Sagan, "1914 Revisited: Allies, Offense, and Instability," *International Security*, vol. 11, no. 2, Fall 1986, pp. 151–75.

CHAPTER TWO
Second-Strike Counterforce

1. Pipes's conclusion, that "the Russians certainly accept the *fact* of deterrence" even though "they regard it as undesirable and transient," was less provocative and alarming than his title. Richard Pipes, "Why the Soviet Union Thinks It Could Fight and Win a Nuclear War," *Commentary*, vol. 64, no. 1, July 1977, p. 29.

2. Colin S. Gray, "Soviet Strategic Vulnerabilities," *Air Force Magazine*, vol. 66, no. 3, March 1979, p. 62, quoted in Aaron L. Friedberg, "A History of U.S. Strategic 'Doctrine'—1945 to 1980," in *Journal of Strategic Studies* vol. 3, no. 3, December 1980, p. 69 n. 41.

3. For example, see Robert L. Arnett, "Soviet Attitudes Towards Nuclear War: Do They Really Think They Can Win?" *Journal of Strategic Studies*, vol. 2, no. 2, September 1979, pp. 172–91.

4. Quoted in *Nuclear War Strategy*, Hearing before the Committee on Foreign Relations, U.S. Senate, 96th Congress, 2d session, September 16, 1980, p. 38 (emphasis added).

5. Quoted in Bernard Brodie, *War and Politics* (London: Cassel, 1974), p. 375; Strobe Talbott (ed.), *Khrushchev Remembers* (Boston: Little, Brown, 1970), p. 518.

6. For example, Marshal Pavel Rotmistrov wrote in 1955: "The duty of the Soviet armed forces is to not permit a surprise attack by an enemy on our country, and in case an attempt is made, not only to repulse the attack successfully, but also to deal to the

enemy simultaneous or even preemptive surprise strikes of terrible crushing power." Rotmistrov, "On the Role of Surprise in Contemporary War," *Military Thought*, no. 2, February 1955, p. 20, quoted by Raymond L. Garthoff, "BMD and East-West Relations," in Ashton B. Carter and David N. Schwartz (eds.), *Ballistic Missile Defense* (Washington, D.C.: Brookings, 1984), p. 290 n. 23. On the early 1960s, see Michael MccGwire, *Military Objectives in Soviet Foreign Policy* (Washington, D.C.: Brookings, 1987), pp. 50–51.

7. Stephen M. Meyer, "Soviet Strategic Programmes and the U.S. SDI," *Survival*, vol. 27, no. 6, November–December 1985, p. 277 (emphasis removed).

8. "Soviets Stage Integrated Test of Weapons," *Aviation Week and Space Technology*, June 28, 1982, pp. 20–21.

9. Department of Defense, *Soviet Military Power 1988*, p. 60.

10. A. N. Kalitayev and others, *Zashchita ot oruzhiya massovogo porazheniya: Spravochnik* (Voyenizdat, 1985), p. 144, quoted by Stephen M. Meyer, "Soviet Nuclear Operations," in Ashton B. Carter, John D. Steinbruner, and Charles A. Zraket, *Managing Nuclear Operations* (Washington, D.C.: Brookings, 1987), p. 514.

11. For contrasting perspectives on this development see Raymond L. Garthoff, "New Thinking in Soviet Military Doctrine," and Jean Quatras, "New Soviet Thinking is Not Good News," both in the *Washington Quarterly*, vol. 11, no. 3, Summer 1988, pp. 131–58 and 171–84; and Stephen M. Meyer, "The Sources and Prospects of Gorbachev's New Political Thinking on Security," *International Security*, vol. 13, no. 2, Fall 1988, pp. 124–63.

12. Makhmut Gareyev, "The Revised Soviet Military Doctrine," *Bulletin of Atomic Scientists*, vol. 44, no. 10, December 1988, p. 30. Vadim Zagladim, a deputy head of the International Department of The Central Committee, also stated that "we proceeded for a long time, for too long, from the possibility of winning a nuclear war." *Pravda*, June 18, 1988, quoted in Graham T. Allison, Jr., "Testing Gorbachev," *Foreign Affairs*, vol. 67, no. 1, Fall 1988, p. 23.

13. Gen. A. Gribkov, *Krasnaya Zvesda*, September 25, 1987, quoted in Alexei Arbatov, "Military Doctrines," The Institute of World Economy and International Relations (IMEMO), *Disarmament and Security 1987 Yearbook* (Moscow: Novosti Press Agency Publishing House, 1988), p. 221.

14. Lt. Gen. V. G. Reznichenko et al. (eds.), *Taktika*, 2d ed.

(Moscow: Voyenizdat, 1987), p. 56, quoted in Garthoff, "New Thinking in Soviet Military Doctrine," p. 157 n. 58.

15. On Soviet civil-military relations and nuclear policy, see David Holloway, *The Soviet Union and the Arms Race* (New Haven: Yale University Press, 1983), pp. 29–64; Condoleezza Rice, "The Party, the Military, and Decision Authority in the Soviet Union," *World Politics*, vol. 40, no. 1, October 1987, pp. 55–81; and Benjamin S. Lambeth, "Contemporary Soviet Military Policy," in Roman Kolkowitz and Ellen Propper Mickiewicz (eds.), *The Soviet Calculus of Nuclear War* (Lexington, MA: Lexington Books, 1986), pp. 25–48.

16. On this point, see Ernest R. May, "Conclusions: Capabilities and Proclivities," in May (ed.), *Knowing One's Enemies: Intelligence Assessment before the Two World Wars* (Princeton: Princeton University Press, 1984), p. 503.

17. The most useful introduction to the uses of organization theory in the study of international relations remains Graham T. Allison, *Essence of Decision* (Boston: Little, Brown, 1971), pp. 67–143. In addition, see Jack S. Levy, "Organizational Routines and the Causes of War," *International Studies Quarterly*, vol. 30, no. 2, June 1986, pp. 193–222.

18. For two prenuclear cases in which military organizations exerted pressure to go to war in a crisis, not because they were confident of victory but because they believed striking quickly provided the best chance of being able to implement their war plans, see Scott D. Sagan, "Origins of the Pacific War," *Journal of Interdisciplinary History*, vol. 18, no. 4, Spring 1988, pp. 914–17; and Sagan, "1914 Revisited: Allies, Offense, and Instability," *International Security*, vol. 11, no. 2, Fall 1986, pp. 166–71.

19. Michael Charleton, *From Deterrence to Defense: The Inside Story of Strategic Policy* (Cambridge, MA: Harvard University Press, 1987), p. 13.

20. Discussions of U.S. command and control vulnerability emphasize the importance of two factors: (1) currently untargetable elements of the system (airborne command posts, covert ground mobile centers, satellites, mobile satellite ground stations, and naval ships at sea); and (2) Soviet uncertainty about the details of the U.S. command and control system and procedures (release authority arrangements and covert communications capabilities). For analyses of these issues see Ashton B. Carter, "Assessing Command System Vulnerability," in Carter et

al. (eds.), *Managing Nuclear Operations*, especially pp. 568–73 and 605–10; and Paul Bracken, *The Command and Control of Nuclear Forces* (New Haven: Yale University Press, 1983), pp. 232–37.

21. See Scott D. Sagan, "SIOP-62: The Nuclear War Plan Briefing to President Kennedy," *International Security*, vol. 12, no. 1, Summer 1987, pp. 22–40, and "SIOP-62 Briefing," ibid., pp. 50–51.

22. Lemnitzer's briefing concluded as follows: "We believe the current SIOP effectively integrates, in a well-planned and coordinated attack, the forces committed. Further, the plan is well designed to meet the objectives prescribed in its preparation. Attainment of these objectives should permit the U.S. to prevail in the event of nuclear war." "SIOP-62 Briefing," p. 51.

23. On the 1961 Berlin crisis contingency planning see Fred Kaplan, *Wizards of Armageddon* (New York: Simon and Schuster, 1983), pp. 294–301; Gregg Herken, *Counsels of War* (New York: Knopf, 1985), pp. 159–60; and Richard K. Betts, *Nuclear Blackmail and Nuclear Balance* (Washington, D.C.: Brookings, 1987), pp. 96–102.

24. At the October 16 Executive Committee meeting, Secretary McNamara—ironically, in an argument in favor of not responding to the Soviet deployment of missiles in Cuba—suggested that the U.S. issue an "ultimatum" to Khrushchev: "*If there is any indication* that they're [the missiles in Cuba] to be launched against this country . . . we will respond directly against the Soviet Union, with a *full nuclear strike*." In his October 22 television address, President Kennedy warned that "it shall be the policy of this nation to regard any nuclear missile launched *from Cuba* against any nation in the Western Hemisphere as an attack by the Soviet Union on the United States, requiring *a full retaliatory response upon the Soviet Union*." "White House Tapes and Minutes of the Cuban Missile Crisis," off-the-record meeting on Cuba, October 16, 1962, *International Security*, vol. 10, no. 1, Summer 1985, p. 193 (emphasis added); and Robert F. Kennedy, *Thirteen Days* (New York: W. W. Norton, 1969), p. 168 (emphasis added).

25. Memorandum: JCS to Secretary of Defense, October 26, 1962, National Security Files (NSF), box 36, Cuba—General, John F. Kennedy Library (JFKL), Boston.

26. "October 27, 1962: Transcripts of the Meetings of the ExComm," *International Security*, vol. 12, no. 3, Winter 1987–1988, p. 63.

27. Report on Exercise Pine Cone, JCS 2311/25, May 22, 1961, p. 140, CCS 3510, Joint and Combined Exercises (February 6, 1961), sec. 2, Records of the Joint Chiefs of Staff, 1961, National Archives.

28. For discussions of Soviet execution and targeting options see Meyer, "Soviet Nuclear Operations," pp. 509–16; William T. Lee, "Soviet Nuclear Targeting Strategy," in Desmond Ball and Jeffrey Richelson (eds.), *Strategic Nuclear Targeting* (Ithaca: Cornell University Press, 1986), pp. 84–108; and Notra Trulock III, "Soviet Perspectives on Limited Nuclear Warfare," in Fred S. Hoffman, Albert Wohlstetter, and David S. Yost (eds.), *Swords and Shields: NATO, the USSR, and New Choices for Long-Range Offense and Defense* (Lexington, MA: Lexington Books, 1987), pp. 53–86.

29. For assessments of ICBM vulnerability see *MX Missile Basing*, Office of Technology Assessment (OTA) (Washington, D.C.: GPO, 1981); William T. Lee and Richard F. Staar, *Soviet Military Policy since World War II* (Stanford: Hoover Institution Press, 1986), pp. 155–70; and Bruce G. Blair, *Strategic Command and Control* (Washington, D.C.: Brookings, 1985), pp. 305–12.

30. See, for example, Louis Rene Beres, "Tilting toward Thanatos: America's 'Countervailing' Nuclear Strategy," *World Politics*, vol. 34, no. 1, October 1981, p. 30; John Edwards, *Superweapon: The Making of the MX* (New York: W. W. Norton, 1982), p. 201; and Charles-Philippe David, *Debating Counterforce* (Boulder, CO: Westview Press, 1987), pp. 90 and 98.

31. See Theodore Draper, *Present History* (New York: Vintage, 1984), pp. 34–63. Secretary Weinberger elaborated on his views in *U.S. Strategic Doctrine*, Hearings before the Committee on Foreign Relations, U.S. Senate, 97th Congress, 2d session, p. 7.

32. This argument has been made most forcefully by Robert Jervis: "It is not clear how this [the threat of a controlled limited attack on hardened targets] would deter the Soviets. Such an American strike would still leave U.S. cities vulnerable." Jervis, *The Illogic of American Nuclear Strategy* (Ithaca: Cornell University Press, 1984), p. 114. Also see pp. 43–46.

33. *U.S. Strategic Doctrine*, p. 7.

34. Weinberger, *Department of Defense Annual Report for FY 1984*, p. 32.

35. Testimony of Gen. Bennie Davis, *Department of Defense Authorization for Appropriations for FY 1986*, Hearings before the

Committee on Armed Services, U.S. Senate, 99th Congress, 1st session, part 7, p. 3740.

36. Department of Defense, *Soviet Military Power 1987*, p. 18.

37. *MX Missile Basing and Related Issues*, Hearings before the Committee on Armed Services, U.S. Senate, 98th Congress, 1st session, April 10–May 3, 1983, p. 382.

38. *Soviet Military Power 1987*, p. 28.

39. Gen. V. Tolubko, *Missile Forces* (in Russian) (Moscow, 1977), p. 34, as quoted in Alexei Arbatov and Alexander Savelyev, "Command, Control, Communications, and Intelligence System as a Factor of Strategic Balance," IMEMO, *Disarmament and Security 1987 Yearbook*, p. 271 (emphasis added). Also note that the statement is suggestive of a launch-on-warning option.

40. Paul H. Nitze, "Assuring Strategic Stability in an Era of Detente," *Foreign Affairs*, vol. 54, no. 2, January 1976, pp. 207–32; and Nitze, "Deterring Our Deterrent," *Foreign Policy*, no. 25, Winter 1976–1977, pp. 195–210. For important critiques of Nitze's analysis see Jan M. Lodal, "Assured Strategic Stability: An Alternative View," *Foreign Affairs*, vol. 54, no. 3, April 1976, pp. 462–81; and Bruce G. Blair and Gary Brewer, "War Games and National Security with a Grain of Salt," *Bulletin of Atomic Scientists*, vol. 35, no. 5, June 1979, pp. 18–26.

41. For evidence that Soviet war planners seek high levels of damage expectancy (.90 or higher) against U.S. ICBMs, see Lee, "Soviet Nuclear Targeting Strategy," pp. 99 and 329 n. 44. ICBMs apparently are an important part of a Soviet reserve force, given the Soviets concerns about the vulnerability of SSBNs and their communications links and the inaccuracy of current Soviet SLBMs.

42. Robert J. Art, "Between Assured Destruction and Nuclear Victory: The Case for the 'MAD-Plus' Posture," in Russell Hardin, John J. Mearsheimer, Gerald Dworkin, and Robert E. Goodin (eds.), *Nuclear Deterrence: Ethics and Strategy* (Chicago: University of Chicago Press, 1985), pp. 121–40; Robert Jervis, "Why Nuclear Superiority Doesn't Matter," *Political Science Quarterly*, vol. 94, no. 4, Winter 1979–1980, pp. 617–33; and Spurgeon M. Keeny, Jr., and Wolfgang K. H. Panofsky, "MAD versus NUTS," in William P. Bundy (ed.), *The Nuclear Controversy* (New York: New American Library, 1985), pp. 3–22.

43. *Draft Memorandum for the President, Recommended FY 1964–*

FY 1968 Strategic Retaliatory Forces, November 21, 1962, p. 9, OSD-FOI.

44. Our understanding of Soviet doctrine on limited nuclear attacks is very uncertain. See Trulock, "Soviet Perspectives on Limited Nuclear Warfare."

45. It is impossible to assess the Soviet leadership's views on *how significant* such damage limitation capabilities would be without evidence of its perceptions of the effects of U.S. retaliation. It is, however, worth remembering here that Secretary of Defense Robert McNamara maintained in 1962 that "there is a tremendous difference, a vital difference, between say, thirty percent fatalities and sixty percent" in a nuclear war. It is not difficult to imagine Soviet authorities holding similar views with respect to limiting damage to the Soviet state and society. Stewart Alsop, "McNamara Thinks about the Unthinkable," *Saturday Evening Post*, December 1, 1962, p. 18.

46. Meyer, "Soviet Nuclear Operations," pp. 510–12.

47. See *Nuclear War Strategy*, p. 9. Also see pp. 38–40.

48. Testimony of William J. Perry, *Department of Defense Appropriations for FY 1981*, Hearings before the Subcommittee on Research and Development, Committee on Armed Services, U.S. Senate, 96th Congress, 2d session, part 5, p. 2865.

49. *Soviet Strategic Force Developments*, Joint Hearing before the Subcommittee on Strategic and Theater Nuclear Forces of the Committee on Armed Services and the Subcommittee on Defense of the Committee on Appropriations, U.S. Senate, 99th Congress, 1st session, June 26, 1985, p. 18.

50. All estimates are from *The Military Balance, 1986–1987* (London: IISS, 1986), pp. 60, 79, and 144–48.

51. Alexander Likhotal and Alexander Pikayev, "France," and Pikayev, "United Kingdom," in IMEMO, *Disarmament and Security 1987 Yearbook*, pp. 157 and 168.

52. Lee, "Soviet Nuclear Targeting Strategy," p. 101.

53. *Nuclear War Strategy*, p. 25.

54. According to Lawrence Gershwin, the National Intelligence Officer for Strategic Programs of the Central Intelligence Agency and National Intelligence Council, "We estimate that there are at least 800, perhaps as many as 1,500, relocation facilities for leaders at the national and regional levels." *Soviet Strategic Force Developments*, p. 17. Donald Latham, Assistant Secretary of Defense for Command, Control, Communications, and

Intelligence has estimated the number of hardened leadership facilities as 1,500 to 2,000. *Department of Defense Appropriations for 1984*, Hearings before the Subcommittee of the Committee on Appropriations, U.S. House of Representatives, 98th Congress, 1st session, part 8, p. 316.

55. *Department of Defense Authorization for Appropriations for FY 1983*, Hearings before the Committee on Armed Services, U.S. Senate, 94th Congress, 2d session, part 7, p. 4673.

56. *Soviet Military Power 1987*, p. 52.

57. George Leopold, "Soviets Dig In to Protect C³ System," *Defense News*, vol. 3, no. 14, April 4, 1988, p. 1. Latham testimony, *Department of Defense Appropriations for 1984*, p. 316.

58. See the discussion in Meyer, "Soviet Nuclear Operations," p. 503.

59. Victor Suvorov, *Inside the Soviet Army* (New York: Berkeley Books, 1984), pp. 178–82; and *Soviet Military Power 1988*, pp. 60–61.

60. *Soviet Strategic Force Developments*, p. 17. According to T. K. Jones, former Deputy Under Secretary of Defense for Research and Engineering, U.S. SLBMs cannot destroy such bunkers. *U.S. and Soviet Union Civil Defense Programs*, Hearings before the Subcomittee on Arms Control, Oceans, International Operations, and Environment, Committee on Foreign Relations, U.S. Senate, 97th Congress, 2d session, p. 55.

61. See Fred Hiatt and Rick Atkinson, "Lab Creating a New Generation of Nuclear Arms," *Washington Post*, June 9, 1986, p. 1; and Edgar Ulsamer, "Missiles and Targets," *Air Force Magazine*, vol. 70, no. 7, July 1987, pp. 69–70.

62. Daniel Ford, *The Button: The Pentagon's Strategic Command and Control System—Does it Work?* (New York: Simon and Schuster, 1985), p. 11.

63. Ibid., p. 127.

64. Department of Defense, *Soviet Military Power 1985*, p. 28; and Meyer, "Soviet Nuclear Operations," pp. 504–5.

65. *Soviet Strategic Force Developments*, p. 17.

66. Art, "Between Assured Destruction and Nuclear Victory," p. 133.

67. Ibid., p. 133.

68. V. D. Sokolovskii, *Soviet Military Strategy* (Englewood Cliffs, NJ: Prentice-Hall, 1963), p. 417.

69. On the leadership evacuation to Kuibyshev in World War

II see Georgi K. Zhukov, *Marshall Zhukov's Greatest Battles* (New York: Harper and Row, 1969), p. 48; and John Erickson, *The Road to Stalingrad* (New York: Harper and Row, 1975), pp. 220 and 228.

70. *Soviet Military Power 1988*, p. 60.

71. Art, "Between Assured Destruction and Nuclear Victory," p. 134.

72. Interview quoted in Herken, *Counsels of War*, p. 307.

73. According to the 1979 testimony of Under Secretary of Defense William Perry, "Avoidance of Enemy's National Command and Control" is embodied in the "operational policy concept requirements" for U.S. targeting doctrine. *Department of Defense Authorization for FY 1980*, Hearing before the Committee on Armed Services, U.S. Senate, 96th Congress, 1st session, part 3, p. 1437.

74. Gen. Larry Welch, quoted in Ulsamer, "Missiles and Targets," p. 74.

75. *Department of Defense Appropriations for FY 1988*, Hearings before a Subcommittee of the Committee on Appropriations, U.S. Senate, 100th Congress, 1st session, part 1, p. 173.

76. See, for example, Colin S. Gray, "Strategic Stability Reconsidered," *Daedalus*, vol. 109, no. 4, Fall 1980, pp. 135–54; and Fred C. Ikle, "The Idol of Stability," *The National Interest*, no. 6, Winter 1986–1987, pp. 75–79.

77. See Jack Snyder and Scott D. Sagan, "The Origins of Offensives and the Consequences of Counterforce," correspondence in *International Security*, vol. 11, no. 3, Winter 1986–1987, pp. 187–98.

78. The threat of a small-scale "decapitation" strike by cruise missiles would remain a serious problem, absent effective arms control restrictions, and will likely require improved surveillance capabilities against cruise missile launches. For a discussion of future warning capabilities against a full-scale stealth bomber or cruise missile attack, see Sidney D. Drell and Thomas H. Johnson, *Technical Trends and Strategic Policy*, Center for International Security and Arms Control Occasional Paper, Stanford University, May 1988, p. 20.

79. See testimony of Gen. John Vessey, *Hearings on S. Con. Res. 26—MX Missile*, Committee on Appropriations, U.S. Senate, 98th Congress, 1st session, pp. 254–55.

80. On targeting Soviet conventional forces see Jan M. Lodal,

"An Arms Control Agenda," *Foreign Policy*, no. 72, Fall 1988, pp. 169–72.

81. Walter Slocombe, "Preplanned Operations," p. 135, and Paul B. Stares, "Nuclear Operations and Anti-Satellites," p. 685, both in Carter et al., *Managing Nuclear Operations*.

82. Albert Carnesale and Charles Glaser, "ICBM Vulnerability: The Cures are Worse than the Disease," *International Security*, vol. 7, no. 1, Summer 1982, pp. 70–85. For a rebuttal, see the testimony of Gen. Larry D. Welch, *Department of Defense Authorization for Appropriations for FY 1987*, Hearings before the Committee on Armed Services, U.S. Senate, 99th Congress, 2d session, part 4, p. 1597.

83. *Soviet Military Power 1988*, p. 17.

84. See Richard Halloran, "Stealth Bomber Takes Shape," *New York Times*, May 16, 1988, p. A9.

85. For an analysis of the implications of START reductions see Michèle A. Flournoy, "START Thinking about a New U.S. Force Posture," *Arms Control Today*, vol. 18, no. 6, pp. 9–14.

86. *Soviet Strategic Force Developments*, p. 8.

CHAPTER THREE
Limited Strategic Defense

1. The speech is reprinted in Steven E. Miller and Stephen Van Evera (eds.), *The Star Wars Controversy* (Princeton: Princeton University Press, 1986), pp. 257–58. Among the most thorough critiques are Sidney D. Drell, Phillip J. Farley, and David Holloway, "Preserving the ABM Treaty: A Critique of the Reagan Strategic Defense Initiative," and Ashton B. Carter, Background Paper, Office of Technology Assessment (OTA), "Directed Energy Missile Defense in Space," both reprinted in *The Star Wars Controversy*, pp. 57–97 and 165–271.

2. On the politics of the March 2, 1983, speech see Gregg Herken, "The Earthly Origins of Star Wars," *Bulletin of Atomic Scientists*, vol. 43, no. 8, October 1987, pp. 20–30.

3. Paul Nitze, "On the Road to a More Stable Peace," address to the Philadelphia World Affairs Council, February 20, 1985, reprinted in Samuel F. Wells, Jr., and Robert S. Litwak (eds.), *Strategic Defenses and Soviet-American Relations* (Cambridge, MA: Ballinger, 1987), pp. 193–99.

4. Early efforts to develop a framework for assessing strategic

stability in an era of mutual limited defense deployments include Office of Technology Assessment, "Ballistic Missile Defense Technologies," in OTA, *Strategic Defenses* (Princeton: Princeton University Press, 1986), pp. 101–16; James A. Thomson, "Deterrence, Stability, and Strategic Defenses," in Fred S. Hoffman, Albert Wohlstetter, and David S. Yost (eds.), *Swords and Shields: NATO, the USSR, and New Choices for Long-Range Offense and Defense* (Lexington, MA: Lexington Books, 1987), pp. 339–56; and Ashton B. Carter, "BMD Applications: Performance and Limitations," in Ashton B. Carter and David N. Schwartz (eds.), *Ballistic Missile Defense* (Washington, D.C.: Brookings, 1984), pp. 98–156.

5. The most important work in favor of deployment of limited strategic defenses has been that of Fred Hoffman, Albert Wohlstetter, and their colleagues at the Pan Heuristics consulting firm. See Fred S. Hoffman, "The SDI in U.S. Nuclear Strategy," and "Ballistic Missile Defenses and U.S. National Security (Hoffman report)," in Miller and Van Evera (eds.), *The Star Wars Controversy*, pp. 3–15 and 273–90. The most detailed critiques of Limited Strategic Defense are Charles L. Glaser, "Do We Want the Missile Defenses We Can Build," in *The Star Wars Controversy*, pp. 98–130; and Peter A. Clausen, "Limited Defense: The Unspoken Goal," in Union of Concerned Scientists (UCS), John Tirman (ed.), *Empty Promise: The Growing Case against Star Wars* (Boston: Beacon Press, 1986), pp. 146–60.

6. James R. Schlesinger, "Rhetoric and Realities in the Star Wars Debate," in Miller and Van Evera (eds.), *The Star Wars Controversy*, p. 18.

7. Harold Brown, "Is SDI Technically Feasible?" in Harold Brown (ed.), *The Strategic Defense Initiative: Shield or Share?* (Boulder, CO: Westview Press, 1987), p. 138.

8. Henry Kissinger, "Reducing the Risk of War," in Zbigniew Brzezinski (ed.), *Promise or Peril: The Strategic Defense Initiative* (Washington, D.C.: Ethics and Public Policy Center, 1986), p. 97.

9. For example, Lt. Gen. James A. Abrahamson, Director of the Strategic Defense Initiative Organization, wrote in 1987: "In March 1983, when the president asked scientists to develop means to render nuclear weapons impotent and obsolete, the question was whether it was possible . . . the question now is no longer whether the President's vision can be made a reality but how and when." James A. Abrahamson and Simon P. Worden,

"Technologies for Effective Multilayer Defenses," in Hoffman et al. (eds.), *Swords and Shields*, p. 193.

10. Caspar W. Weinberger, "U.S. Defense Strategy," *Foreign Affairs*, vol. 64, no. 4, Spring 1986, pp. 681 and 684 (emphasis added).

11. Reprinted in OTA, *Strategic Defenses*, p. 307.

12. Richard K. Betts, "Innovation, Assessment, and Decision," in Betts, *Cruise Missiles: Technology, Strategy, Politics* (Washington, D.C.: Brookings, 1981), p. 3.

13. For very useful summaries see Brown, "Is SDI Technically Feasible?" pp. 122–32; Aspen Strategy Group, *The Strategic Defense Initiative and American Security* (Lanham, MD: University Press of America, 1987), pp. 13–24; and Michael M. May, "Technical Feasibility of the SDI," in Wells and Litwak (eds.), *Strategic Defenses and Soviet-American Relations*, pp. 125–40.

14. A published report of the Committee of Soviet Scientists for Peace, Against the Nuclear Threat, *The Large-Scale Anti-Missile System and International Security* (Moscow, February 1986), presents the Soviet Union's public position on countermeasures. For discussion of Soviet countermeasures see Benjamin Lambeth, "Soviet Perspectives on the SDI," in Wells and Litwak (eds.), *Strategic Defenses and Soviet-American Relations*, pp. 56–61; Stephen Meyer, "Soviet Strategic Programmes and the U.S. SDI," *Survival*, vol. 27, no. 6, November–December 1985, pp. 274–92; and David Holloway, "The SDI and The Soviet Union," in Franklin A. Long, Donald Hafner, and Jeffrey Boutwell (eds.), *Weapons in Space* (New York: W. W. Norton, 1986), pp. 268–73. Useful Western analyses of countermeasures include OTA, "Ballistic Missile Defense Technologies," pp. 170–78; and Richard L. Garwin, "The Soviet Response: New Missiles and Countermeasures," in UCS, *Empty Promise*, pp. 129–46.

15. Richard Halloran, "Higher Budget Foreseen for Advanced Missiles," *New York Times*, May 18, 1983, p. 11, quoted in Drell, Farley, and Holloway, "Preserving the ABM Treaty," p. 90.

16. Department of Defense, *Soviet Military Power 1988*, p. 51.

17. Ibid., pp. 51 and 53.

18. Carter, "Directed Energy Missile Defense in Space," p. 253.

19. Ashton B. Carter, Introduction to Herbert York, *Does Strategic Defense Breed Offense?* Center for Science and International

Affairs Occasional Paper (Lanham, MD: University Press of America, 1987), p. 4.

20. See, for example, George A. Keyworth's discussion of stability in "The Case for Strategic Defense: An Option for a Disarmed World," *Issues in Science and Technology*, vol. 1, no. 1, Fall 1984, pp. 41–42.

21. Robert S. McNamara, "The Dynamics of Nuclear Strategy," *Department of State Bulletin*, vol. 57, no. 1476, October 9, 1967, p. 450. See Fred C. Ikle, "Nuclear Strategy: Can There Be a Happy Ending?" *Foreign Affairs*, vol. 63, no. 4, Spring 1985, p. 824; and Kenneth L. Adelman, "SDI: Setting the Record Straight," reprinted in Brzezinski (ed.), *Promise or Peril: The Strategic Defense Initiative*, p. 204.

22. Michael R. Gordon, "Nunn Seeks Shield for Missiles Fired in Error," *New York Times*, January 20, 1988, p. 1.

23. Department of Defense, *Soviet Military Power 1987*, p. 33.

24. Ibid.

25. See Theodore A. Postol, *The Implications of Accidental Launch Protection Systems for U.S. Security*, Hearing before the Panel on the Strategic Defense Initiative of the Committee on Armed Services, U.S. House of Representatives, April 20, 1988, forthcoming. Also see Anne H. Cahn, Martha C. Little, and Stephen Daggett, "Nunn and Contractors Sell ALPS," *Bulletin of Atomic Scientists*, vol. 44, no. 5, June 1988, pp. 10–12.

26. For further discussion of Soviet and American accidental war prevention measures see chapter 4.

27. "Soviets Goofed, Told Mars Probe to 'Commit Suicide,' " *San Francisco Chronicle*, September 10, 1988, p. A-11.

28. On French, British, and Chinese nuclear weapons safety procedures see Dan Caldwell, "Permissive Action Links," *Survival*, vol. 29, no. 3, May–June 1987, pp. 224–38. On British and French nuclear targeting policy see Lawrence Freedman, "British Nuclear Targeting," and David S. Yost, "French Nuclear Targeting," in Desmond Ball and Jeffrey Richelson (eds.), *Strategic Nuclear Targeting* (Ithaca: Cornell University Press, 1986), pp. 109–58. On China's nuclear strategy see Gerald Segal, "China's Nuclear Posture for the 1980s," *Survival*, vol. 23, no. 1, January–February 1981, pp. 11–17.

29. Cahn et al., "Nunn and Contractors sell ALPs," p. 11.

30. Kissinger, "Reducing the Risk of War," in Brzezinski (ed.), *Promise or Peril*, p. 98.

31. On this point see Richard K. Betts, "Heavenly Gains on Earthly Losses? Toward A Balance Sheet For Strategic Defense," in Brown (ed.), *The Strategic Defense Initiative: Shield or Snare?* p. 244.

32. On the proliferation of ballistic missile technology see Aaron Karp, "Ballistic Missiles in the Third World," *International Security*, vol. 9, no. 3, Winter 1984–1985, pp. 166–95; and Karp, "The Frantic Third World Quest for Ballistic Missiles," *Bulletin of Atomic Scientists*, vol. 44, no. 5, June 1988, pp. 14–19.

33. On the debate over the utility of ICBMs see the "President's Commission on Strategic Forces" (the Scowcroft report), March 1984; Albert Carnesale and Charles Glaser, "ICBM Vulnerability: The Cures Are Worse than the Disease," *International Security*, vol. 7, no. 1, Summer 1982, pp. 70–85; and Russel E. Dougherty, "The Value of ICBM Modernization," *International Security*, vol. 12, no. 2, Fall 1987, pp. 163–72.

34. See, for example, Clausen, "Limited Defense," p. 153.

35. On mobility alternatives see OTA, *MX Missile Basing* (Washington, D.C.: GPO, September 1981); Donald A. Hicks, "ICBM Modernization: Consider the Alternatives," *International Security*, vol. 12, no. 2, Fall 1987, pp. 173–81; and Jan M. Lodal, "SICBM Yes, HML No," ibid., pp. 182–86.

36. "Ballistic Missile Defenses and U.S. National Security," p. 289. Also see William E. Odom, "The Implications of Active Defense of NATO for Soviet Military Strategy," in Hoffman et al. (eds.), *Swords and Shields*, p. 172; and Albert Wohlstetter, "The Political and Military Aims of Offense and Defense Innovation," in *Swords and Shields*, p. 28.

37. For similar arguments see Glaser, "Do We Want the Missile Defenses We Can Build?" p. 108; and John C. Toomay, "The Case for Ballistic Missile Defense," in Long et al. (eds.), *Weapons in Space*, p. 227.

38. Cahn et al. "Nunn and Contractors Sell ALPS," p. 11.

39. "Ballistic Missile Defenses and U.S. National Security," p. 286 (emphasis in original).

40. Fred S. Hoffman, "Imperfect Strategies, Near-Perfect Defenses, and the SDI," in Hoffman et al. (eds.), *Swords and Shields*, p. 220.

41. Paul Kozemchak, "New Guidance for Nuclear and Nonnuclear Weapons," in Hoffman et al. (eds.), *Swords and Shields*, p. 277. For a similar argument see Abrahamson and Worden,

"Technologies for Effective Multilayer Defenses," in *Swords and Shields*, pp. 179–80.

42. The only major exceptions today would be U.S. launch failures due to technical reliability defects and the small number of ICBMs or SLBMs destroyed by the Moscow ABM system.

43. See William T. Lee, "Soviet Nuclear Targeting," in Ball and Richelson (eds.), *Strategic Nuclear Targeting*, pp. 84–108; and Notra Trulock III, "Soviet Perspectives on Limited Nuclear Warfare," in Hoffman et al. (eds.), *Swords and Shields*, pp. 53–85.

44. Hoffman, "The SDI in U.S. Nuclear Strategy," p. 11.

45. Philip Taubman, "Gorbachev Says Soviet Test Halt Is Again Extended," *New York Times*, August 19, 1986, pp. A-1, A-13; Committee of Soviet Scientists for Peace, Against the Nuclear Threat, *The Large-Scale Anti-Missile System and International Security*, p. 77.

46. See Meyer, "Soviet Strategic Programmes and the U.S. SDI," pp. 274–92; Bruce Parrott, "Soviet Policy toward BMD and SDI," in Brown (ed.), *The Strategic Defense Initiative: Shield or Snare?* pp. 211–20; and Don Oberdorfer, "Military Response Planned to 'Star Wars' Soviet Says," *Washington Post*, March 8, 1985, p. A-1. For the arguments of opponents to this view see Raymond L. Garthoff, "New Thinking in Soviet Military Doctrine," *Washington Quarterly*, vol. 11, no. 3, Summer 1988, pp. 131–58.

47. Interview with Viktor Afanasyev in *Die Presse*, Vienna, January 29, 1985, as quoted in Lambeth, "Soviet Perspectives on the SDI," p. 67. Also see Philip Taubman, "Moscow Says Its A-Test Halt Is Militarily Beneficial to U.S.," *New York Times*, August 26, 1986, p. A4.

48. See Odom, "The Implications of Active Defense of NATO for Soviet Military Strategy," p. 160.

49. *Pravda*, March 27, 1983, as quoted in OTA, "Ballistic Missile Defense Technologies," appendix K, p. 312. Roald Sagdeyev, Director of The Institute of Space Research of the USSR Academy of Sciences, argued similarly in April 1984: "A space-based defense system would prove to be extraordinarily destabilizing. When those who command such a system understand that it does not provide 100 percent protection, they might be seduced by the idea of attempting a first strike." *U.S. News and World Report*, April 23, 1984, p. 50, quoted in "Ballistic Missile Defense Technologies," appendix K, p. 312.

50. "Excerpts of Interview with Soviet Armed Forces Chief of Staff," *New York Times*, October 30, 1987, p. 4.

51. March 23, 1983, Speech on Defense Spending and Defensive Technology, in Miller and Van Evera (eds.), *The Star Wars Controversy*, p. 258.

52. Colin S. Gray, *Strategic Defense and National Security*, Hearings on H.R. 3073, Committee on Armed Services, Nov. 10, 1983, House of Representatives, 98th Congress, 1st session, p. 116.

53. According to the Department of Defense, the SA-10 and SA-X-12B/Giant Systems "may have the potential to intercept some types of strategic ballistic missiles. Both systems are expected to have widespread deployments." *Soviet Military Power 1987*, p. 50. For an analysis of Soviet defenses, see David S. Yost, "Strategic Defenses in Soviet Doctrine and Force Posture," in Hoffman et al. (eds.), *Swords and Shields*, pp. 123–57.

CHAPTER FOUR
Accidental War and Operational Arms Control

1. Among the leading scholars on this subject, there is a striking consensus that the "purely" accidental war problem has been essentially solved. Paul Bracken has concluded that the "pure accidental war . . . is a virtual impossibility today." Bruce Blair has similarly argued that "the high priority assigned to negative control would seem to warrant high confidence in peacetime safeguards against accidental or unauthorized use of nuclear weapons." Finally, Ashton Carter, John Steinbruner, and Charles Zraket have concluded that "peacetime control has received attention commensurate with its importance. Weapons designs and procedural rules have evolved to preserve effective control over the sizable, globally dispersed operations that are routine in peacetime, and these have been completely successful in the sense that no accidental or unauthorized nuclear explosion has occurred." Paul Bracken, "Accidental Nuclear War," in Graham T. Allison, Albert Carnesale, and Joseph S. Nye, Jr. (eds.), *Hawks, Doves, and Owls* (New York: W. W. Norton, 1985), p. 39; Bruce G. Blair, *Strategic Command and Control: Redefining the Nuclear Threat* (Washington, D.C.: Brookings, 1985), p. 286; and Ashton B. Carter, John D. Steinbruner, and Charles A. Zraket (eds.), *Managing Nuclear Operations* (Washington, D.C.: Brookings, 1987), p. 9.

2. The views of senior U.S. military officers were studied in a 1984 Gallup poll. It reported that only 13 percent of senior generals and admirals stated that they were concerned either "a great deal" or "a fair amount" about the possibility of "a war resulting from an accidental detonation of a nuclear weapon." Similarly, only 16 percent expressed high or moderate concerns about war started by "a direct nuclear attack by the Soviet Union on the U.S." In contrast, 54 percent expressed great or a fair amount of concern about conventional war escalating to nuclear war. *Newsweek*, July 9, 1984, p. 37.

3. The only known exception occurred at the height of the Korean War when nine nuclear weapons were transferred to the Air Force in preparation for potential use. See Roger M. Anders (ed.), *Forging the Atomic Shield: Excerpts from the Office Diary of Gordon E. Dean* (Chapel Hill: University of North Carolina Press, 1987), p. 137.

4. David Alan Rosenberg, "The Origins of Overkill: Nuclear Weapons and American Strategy, 1945–1960," *International Security*, vol. 7, no. 4, Spring 1983, p. 42. The stockpile estimate is based on the figures given in Thomas B. Cochran, William M. Arkin, and Milton M. Hoenig, *U.S. Nuclear Forces and Capabilities*, vol. 1 of *Nuclear Weapons Data Book* (Cambridge, MA: Ballinger, 1984), p. 15.

5. Peter Stein and Peter Feaver, *Assuring Control of Nuclear Weapons*, Center for Science and International Affairs Occasional Paper, no. 2 (Lanham, MD: University Press of America, 1987), pp. 30–31.

6. Ibid., pp. 39 and 83. Also see John T. McNaughton, "Arms Restraint in Military Decisions," *Journal of Conflict Resolution*, vol. 7, no. 3, September 1963, pp. 228–34.

7. On Soviet locking devices see Stephen M. Meyer, "Soviet Nuclear Operations," in Carter et al. (eds.), *Managing Nuclear Operations*, pp. 491–93. For a survey of the PAL-type programs of other nuclear powers see Dan Caldwell, "Permissive Action Links," *Survival*, vol. 29, no. 3, May–June 1987, pp. 224–38.

8. Stein and Feaver, *Assuring Control of Nuclear Weapons*, pp. 53–77.

9. *Department of Defense Authorization for Appropriations for FY 1986*, Hearings before the Committee on Armed Services, U.S. Senate, 99th Congress, 1st session, part 7, Strategic and Theater Nuclear Forces, pp. 3857–58. Also see Donald R. Cotter, "Peace-

time Operations," in Carter et al. (eds.), *Managing Nuclear Operations*, p. 52.

10. Memorandum by the Chief of Staff, U.S. Air Force, for the Joint Chiefs on Launching of the Strategic Air Command Alert Force, March 10, 1958, CSAFM-72-58, enclosure to JCS 1899/393, February 20, 1958, Note by the Secretaries to the Joint Chiefs of Staff on CINC NORAD Comments on WSEG 33, Phase II, CCS 381 US (5-23-46) (sec. 94) RG 218, Records of the Joint Chiefs of Staff, 1958, National Archives.

11. Thomas S. Power, *Design for Survival* (New York: Coward-McCann, 1964), pp. 156–57. The other indications that the BMEWS warning was a false alarm were BMEWS reports of unreasonable ICBM speeds and erratic times-of-impact estimates. See Gen. Laurence S. Kuter, Oral History, Air Force Historical Research Center, Maxwell AFB, Montgomery, AL, pp. 601–3.

12. Memorandum for the Secretary of Defense, August 8, 1961, DJSM-926-61, CCS 4615 (April 3, 1961), sec. 2, RG 218, Records of the Joint Chiefs of Staff, 1961, National Archives; and Power, *Design for Survival*, p. 157.

13. For an excellent discussion of U.S. warning systems see John C. Toomay, "Warning and Assessment Sensors," in Carter et al. (eds.), *Managing Nuclear Operations*, pp. 293–311.

14. Ground-based nuclear detection sensors outside Air Force bases and near U.S. cities were originally deployed in the 1950s to provide information that a nuclear bomb had exploded nearby. The Vela satellite program provided some additional detection capability starting in 1963, and the current NAVSTAR satellite system includes multiple nuclear detection systems. Ibid., pp. 294 and 309–10.

15. JCS 2019/245, September 10, 1957, appendix, CINCLANT letter 00049/54, August 5, 1957, Declassified Documents Reference Collection, Carrollton Press, 1980, no. 273A; and Rosenberg, "Origins of Overkill," pp. 43 and 48–49.

16. Gen. Thomas White to Gen. Thomas Power, November 22, 1957, Thomas D. White Papers, box 41, 1957 General File, Library of Congress. (Also available at the National Security Archives, Washington, D.C.)

17. *Memorandum to the President, Policies Previously Approved in NSC Which Need Review*, NSC Meetings 1961, January 30, 1961, folder 2, box 313, National Security Files (NSF), John F. Kennedy Library (JFKL), Boston.

18. The best discussion of the delegation issue is Paul Bracken, "Delegation of Nuclear Command Authority," in Carter et al. (eds.), *Managing Nuclear Operations*, pp. 352–72. For a discussion of the legal issues involved, see *Authority to Order the Use of Nuclear Weapons*, Congressional Research Service Report prepared for the Subcommittee on International Security and Scientific Affairs of the Committee on International Relations, December 1, 1975 (Washington: GPO, 1975).

19. Harold Brown, *Thinking about National Security* (Boulder, CO: Westview Press, 1983), p. 79. That genuine capabilities for such devolution exist was suggested in the following comments made by Gen. Thomas Stafford, Deputy Chief of Staff of the Air Force for Research, Development, and Acquisition, and Dr. S. L. Zeiberg, Deputy Under Secretary of Defense for Strategic and Space Systems, in 1979 congressional hearings on the requirements for U.S. attack assessment systems:

Mr. Murtha: What is the difference? What are you going to do? If you only have [deleted] minutes, what difference does it make?

General Stafford: Sir, the difference is if you know specifically [deleted] is under attack, there is no doubt that they are attacking high value really non-military targets [deleted] and the response of our forces would be different than if they were attacking only military targets. Also we would relay the command to our airborne command post. In other words, we would [deleted].

Dr. Zeibert: It is also very critical to know whether the [deleted] because then we need to start the devolution chain.

(*Department of Defense Appropriations for 1980*, Hearings before a Subcommittee of the Committee on Appropriations, U.S. House of Representatives, 96th Congress, 1st session, part 3, p. 878).

20. For an excellent discussion of "tight coupling" of modern Soviet and American nuclear command and control systems, see Paul Bracken, *The Command Control of Nuclear Forces* (New Haven: Yale University Press, 1983), pp. 59–65.

21. See Milton Leitenberg, "Accidents of Nuclear Weapons and Nuclear Delivery Systems," *SIPRI Yearbook of World Arma-*

ments, 1968–1969 (New York: Humanities Press, 1970), pp. 261–62.

22. Robert S. McNamara, interview with author, July 9, 1987.

23. For more detailed descriptions of this event see *Strategic Warning System False Alerts*, Hearings before the Committee on Armed Services, U.S. House of Representatives, 96th Congress, 2d session; *Recent False Alerts from the Nation's Missile Attack Warning System*, Report of Senators Gary Hart and Barry Goldwater to the Committee on Armed Services, U.S. Senate, 96th Congress, 2d session; and *Failures of the North American Aerospace Defense Command's (NORAD) Attack Warning System*, Hearings before a Subcommittee of the Committee on Government Operations, U.S. House of Representatives, 97th Congress, 1st session.

24. That the Pacific Command's Airborne Command Post took off while the Atlantic Command's did not, is a good example of the effect of the requirement for human evaluation of warning: officers of the two commands differed on how best to respond to the incoming warning information.

25. History of the 6595th Aerospace Test Wing, October 22, 1962–November 22, 1962, FOI.

26. Ibid, pp. 2 and 7. SAC had approved of the test launch, but there is no record of special JCS or OSD test approval during the crisis.

27. The paragraph is based on Raymond L. Garthoff, *Reflections on the Cuban Missile Crisis* (Washington, D.C.: Brookings, 1987), pp. 39–41. Garthoff, then a State Department intelligence officer, was told about the event by a CIA officer soon afterward. He cannot today confirm it through unclassified sources, but he believes the account to be true.

28. Col. Charles Maultsby, interview with author, September 15, 1988.

29. For more details, see Scott D. Sagan, "Nuclear Alerts and Crisis Management," *International Security*, vol. 9, no. 4, Spring 1985, pp. 118–21. On October 22, as part of the crisis alert, six F-102s with nuclear "Falcon" air-to-air missiles were deployed to both Galena and Eilson Air Force bases. Extracts from the Command Post Log, from Alaskan NORAD Region, Regional Historical Report, July 1–December 1962, p. 1, K-484-.011-1, Air Force Historical Research Center, Maxwell AFB, AL.

30. Theodore C. Sorensen, *Kennedy* (New York: Harper and Row, 1965), p. 713. This fear was not unfounded in 1962. SIOP-

63 included specific "prestrike reconnaissance" missions. JSTPS memorandum, JPM to JDD, March 29, 1962, General Format for SIOP-63, CCS 3105 (Joint Planning) (March 8, 1961) (3) (sec. 2), Records of the Joint Chiefs of Staff, 1961, RG 218, National Archives.

31. Robert F. Kennedy, *Thirteen Days* (New York: W. W. Norton, 1969), p. 210.

32. See Sagan, "Nuclear Alerts and Crisis Management," pp. 129–30; and Marc Trachtenberg, "The Influence of Nuclear Weapons in the Cuban Missile Crisis," *International Security*, vol. 10, no. 1, Summer 1985, pp. 156–61.

33. Report on Exercise Pine Cone, JCS 2311/25, May 22, 1961, p. 140, 3510 Joint and Combined Exercises, February 6, 1961, sec. 2, Records of the Joint Chiefs of Staff, 1961, RG 218, National Archives. The existence of a decision in an exercise does *not*, of course, prove that a similar decision would have been taken in a real crisis.

34. Indeed, there are significant differences in the accounts of the October 27 conversation given by Robert Kennedy and Nikita Khrushchev, though the degree to which the differences are due to errors in the writer's memories, and not miscommunication in 1962, is not clear. For that, one would have to be able to compare Dobrynin's cable to Moscow with Kennedy's memorandum of conversation. For accounts see Kennedy, *Thirteen Days*, pp. 107–9; Strobe Talbott (ed.), *Khrushchev Remembers* (Boston: Little, Brown, 1970), pp. 497–98; and Anatolii Gromyko, "The Caribbean Crisis, Part 2," reprinted in Ronald R. Pope (ed.), *Soviet Views of the Cuban Missile Crisis* (Washington, D.C.: University Press of America, 1982), pp. 215–16.

35. Robert Kennedy's account suggests that it took thirty minutes for Dobrynin to get to the Justice Department. Gromyko adds that Kennedy gave Dobrynin the President's personal phone number at the White House, apparently to reduce the time involved for a reply. Kennedy, *Thirteen Days*, p. 107. Also see, however, Raymond L. Garthoff, "Cuban Missile Crisis: The Soviet Story," *Foreign Policy*, no. 72, Fall 1988, p. 75.

36. Details of the DCL are described in Sally K. Horn, "The Hotline," in John Borawski (ed.), *Avoiding War in the Nuclear Age* (Boulder, CO: Westview Press, 1986), pp. 44–48.

37. Secretary of Defense Weinberger's April 1983 report to Congress, "Direct Communications Links and Other Measures

to Enhance Stability," is reprinted in Barry M. Blechman (ed.), *Preventing Nuclear War: A Realistic Approach* (Bloomington: Indiana University Press, 1985), pp. 172–85.

38. See Michael M. May and John R. Harvey, "Nuclear Operations and Arms Control," in Carter et al. (eds.), *Managing Nuclear Operations*, p. 715.

39. The Interim Report of the Nunn-Warner Working Group on Nuclear Risk Reduction is reprinted in Blechman (ed.), *Preventing Nuclear War*, pp. 167–71. Also see Richard K. Betts, "A Joint Nuclear Risk Control Center," in *Preventing Nuclear War*, pp. 65–85.

40. The text of the September 15, 1987, agreement is printed in *Arms Control Today*, vol. 17, no. 8, October 1987, pp. 28–29.

41. *Defense Department Authorization for Appropriations for FY 1986*, p. 3906.

42. For an examination of why this is the case see Charles Perrow, *Normal Accidents* (New York: Basic Books, 1984).

43. "Direct Communications Links and Other Measures to Enhance Stability," p. 178.

44. May and Harvey, "Nuclear Operations and Arms Control," pp. 710–11.

45. "Soviets Stage Integrated Test of Weapons," *Aviation Week and Space Technology*, June 28, 1982, pp. 20–21.

46. Blair, *Strategic Command and Control*, p. 289. The proposal was recently seconded in Morton H. Halperin, *Nuclear Fallacy: Dispelling the Myth of Nuclear Strategy* (Cambridge, MA: Ballinger, 1987), p. 83. It should be noted that Blair views this proposal as a long-term goal, requiring significant restructuring of U.S. forces and command and control, and not a near-term policy option.

47. Testimony of Gen. Bennie Davis, in *MX Missile Basing System and Related Issues*, Hearings before the Committee on Armed Services, U.S. Senate, 98th Congress, 1st session, April 10–May 3, 1983, p. 416.

48. See Davis Testimony, *MX Missile Basing*, p. 417, and testimony of Gen. Robert T. Herres, in *Our Nation's Nuclear Warning System: Will It Work If We Need It?* Hearing before a Subcommittee of the Committee on Government Operations, House of Representatives, 99th Congress, 1st session, p. 72. Under the scenario posited here, there would be at least five different warning systems reporting the existence of the attack: DSP satellites, BMEWS

Radar, PARCS (Perimeter Acquisition Radar Attack Characterization System) Radar, PAVE PAWS Radar, and Nuclear Detection Systems.

49. In addition, Slocombe suggests that "Soviet targets should be narrowly defined, including, or possibly even confined to, Soviet ICBMs." Walter Slocombe, "Preplanned Operations," in Carter et al. (eds.), *Managing Nuclear Operations*, p. 135. For differing assessments of the technical feasibility of such a Launch Under Attack option see Ashton B. Carter, "Assessing Command System Vulnerability," in *Managing Nuclear Operations*, pp. 578–82; and Blair, *Strategic Command and Control*, pp. 234–38.

50. In April 1983, Under Secretary of Defense (Policy) Fred C. Ikle stated: "It is our policy not to explain in detail how we would respond to a missile attack, to increase the uncertainties in the minds of Soviet planners. However, the United States does not rely on its capacity for launch on warning or launch under attack to ensure the credibility of its deterrent." Hedrick Smith, "Colonel Stirs Questions on MX Firing Doctrine," *New York Times*, April 8, 1983, p. D-15.

51. Although current U.S. airborne command posts have the ability to launch the ICBMs independently if the Launch Control Centers are destroyed in an attack, they lack the capability to retarget the forces. Carter, "Assessing Command System Vulnerability," p. 578.

52. *Nuclear War Strategy*, Hearing before the Committee on Foreign Relations, U.S. Senate, 96th Congress, 2d session, September 16, 1980, p. 18.

53. Ibid. It is worth noting that Blair, the major advocate for a more delayed retaliation policy, also writes: "From the perspective of a conservative Soviet planner, the capability of the United States to launch-on-warning is probably very credible. The advantage of this perception to the United States is that it reduces the appeal of Soviet preemption." *Our Nation's Nuclear Warning System*, p. 43.

54. According to the work of Sidney D. Drell and Thomas H. Johnson, "An individual cruise missile or ALCM carrier might escape detection for all or a substantial portion of its flight. However, technology exists to detect with confidence and to provide some tracking information on large numbers of such targets in flight against ground clutter; and advanced means exist for processing such signals from rapidly moving targets against the

background reflected from static ground targets." Sidney D. Drell and Thomas H. Johnson, *Technical Trends and Strategic Policy*, Center for International Security and Arms Control Occasional Paper, Stanford University, May 1988, p. 20. Also see Department of Defense, *Soviet Military Power 1988*, p. 102.

55. In 1988 the Soviets moved some of their Yankee-class submarines away from the U.S. East Coast and closer to Europe, apparently to compensate for the reductions in SS-20 missiles under the INF treaty. According to Pentagon officials, "Such submarines are now only occasionally deployed off United States coasts." Michael R. Gordon, "Soviets Cut Back Ship Deployments in Distant Waters," *New York Times*, July 17, 1988, pp. 1 and 5.

56. May and Harvey, "Nuclear Operations and Arms Control," p. 720.

57. Unconfirmed reports emerged in September 1988 suggesting that some Soviet SLBM launches *might* have been tested on "short-range, short-time-of-flight trajectories." Even if these initial reports turn out to be accurate, however, a test ban is not ruled out since extensive testing would be required to ensure the reliability and accuracy of severely depressed trajectory SLBMs. "USSR: New Major Book on Soviet Navy," Office of Naval Intelligence Public Release, September 1988.

58. For further discussion see May and Harvey, "Nuclear Operations and Arms Control," pp. 720–22, and Kurt Gottfried and Bruce G. Blair (eds.), *Crisis Stability and Nuclear War* (New York: Oxford University Press, 1988), pp. 105–6.

59. May and Harvey, "Nuclear Operations and Arms Control," p. 720. They correctly note, however, that even with imperfect detection, an element of stability would be produced since "a side that wished to gain advantage by illegally stationing one or more of its SSBNs within a standoff zone would have to weigh the negative consequences of detection by the other side, and thus might be deterred." On SSBN standoff zone verification issues also see Alan J. Vick and James A. Thomson, "The Military Significance of Restrictions on the Operations of Strategic Nuclear Forces," in Blechman (ed.), *Preventing Nuclear War*, p. 122.

60. According to *New York Times* military correspondent Richard Halloran, U.S. Navy officers report "they can account for most of the two dozen Soviet submarines in the North Atlantic, the Caribbean and the Mediterranean at any one time, but are

less confident about those in the Pacific and Indian Oceans."
Halloran reports, moreover, that the U.S. has an SSN following
behind each of the two to three Soviet SSBNs that are stationed
five hundred to a thousand miles off each of the U.S. coasts.
Richard Halloran, "A Silent Battle Surfaces," *New York Times
Magazine*, December 7, 1986, pp. 94 and 98. Halloran appears to
be discussing Yankee-class SSBNs, however, not the far more
quiet Delta and Typhoon-class submarines.

61. Stein and Feaver, *Assuring Control of Nuclear Weapons*, pp.
99–103; Allison, Carnesale, and Nye (eds.), *Hawks, Doves, and
Owls*, pp. 233–34; The American Academy of Arts and Science
and the Cornell University Peace Studies Program (Desmond Ball
et al.), *Crisis Stability and Nuclear War* (Ithaca: Cornell University
Peace Studies Program, 1987), p. 76. Also see Lawrence Meyer,
"AF Locks System Urged for Navy's Nuclear Missiles," *Los Angeles Times*, October 14, 1984, pp. 1–2.

62. For evidence of possible delegated authority to SSBN commanders in the 1960s, see Blair, *Strategic Command and Control*, p.
101.

63. See Sagan, "Nuclear Alerts and Crisis Management," pp.
129–34. The most complete description of current U.S. nuclear
alerting procedures is in Bruce G. Blair, "Alerting in Crisis and
Conventional War," in Carter et al. (eds.), *Managing Nuclear Operations*, pp. 75–120.

64. Precisely such a development occurred during a simulated
war game broadcast by ABC's "Nightline" ("The Crisis Game,"
November 23–24, 1983). Some of the American decision makers
argued against alerting American nuclear forces, in response to a
Soviet invasion of Iran and intelligence that Soviet ballistic missile submarines had been sent to sea, fearing that an American
alert would be provocative. Although the "President" did, in the
end, order U.S. forces to be placed on alert, it is worth noting
that there was strong sentiment in the control group, playing the
Soviet leadership, to escalate the crisis further if the U.S. had
reacted passively to the Soviet alert measures. Interviews with
participants.

65. Desmond Ball, "Soviet Strategic Planning and the Control
of Nuclear War," in Roman Kolkowitz and Ellen Propper Mickiewicz (eds.), *The Soviet Calculus of Nuclear War* (Lexington, MA:
Lexington Books, 1986), p. 61; Colin S. Gray, *Nuclear Strategy and
National Style* (Lanham, MD: Hamilton Press/Abt Books, 1986), p.

167 n. 84; and Richard Pipes, *Survival is Not Enough* (New York: Simon and Schuster, 1984), p. 225.

66. U.S. alert levels are given in the following sources: Department of Defense *Authorization for Appropriations for FY 1987*, Hearings before the Committee on Armed Services, U.S. Senate, 99th Congress, 2d session, p. 1570; *MX Missile Basing*, p. 418; and Cotter, "Peacetime Operations," pp. 24–25. Soviet alert levels are found in the following sources: John M. Collins, *U.S.-Soviet Military Balance, 1980–1985* (Washington, D.C.: Pergamon-Brassey's, 1985), p. 54; and *The Allocation of Resources in the Soviet Union and China*, Joint Economic Committee, 96th Congress, 1st session, part 7, p. 199.

67. According to DIA congressional testimony, "Soviet ICBMs, like U.S. ICBMs, are fully manned and on normal readiness conditions on a routine basis. Most, if not all, Soviet ICBMs could be launched within minutes of a valid launch order." *The Allocation of Resources in the Soviet Union and China*, part 7, p. 199.

68. Gen. Bennie Davis testimony, *MX Missile Basing and Related Issues*, p. 418; Cotter, "Peacetime Operations," pp. 24–25.

69. *The Allocation of Resources in the Soviet Union and China*, part 7, p. 199.

70. John M. Collins, *U.S.-Soviet Military Balance, 1980–1985* (Washington, D.C.: Pergamon-Brassey's, 1985), p. 54. Also see Meyer, "Soviet Nuclear Operations," p. 494.

71. See Carter, "Assessing Command System Vulnerability," pp. 570 and 607–8. Note, furthermore, that Carter's assumptions about eventual U.S. reconstitution and retaliation do not appear to include the possibility of Soviet follow-on nuclear attacks.

72. Richard H. Ellis, "Strategic Connectivity," Incidental Paper, Seminar on Command, Control, Communications, and Intelligence, Guest Presentations, Spring 1982, Program on Information Resources Policy, Harvard University, p. 5. The widely dispersed current alert authority can be traced to the 1959 JCS development of uniform readiness conditions. According to SM-833-59, a JCS memorandum (August 25, 1959, revised March 30, 1964), "In circumstances which preclude prior consultation with the Joint Chiefs of Staff, each commander of a unified or specified command is authorized to advance the readiness of the forces in his command." CCS 3180 (Emergency Readiness Plans) (April 20, 1959) Records of the Joint Chiefs of Staff, 1959, RG 218, National Archives.

73. See, for examples of such actions, Sagan, "Nuclear Alerts and Crisis Management," pp. 118–22.

74. JCS 1899/402, May 1, 1958, Report of the Joint Strategic Plans Committee to the Joint Chiefs of Staff, "Positive Control," presentation to NSC, CCS 381, U.S. (5-23-46) (sec. 97), p. 2619, Records of the Joint Chiefs of Staff, 1958, RG 218, National Archives.

75. See Sagan, "Managing Nuclear Alert Operations," forthcoming, RAND Corporation.

76. Col. Charles Maultsby, interview with author, September 15, 1988.

77. See Stein and Feaver, *Assuring Control of Nuclear Weapons*, p. 83; and Paul Bracken and Martin Shubik, "Strategic War: What Are The Questions and Who Should Ask Them?" *Technology in Society*, vol. 4, no. 3, p. 173.

78. Raymond L. Garthoff, "The Accidents Measures Agreement," in Borawski (ed.), *Avoiding War in the Nuclear Age*, pp. 60–61.

79. "Soviets Run to Air-Raid Shelters in False Alert" *San Francisco Chronicle*, April 29, 1988, p. A35.

80. Seymour Hersh, *The Target Is Destroyed* (New York: Vintage Books, 1987), p. 13.

81. This issue was originally raised in Bracken and Shubik, "Strategic War: What Are The Questions and Who Should Ask Them?" p. 173.

CHAPTER FIVE
A Delicate Balancing Act

1. Joseph S. Nye, Jr., "Reducing Nuclear Weapons," in Brent Scowcroft, R. James Woolsey, and Thomas H. Etzold (eds.), *Defending Peace and Freedom* (Lanham, MD: University Press of America, 1988), p. 143.

2. Arthur A. Stein, "Strategy as Politics, Politics as Strategy: Domestic Debates, Statecraft, and Star Wars," in Roman Kolkowitz (ed.), *The Logic of Nuclear Terror* (Boston: Allen and Unwin, 1987), p. 194.

3. For an analysis of the 1983 decision see Gregg Herken, "The Earthly Origins of Star Wars," *Bulletin of Atomic Scientists*, vol. 43, no. 8, October 1987, pp. 20–28.

4. For a thoughtful review of the problems involved in a world

with small nuclear arsenals, see James N. Miller, Jr., "Zero and Minimal Nuclear Weapons," in Joseph S. Nye, Jr., Graham T. Allison, and Albert Carnesale (eds.), *Fateful Visions: Avoiding Nuclear Catastrophe* (Cambridge, MA: Ballinger, 1988), pp. 11–32.

5. *U.S.-USSR Strategic Policies*, Hearings before the Subcommittee on Arms Control, International Law, and Organization of the Committee on Foreign Relations, U.S. Senate, 93d Congress, 2d session, March 4, 1974, p. 9 (emphasis added).

6. Scott D. Sagan, "Nuclear Alerts and Crisis Management," *International Security*, vol. 9, no. 4, Spring 1985, pp. 102–6.

7. Alexander M. Haig, Jr., *Caveat* (New York: Macmillan, 1984), pp. 157–61; and "Weinberger Quarrels with Haig's Account," *New York Times*, March 29, 1984, p. 25.

Index